NATIONAL SECURITY MANAGEMENT

A MODERN DESIGN FOR DEFENSE DECISION

A McNamara-Hitch-Enthoven Anthology

Edited by
Samuel A. Tucker

INDUSTRIAL COLLEGE OF THE ARMED FORCES
WASHINGTON, D.C.
1966

INDUSTRIAL COLLEGE OF THE ARMED FORCES
Washington, D.C.

AUGUST SCHOMBURG, Lt. Gen., USA
Commandant

J. J. APPLEBY, Rear Admiral, USN
Deputy Commandant

G. F. SMALE, Captain, USN
Director, Correspondence School

FOREWORD

Since his assumption of office in January 1961, Secretary of Defense Robert S. McNamara has stressed the need for a sound planning-programming-budgeting system as a key instrument in managing the manifold and far-flung activities of the Defense establishment. In essence, that system is directed to the realization of one objective—the most effective allocation of the resources available to Defense. This has always been the major concern and central management problem of the Secretary of Defense as, indeed, it is of the heads of all government departments and agencies. The unique feature of Mr. McNamara's approach, which President Johnson has recently prescribed for government-wide application, has been his quest for alternatives and his emphasis on analysis of cost and effectiveness in deciding on the best mix of force structures and weapon systems needed for the national defense.

Much is being written these days on the management "revolution" in the Pentagon. Actually, Mr. McNamara's innovations draw deeply on the past; they represent an extension of techniques of economic analysis long used in industry and of the systematic discipline employed in military operations research since World War II. As Mr. McNamara has suggested, "systems analysis" may perhaps best be characterized as "quantitative common sense." Quantitative approaches to decision-making do not deny the role of value judgments; instead, these techniques can contribute to the factual and analytical basis for informed and reflective judgment. What is new and striking about Mr. McNamara's approach is his insistence on a more systematic application of objectivity, logic, and explicit analysis of the issues and alternatives in considering the best defense policies to attain national security objectives.

This compilation embodies the thinking of the three principal architects of the contemporary approach to decision making: Defense Secretary McNamara; Charles J. Hitch, Assistant Secretary of Defense (Comptroller), now Vice President—Business and Finance, University of California; and Alain C. Enthoven, Assistant Secretary of Defense (Systems Analysis). The selections are focused not on a detailed account of techniques and methodologies, but on some of the broader aspects of this emerging discipline—its essential characteristics, its applications, its strengths, and, indeed, its present limitations. They get at the heart of basic questions of vital concern to us all: How are the fundamental choices of strategies and weapons systems to be made? What considerations must be weighed and what kind of information is needed to solve the complex problems of choice in making decisions? And what are the roles of the Secretary of Defense and his principal military and civilian staff advisers who, with the President and Congress, must bear the ultimate responsibility for decisions on our defense posture?

The Industrial College is proud to present this McNamara-Hitch-Enthoven Anthology as a part of its continuing effort to develop a corps of military and civilian officials who will be better informed and better equipped to meet present and future challenges to our national security.

AUGUST SCHOMBURG
Lieutenant General, USA

Industrial College of the Armed Forces
Washington, D. C.
11 July, 1966

CONTENTS

ILLUSTRATIONS

INTRODUCTION

In everyday speech, the words "budget" and "budgeting" carry largely negative connotations, evoking images of unwelcome financial constraints and of dreary numerical tabulations. Yet despite its lack of glamour, budgeting is an essential tool for the management of large enterprises. It is first and foremost a planning process, through which the manager allocates the available resources to the working units of his organization. Ideally, a budget should convert goals, programs, and priorities into monetary terms following rational economic analysis and decision on the optimum means of accomplishing an agency's objectives. Moreover, budgeting is an important device for the review and control of the activities of the component parts of an organization, to the end that over-all purposes and not parochial ones are served. Thus, modern budgeting is inextricably linked to the formulation of policy and the orderly execution of programs.

In the Federal Government, the use of the budget process as a positive instrument for these purposes is of comparatively recent origin and is still evolving. Of course, from the early days of the Republic, the Congress used its power to appropriate funds as a means for exerting control over the activities of the Executive Branch. It did not, however, employ the power of the purse to promote executive responsibility nor the comprehensive review of programs. The lack of systematic budgeting as understood today was acceptable during most of the nineteenth century when the country's economy was based primarily on agriculture, when its foreign interests and commitments were small, and when Federal activities were limited in scope and impact. But such haphazard procedures became increasingly inadequate as industrialization and urbanization proceeded and the tasks of government expanded. New conditions required new institutions; three Presidential commissions served as the catalysts in producing needed budgetary reforms.

The first of these groups was President Taft's Commission on Economy and Efficiency. Its report in 1912 called for a comprehensive executive budget, with expenditures classified by function. It also proposed that the President, his department heads, and their bureau chiefs be given greater authority and discretion in applying funds to programs—and that they be held responsible for operating results. These recommendations pointed the way to more effective budgeting and direction of public policy, but the first steps toward implementation were delayed until 1921, when the Congress enacted the Budget and Accounting Act.

This legislation established the Bureau of the Budget in the Treasury Department and required the submission of a comprehensive budget. Initially, the bureau concentrated much of its attention on the promotion of economy in government, particularly in "housekeeping" activities, rather than on the broader questions raised by the Taft Commission. The new agency did, however, assist the Harding, Coolidge, and Hoover Administrations in reducing Federal expenditures during the 1920's when the political slogans of the day were "Back to Normalcy," "Less Government in Business," and "The Business of America Is Business."

The depression of 1929 produced a marked change in what people expected of the Federal Government and of the President. Of course, the economic situation was considered a temporary emergency and the increasing involvement of the Government in the economic life of the Nation as a mere expedient. Yet remedial programs and new agencies proliferated, while coordination was often inadequate. A second fact-finding group, President Roosevelt's Committee on Administrative Management, proposed organizational changes to correct such deficiencies and also recommended that the Chief Executive be given greater administrative authority and more staff assistance so that he could be master in his own house. One of the Committee's recommendations resulted in the transfer of the Bureau of the Budget to the newly established Executive Office of the President in 1939 and an increase in its size and authority. Thus, it began to exercise a more important and a more effective role in coordinating Federal activities and in assisting the President to formulate and enforce public policy through budgeting.

Even after these changes, however, the Federal budget continued to reflect Congressional emphasis on organizational entities and subentities and on line items of expenditure, rather than broad programmatic content. The third of the Presidential commissions, the first Hoover Commission on Organization of the Executive Branch of the Government, appointed by President Truman in 1947, reviewed the situation and repeated the call for budgetary reform. It proposed ". . . the adoption of a budget based upon functions, activities, and projects: this we designate a 'performance budget.' " Such a budget presentation would focus attention on the work to be done and not on expenditures for personnel, supplies, travel, services, and the like.[1]

This recommendation was advanced in 1949 at a time when military expenditures had become and seemed likely to remain a major component of the Federal budget as a result of World War II and the subsequent cold war. In addition, at this time the Secretary of Defense, in his new position, was struggling with the many problems of integrating military policies and activities. In these circumstances, the torch of budgetary reform passed to the Department of Defense.

Amendments in 1949 to the National Security Act of 1947 reflected the work and proposals of the Hoover Commission. The Secretary of Defense was given greater authority over financial management in the department, and the Congress also required that he submit "performance" budgets thereafter. Accordingly, the budget and accounting structures of the military departments were simplified and made more uniform. Broad classifications such as Personnel, Operation and Maintenance, Procurement, Research and Development, and Construction replaced antiquated appropriation categories under which the technical services of the Army and the naval bureaus had received and administered their own separate appropriations. This change had the advantage of permitting comparisons between the military Services and separated the one-year accounts from the longer range ones— but the results fell short of being a true performance budget.

Criticism of Defense budgeting was heard with increasing frequency in the late 1950's. It was voiced within the Executive Branch, by members of the Congress, and by private citizens. The lines of dissent and the reasons given for them were diverse. Many critics stressed the importance to national security of assuring that foreign, economic, and military policies were properly coordinated and that imbalances in the force structure were eliminated. For example, the Rockefeller report on the problems of U.S. defense recommended in 1958 that a start be made toward a budgetary system that "corresponds more closely to a coherent strategic doctrine. It should not be too difficult, for example, to restate the presentation of the Service budgets, so that instead of the present categories of 'procurement,' 'operation and maintenance,' 'military personnel,' etc., there would be a much better indication of how much goes, for example, to strategic air, to air

---

[1] Commission on Organization of the Executive Branch of the Government, *Budgeting and Accounting: A Report to the Congress* (Washington: Government Printing Office, 1949), p. 8.

defense, to antisubmarine warfare, and so forth."[2] General Maxwell D. Taylor expressed similar views—

> The three services develop their forces more or less in isolation from each other, so that a force category such as the strategic retaliatory force, which consists of contributions of both the Navy and the Air Force, is never viewed in the aggregate. Similarly, it is impossible to tell exactly how much continental air defense is being obtained from the defense budget since this is another category to which several services contribute. In other words, we look at our forces horizontally when we think of combat functions but we view them vertically in developing the defense budget.[3]

Other critics hoped that more meaningful fiscal presentations would permit reductions in the Defense budget and more rational use of resources. For example, the House Appropriations Committee reported in 1959 that—

> The Joint Chiefs of Staff should look at what is available for what purposes and attempt to match it with the needs. As an example, the Joint Chiefs should take a look at the combined forces of the Marine Corps and the Army. It is not a question of combining the Army and the Marine Corps. It is merely a question of looking at the combined strength and the combined capability of these two great forces in making the final determination as to what our ground force should be in providing for our commitments throughout the world.[4]

During the following year, the same Committee showed its interest in preventing the costly false starts that had plagued military research and development programs:

> The present system should be revised to permit the orderly development of alternative approaches to weapons systems on a development basis only. The system should recognize the necessity to eliminate alternatives at the time a decision is made for quantity production. It is this decision that is all-important. At this point there should be a full evaluation of (1) the military potential of the system in terms of need and time in relation to other developments, by all the military services, and (2) its follow-on expenditure impact if approved for quantity production.[5]

Whatever the reasons, the calls for budgetary reforms were being sounded in growing volume. More than improvements in techniques were needed. As the staff of the Senate Subcommittee on National Policy Machinery expressed it:

---

2 Rockefeller Brothers Fund. *International Security: the Military Aspect*, report of Panel II of the Special Studies Project. (Garden City, N.Y.: Doubleday, 1958), pp. 58-59.

3 Maxwell D. Taylor, *The Uncertain Trumpet* (New York: Harper & Bros., 1959), p. 123.

4 U.S. Congress, House. Report No. 408. Committee on Appropriations, *Report on Department of Defense Appropriations Bill, 1960;* 86th Congress, 1st Session (Washington: Government Printing Office, 1959), p. 11.

5 U.S. Congress, House. Report No. 1561. Committee on Appropriations, *Report on Department of Defense Appropriations Bill, 1961;* 86th Congress, 2d Session (Washington: Government Printing Office, 1960), p. 25.

*There are better ways to make the budget process a more effective
instrument for reviewing and integrating programs and performance
in the area of national security.* There is need to return to the earlier
tradition which regarded the budgetary process as a key program
management tool of the President.[6]

Nor was President Eisenhower in fundamental disagreement.
In his final budget message to the Congress, he affirmed that "the
budget process is perhaps our most significant device for planning, controlling, and coordinating our programs and policies as
well as our finances. Thus, the President and the Congress will
always need to give attention to the improvement and full utilization of the budget system."[7]

While the specific proposals for change reflected problems current at the time, they also constituted the latest stage in the long-
standing effort to adjust government institutions to new roles
as conditions changed. The post-World War II situation had
required the United States to take a greatly expanded part in
international affairs. The adjustment to this demand, difficult
in itself, was further complicated by the scientific and technological revolution that was taking place concurrently. Seen in this
perspective, the budgetary reforms of 1961 and subsequent years
were a continuation of the traditional search for better government.

The introduction of any major innovation requires not only a
recognition of the need for change but also the availability of
the tools for an effective solution. Both were present by 1961.
The economic theory of price and allocation, a branch of moral
philosophy in Adam Smith's day, had been reduced to mathematical terms and made into a usable instrument for quantitative
analysis of problems of choice. In the late 1940's, the Air Force
established Project RAND and Mr. Charles J. Hitch began to
assemble the Economics Division of the RAND Corporation.
During the 1950's, this group began applying economic analysis
to the choice of weapon systems and strategies, as a research
tool, to the point that, by 1961, it was ready for use as a working
management technique in the Defense Department. This work
was summarized by Hitch and Roland McKean in their book,
The Economics of Defense in the Nuclear Age.[8] The 1940's and
1950's also saw the rapid development of many other tools of

6 U.S. Congress, Senate. Subcommittee on National Policy Machinery of the Committee
on Government Operations. Committee print, *Organizing for National Security: Super-
Cabinet Officers and Super Staffs,* 86th Congress, 2d Session (Washington: Government
Printing Office, 1960), p. 9.

7 *Public Papers of the Presidents of the United States: Dwight D. Eisenhower, 1960-61*
(Washington: Government Printing Office, 1961), p. 1023.

8 Harvard University Press, Cambridge, 1960.

analysis that might be grouped under the general title of "Decision Theory." The list includes statistical decision theory, theory of games, linear programming and its extensions, etc. Operations research, a new discipline in World War II, was expanding beyond the solution of tactical problems and analysis of single weapons to constantly broader fields, particularly under the influence of economists, who contributed their deceptively simple technique of isolating a problem, "arraying alternatives, estimating the utilities and cost of each, and choosing the alternative that yields the greatest excess of utilities over costs."[9] The digital computer, a classified project in World War II, had achieved capabilities to store and display vast amounts of information and to do computations of a scale undreamed of only a few years earlier.

The most important contributors to these developments included the military Services, whose far-sighted policies on research led them to support most of these advances, especially at the Air Force Project RAND and through the Office of Naval Research. In addition, the improvements made over the years in public administration, budgeting, and accounting provided the essential base for the application of the new concepts.

Thus, by 1961 there was a general recognition of the need for change. The conceptual tools had been developed. Congressional leaders had expressed desire for reform. Many military officers were ready and able to participate in the program. The arrival of Mr. McNamara as Secretary of Defense in January 1961 resulted in a concerted and intensive effort to focus these new developments on the vital and complicated issues of U.S. national security in the 1960's. As the first Secretary of Defense educated in the modern tools of management analysis, he made it clear to the Department that he wanted all its problems approached in a logical, analytical way. His philosophy of managerial leadership and initiative, described on pages 11–19, coupled with his remarkable energy, provided the "drive" for establishing the new system quickly and effectively.

Arguments about such peripheral matters as "inexperienced civilians" or "centralization" should not be allowed to obscure the fact that the years since 1961 have seen a great cooperative effort to overhaul the decision-making machinery of the Department. The result has been greatly improved procedures for planning, programming, and budgeting as well as for the realistic analysis of the complex problems of decision. Their application in the Department of Defense has made the budgetary process

---

[9] Charles J. Hitch, *The Uses of Economics*, RAND Publication P-2179-RC, Nov. 17, 1960, pp. 2-3.

a much more effective means for weighing alternatives, selecting optimum strategies, and building the necessary force structure. The objectives and methods of this new system are the subject of the selections that compose this anthology.

The practical application of these tools to the problems of decision in the Defense Department remains much more a matter of judgment and common sense and much less of esoteric techniques than most of the published literature would suggest. The value of the development of these tools has been not in their rigid mechanical application but in providing a new way of looking at problems.

As its practitioners are the first to stress, the present techniques of systems analysis are still in an early stage of development; improvements are continually being sought to increase the utility of the system to management. Yet the current planning-programming-budgeting procedures and concepts of systems analysis have already proved so useful that President Johnson in August 1965 directed their extension on a Government-wide basis "to present us with the alternatives and the information on which we can, together, make better decisions." (See App. I, pages 213–214).

Procedures and techniques are not substitutes for wisdom and judgment. They are, however, aids to the effective exercise of these faculties. Their use will assist the Nation to govern itself more effectively and to achieve its national objectives more efficiently. In President Johnson's words, "The people will be the beneficiary."

ALAIN C. ENTHOVEN

PART I

THE BUDGET AS A MANAGEMENT TOOL FOR INTEGRATING NATIONAL AND DEFENSE POLICY

Part I is composed of five selections that illustrate the interlocking relationship between decisions on national policy and decisions on the Federal budget. Its theme was concisely stated by Secretary of Defense Robert S. McNamara: "I consider the budget nothing more and nothing less than the quantitative expression of a plan or a policy. So in developing the budget I propose to start with the plan or the policy and translate it into quantitative terms, terms of benefit and cost." Consequently, one of the Secretary's objectives has been to improve the process through which policy decisions are converted into budgetary programs.

In the opening selection, Mr. McNamara reflects on his role as the agent of the President in translating policy into action; he reports on the progress being made in installing the improved budgetary system; and he discusses the participation of the Joint Chiefs of Staff and other senior military leaders in the deliberations that precede policy decisions. The central question—how much is enough?—and how the new budget system assists in providing answers are treated in selection 2, a speech given by the Secretary in 1963 to newspaper editors.

The relationship between decisions on national policy and on budget levels and force structures has been of continuing interest to the Congress. The Jackson Committee (Subcommittee on National Policy Machinery, Committee on Government Operations, U.S. Senate) explored this matter with Mr. McNamara in August 1961; an excerpt from his testimony has been included as selection 3. In addition, in his annual statements on the Defense budget presented before the House and Senate Armed Services and Appropriations Committees, the Secretary has customarily reviewed the policy considerations that dictate the recommended budget levels. The introductory portion of the statement on the fiscal year 1965 request and an excerpt from the subsequent close questioning of the Secretary by members of the House Appropriations Committee are included as selection 4 to illustrate both the rationale for the budget and the extent of Congressional concern about the process through which decisions are reached.

The relationship of the Defense budget to the total economic program of the Federal Government, as well as to other national security policies, was discussed by the then-Assistant Secretary of Defense (Comptroller), Mr. Charles J. Hitch, in a lecture before the National War College and the Industrial College of the Armed Forces in 1964. A portion of his remarks completes Part I.

1

MANAGING THE DEPARTMENT OF DEFENSE*
By Robert S. McNamara

When the President first asked that I accept appointment as the Secretary of Defense in his Cabinet, my immediate reaction was to question my own competency. I had very little experience in the Government—no experience at the level to which the President proposed to appoint me. Even my limited exposure to the workings of the Pentagon as an officer in the headquarters of the then Army Air Force during World War II was some 15 years behind me.

What was the climate in the Pentagon? What kind of a job was being the Secretary of Defense? Could I—or for that matter could anyone—truly manage the Department of Defense?

I expressed my doubts to the President and seriously questioned whether he would be wise in making the appointment.

The President said he was not aware of any school for cabinet officers.

It was after this that I called upon my predecessor, the Honorable Thomas S. Gates, Jr. Mr. Gates briefed me thoroughly on his own experience as Secretary of Defense. I learned that he first came into office as Under Secretary of the Navy in the Defense Department in 1953, just after a committee headed by Nelson Rockefeller had examined the powers of the Secretary of Defense and reported to Congress, as follows:

> The Secretary of Defense has by statute full and complete authority over the Department of Defense, all its agencies, subdivisions and personnel subject only to the President. . . . There are no separately administered preserves in the Department of Defense. . . . The Secretaries of the Military Departments, the Joint Chiefs of Staff, all officers and other personnel are *under* the Secretary of Defense. . . . His power extends to all affairs and activities of the Department of Defense.

Counsel for the Rockefeller Committee observed: "It remains only to sweep away the annoying challenges to that authority from time to time."

During his 6 years as Under Secretary and Secretary of the the Navy, and thereafter during his 2 years as Deputy Secretary

---

*Reprinted from *Civil Service Journal*, Vol. 4, No. 4, April-June 1964, pp. 1-5.

and Secretary of Defense, Mr. Gates had worked to establish the sort of control that Congress had authorized.

But just what did this control really involve? We have some 3,700,000 people in the Department of Defense—2,700,000 in uniform and 1,000,000 civilian employees—located all over the world. The Department spends over $50 billion a year—over half of the Federal Government budget. Its inventory of real property and equipment is worth over $150 billion. Its major installations—some 600 of them in the United States alone—are in reality municipalities with all of the housing, the utilities systems, maintenance and transportation requirements, policing needs, and schools and hospitals typical of our small cities. The Department operates, for support of its forces, airlines, shipping lines, a communication system, supply distribution systems, and maintenance establishments, each of which represents a major management task in its own right. It procures annually over four million different items of equipment and supplies.

The sheer magnitude of the task as it unfolded made me question whether I or anyone could really manage the Department.

On reflection, it became clear that either of two broad philosophies of management could be followed by a Secretary of Defense. He could play an essentially passive role—a judicial role. In this role the Secretary would make the decisions required of him by law by approving recommendations made to him. On the other hand, the Secretary of Defense could play an active role providing aggressive leadership—questioning, suggesting alternatives, proposing objectives, and stimulating progress. This active role represents my own philosophy of management. In talking with Mr. Gates and thinking about his experiences, I became convinced that there was room for and need of this kind of management philosophy in the Department of Defense.

In my preparation I read a report published the previous month by Senator Henry Jackson's Subcommittee. It recommended "more vigorous implementation of the broad powers already vested in the Secretary of Defense." I knew full well that this view was not unanimously shared either in or out of the Pentagon.

The creation of the Department of Defense resulted from the clear recognition that separate land, sea, and air warfare is gone forever. The National Security Act of 1947 and its various amendments, down through the Department of Defense Reorganization Act of 1958, established the Department and the basis for its operations. Changes in the overall organization and in the character and disposition of our military forces have taken place on an evolutionary basis in response to Congressional action represented by this legislation. In essence, the three military departments (the Army, the Navy [including the Marines], and the Air Force) have been preserved as separate organizational entities to train, supply, and support the land, sea, and air forces. The forces for the most part, however, are assigned to unified and specified combatant commands, the commanders of which by law exercise full operational command of the forces assigned to them.

The function of these commands was to carry out wartime strategic missions assigned to them by the President through the Secretary of Defense and the Joint Chiefs of Staff. The ultimate responsibility rests with the President. Immediate command of the forces is in the hands of the unified and specified commanders subject to the instructions issued by the President. I, as Secretary of Defense, act as agent for the President.

As I saw it, the changes which had been made since 1947 had recognized two highly significant facts. First, it is clear that our international political problems and our military problems are now indivisible. On the one hand we have global commitments growing out of our position of world leadership. On the other, the vast strides made in communications and means of transportation have shrunk both the time and distance factors which influence our relationships throughout the world. The need is for a capability to react quickly with both strength and restraint. The importance of any action which the United States may take anywhere in the world is so great that it must be carefully considered and decided upon at the highest levels of our Government. Second, it is equally clear that the role of the Joint Chiefs of Staff has significantly changed. No longer is their influence greatest as chiefs of their respective Services. Rather, as members of the Joint Chiefs of Staff in the command channel from the President to the Unified and Specified Commanders, their greatest influence is in the strategic dispositions and employment of our combined forces deployed throughout the world.

Each of these changes was fundamental to the relationships of the leadership in the Department of Defense. Each necessitated a rethinking of old concepts and a new approach to traditional ways of doing things.

PLANNING-PROGRAMMING-BUDGETING

The President's charge to me was a two-pronged one—to determine what forces were required and to procure and support them as economically as possible. As I have described, this had to be done in an atmosphere of necessary change already in process. The decisions required were and are numerous, complex, and of the greatest importance. But the mechanism of decision-making left something to be desired from my viewpoint—the viewpoint of active managership.

We had to begin with a thorough reexamination and analysis of the contingencies we might face worldwide. I considered that we were too slow to develop the alternatives and the decisions as to the numbers and types of forces we really needed.

Our problems of choice among alternatives in strategy and in weapon systems have been complicated enormously by the bewildering array of entirely workable alternative courses which our technology can support. We believe the Nation can afford whatever investment in national security is necessary. The difficult question is "What is required?" It is far more difficult to build a defense program on this kind of foundation than it is to set a budget ceiling and then squeeze into it whatever programs you can. However difficult, this is exactly what we set out to do.

We first took a major step forward in the development of our planning, programing, and budget process.

To be really meaningful the defense program must be looked at in its entirety with each of its elements considered in light of the total program. This can only be done at the Department of Defense level. For example, the size of the POLARIS force cannot be determined in terms of the Navy shipbuilding program or even the entire Navy program, but can be validly judged only in relation to all of the other elements of the Strategic Retaliatory Forces —the B–52's, the ATLAS, the TITAN, and the MINUTEMAN ICBM's. Similarly, the requirement for Air Force tactical fighters cannot be determined independently of the requirement for Army ground forces.

To make such a review a reality, a 5-year program was devised presenting the proposed force structure and cost projections in terms of the principal missions of the Defense Department.

In our approach we show just what we are planning to spend on each mission, such as for the strategic retaliatory forces, continental air and missile defenses, general purpose forces (primarily for limited wars), research and development, etc. These categories are further broken down into individual systems and projects. For each mission, you can see how many planes we plan to have, how much investment is involved, what the expected operating costs are, how many personnel are involved. In each case, competing programs and systems are judged on the basis of their contribution to the mission to be accomplished and to the Defense effort as a whole. Balance within a given program and within the entire effort is sought, always with a single overriding objective—the defense of the Nation.

The judgment inherent in this balancing of programs and systems can no longer be intuitive or rely on past experience alone. The range of choice is too broad; the number and type of alternatives too great.

In the selection of weapon systems, in the design of forces, and in determination of the level of the national defense effort, therefore, we are making greater use of a technique called *systems analysis*. Perhaps it is best described as "quantitative common sense."

Systems analysis takes a complex problem and sorts out the tangle of factors. It aims to assist the decision-maker by furnishing him with quantitative estimates of the effectiveness and costs of each of the alternative courses which he could choose. Confronting a multiplicity of options we have turned to analytical techniques to assist us in our choice.

These were two of the primary management tools we put to work—a mission-oriented planning and programing process to assist in defining and balancing the total effort, and systems analysis to assist in the selection of specific weapons systems and courses of action from among potential alternatives. But management tools and techniques are only that—they assist, but *only* assist, in the decision-making process.

I am sure that no significant military problem will ever be *wholly* susceptible to purely quantitative analysis. But every piece of the total problem that can be quantitatively analyzed removes one more piece of uncertainty from our process of making a choice. There are many factors which cannot be adequately quantified and which therefore must be supplemented with judgment seasoned by experience. Furthermore, experience is necessary to determine the relevant questions with which to proceed with any analysis.

I would not, if I could, attempt to substitute analytical techniques for judgment based upon experience. The very development and use of those techniques have placed an even greater premium on that experience and judgment, as issues have been clarified and basic problems exposed to dispassionate examination. The better the factual basis for reflective judgment, the better the judgment is likely to be. The need to provide that factual basis is the reason for emphasizing the analytical technique.

ROLE OF MILITARY LEADERS

There has been some intimation, I know, that I have usurped the decision-making prerogatives of our military leaders. I think they would be the first to say that this is not so. To the contrary, I have encouraged the Joints Chief of Staff to express themselves openly and free of the restraints of their service connections in the interest of the soundest possible defense program for the country. My effort has been to provide to our military leaders and my civilian associates, through every scientific, technical, and management tool available, the best factual basis for judgment which can be produced. But then, that very judgment born of experience must be brought into play.

On many major issues, backgrounds of varied experience lead to different judgments and conclusions as to the best course of action. I am gratified that this is the case! Too often has honest difference been resolved by compromise in the interest of unanimity with the result that the strongest elements favoring each position are lost in the process. The accumulation of individual and collective judgments, however, cannot be substituted for decision. It can only facilitate it, if the philosophy of active management is to be followed. In some cases service interests are involved inevitably. The judgments brought to bear reflect experiences characteristic of the historic viewpoints of particular services. These cases are rare, fortunately, but when they occur they are fraught with controversy. In such circumstances the decision must be mine. Obviously, a decision made in these circumstances cannot satisfy every differing viewpoint—it cannot please every protagonist—but it must be made. I am charged by law with the decision-making responsibility—and I have no hestitancy in making the required decisions, always, of course, subject to the approval of the President.

We must encourage honest differences in views in our deliberations. The exposing of differences and examination of the argumentation supporting these differing views provide the insight necessary for wise decisions—and the times demand the wisest decisions which can be made. It goes without saying, perhaps, that once a decision has been made we all must close ranks and support it.

My constant association with the Joint Chiefs of Staff and my frequent contacts with our senior commanders have served to heighten my admiration for them and their staffs—our military colleagues. Their dedication and ability are unquestioned. The perception and insight with which they approach questions of the gravest magnitude should be as great a source of satisfaction to every American as it is to me.

In my weekly discussions of major issues with the Joint Chiefs of Staff we are frank and candid in our expressions of views. The views of each of us, I know, are influenced by these discussions. Our direct contact is growing closer than that contact has ever been before between the Joint Chiefs of Staff and a Secretary of Defense. Before submitting my views to the Congress on any major issue, before making my annual program and budget presentation to the President and to Congress, and, in fact, before I submit a memorandum to the President on an important matter, I solicit, welcome, and consider the views of the Joint Chiefs of Staff. This is as it should be.

I should add that it is not uncommon to find adherents and opponents of a particular view both among my military advisors and my civilian advisors. Rarely, if ever, is there a division of views along military and civilian lines in the Defense Department—there is a consideration of views and judgments and a decision in the interest of the defense of the Nation.

ACCOMPLISHMENTS AND PROSPECTS

We have had an immense buildup in the military strength of this country in the past 2½ years, but every major decision affecting it was born of controversy within the Defense Department—controversy in the sense of honest difference in views, that is.

During that period, we increased the number of warheads in our strategic nuclear alert forces by 100 percent. We increased the number of combat-ready Army divisions by 45 percent. We increased the number of tactical fighter wings by 30 percent; we increased the expenditures for new Navy ship construction to modernize the fleet by 100 percent. We increased by over 300 percent the size of the forces trained to counter the campaigns of subversion and covert aggression and guerrilla operations which the Communists are emphasizing. Note that the increases are widely different in size. Each of the decisions involved in achieving these increases was the subject of careful analytical evaluation and equally careful and soul-searching judgment—differences of opinion were encouraged to sharpen our focus on issues and help in reaching decision.

I am convinced that the defense program has moved ahead. I think we can appraise our progress in terms of the immediate combat-readiness and size of the forces we now have. I am fully aware that the application of my management philosophy—that of active management at the top—has caused some wrenching strains in the Department as new thought-patterns have been substituted for old. I am convinced, nevertheless, that the strains have been worth it and that the Department has taken on the vital outlook which I believed it should in the interest of the best defense for the Nation.

It has been suggested in some quarters that I am unwilling to decentralize decision-making authority. Nothing could be farther from the truth. I strongly believe in the pyramid nature of decision-making and that, within that frame, decision-making should be pushed to the lowest level in the organization that has the ability and information available to apply approved policy. The defense effort is entirely too big, too complex, and too geographically dispersed for its operations to be managed from a single control point. Our effort has been to create a framework of policy within which meaningful decentralization of operations can be accomplished. However, before we can effectively decentralize we must develop an organizational structure which will permit us to proceed to true decentralized decision-making rather than to management anarchy.

Too often responsibility and authority have been so fragmented by overlapping and diffused organizational arrangements within the Department as to make it virtually impossible to pinpoint responsibility. In such situations decentralization of decision-making authority is unwise, if not impossible. As a matter of fact, in these circumstances decisions must be made at higher levels in the Department—often at the very top—because no one else has the clear authority to make them. The organization itself must be so structured as to clearly define the lines of authority and responsibility. We completed the development of the Defense Communications Agency which already had been set up and established additional Department-wide agencies such as the Defense Supply Agency and the Defense Intelligence Agency to accomplish exactly those purposes. This has permitted us to begin the decentralization of decision-making that we want.

Before I finish my tour of duty in the Department of Defense, I hope we will have established an approach to the job—a philosophy of management and a foundation of military security —that my successors will be able to build upon and strengthen. I think each large organization goes through a period of evaluation when the patterns of the future are formed, when the intellectual framework for decisions is established, when the administrative techniques are sharpened, when the organization structure takes shape. I believe that the Department of Defense is in such a period today.

We have expressed a management philosophy and developed a management concept which we are following, and from which we are trying to establish procedures. We believe the Department, the Congress, and the country will benefit from this effort as we pursue the basic objective—the defense of the Nation.

2

DECISION-MAKING IN THE DEPARTMENT OF DEFENSE*

By Robert S. McNamara

What I want to talk to you about is the problem of decision-making in the Defense Department, and the way we are trying to approach the problem.

The Department of Defense is responsible for spending nearly 10% of the national income of this country. It employs 3.7 million Americans directly, in and out of uniform, and millions more indirectly in every aspect of our economic life. It absorbs over half of every tax dollar, as it has done for over a decade.

All of this is well enough known. If anything, the potential dangers of this so-called "military-industrial complex" have been overstated rather than understated in recent months. But at risk of repeating the obvious, let me point out once again that this unavoidably vast establishment exists for one purpose and one purpose only: to act as the servant of United States foreign policy. Our responsibility is to provide this nation with the means to safeguard its legitimate interests and to meet its commitments at home and around the world. The Defense Department exists to serve that purpose, and to serve none other.

Yet, although it is easy enough to say in a few words what our purpose is, the translation of this purpose into decisions on force levels, on contingency war planning, on weapons developments— and cancellations—on reorganizations, on all the range of decisions which shape our defense establishment, cannot be readily or easily deduced from the general principles. You probably remember General Marshall's shrewd remark: "Don't ask me to say we agree in principle; that just means we haven't agreed yet."

What I want to do is to outline . . . how we are trying to translate these general principles, on which all Americans would agree our defense policy should be based, into specific decisions that will effectively carry through those general principles. These specific decisions will inevitably and properly remain the subject of searching, even harsh, criticism. We are, after all, dealing with issues which could affect the very life of this nation, indeed the life of a great part of this planet. We cannot and do not claim

---

*From Remarks before the American Society of Newspaper Editors at the Statler-Hilton Hotel, Washington, D. C., 20 April 1963, DOD Press Release No. 548–63, with omissions.

infallibility. Only the future can tell when and where we have been right, when and where we have been wrong. We can only do our best to approach these problems as sensibly and realistically as we know how.

Let me start with two points which seem to me axiomatic. The first is that, at least within any range of defense spending that is likely to appear at all desirable in the foreseeable future, the United States is well able to spend whatever it needs to spend on national security. The second point is that this ability does not excuse us from applying strict standards of effectiveness and efficiency to the way we spend our defense dollars.

· · · · · · · · · · · · · · ·

Every dollar we spend inefficiently or ineffectively is not only an unnecessary addition to the arms race which threatens all mankind, but an unfair burden on the taxpayer, or an unwise diversion of resources which could be invested elsewhere to serve our national interests at home or abroad, or a dollar that could, even if kept in the military budget, be invested in something that would better strengthen our military posture. The fact that we cannot be poor enough to grudge the price of our own survival does not mean we are rich enough to squander our resources in the name of national security.

I do not mean to suggest that we can measure national security in terms of dollars—you cannot price what is inherently priceless. But if we are to avoid talking in generalities, we must talk about dollars: for policy decisions must sooner or later be expressed in the form of budget decisions on where to spend and how much.

· · · · · · · · · · · · · · ·

BUDGETARY REFORMS

It is ... in the ... area ... of increasing the effectiveness and efficiency of our military establishment that controversy has developed. Not that there was much disagreement about the need: for years everyone who has thought seriously about the Department of Defense has felt that major improvements were needed. The solutions offered ranged from drastic proposals for complete unification of the armed forces to vague suggestions about "cutting the fat out of the military budget."

Thus, there was a national consensus here that reforms were in order. But there was no consensus on just what should be done. And there was an additional and inevitable human problem. For these reforms would necessarily take the shape of changes in the traditional ways of doing things, and limitations on the customary ways of spending defense money. It is inevitable that people will take more easily to suggestion that they should have more money to spend, as in the improvement of our nuclear and non-nuclear capabilities, than to suggestions that they must spend less, or that they must abandon established ways of doing things. Yet the very substantial increases in the budget which we felt necessary added a further strong incentive, if any were needed, to move ahead on these problems of increasing efficiency and effectiveness.

The first and most important thing to notice about the effort in this area is what it is *not*. It is *not* an effort to save dollars at the expense of military effectiveness. What we are trying to do can be divided into two parts: the first is essentially a series of management reforms of the kind you will find in any well-run organization, an effort which is in large part covered by the formal Five Year Cost Reduction Program we set up in July 1962. The common characteristic of reforms in this part of the effort is that they have very little, if anything, to do with military effectiveness, one way or the other. They neither increase nor decrease our military effectiveness; they merely save money by introducing more efficient methods of doing things.

. . . .

The second, and really the more important, part of the effort does bear directly on military effectiveness. Although dollar savings are sometimes an important by-product, here the essential point is to increase military effectiveness. For example, we found that the three military departments had been establishing their requirements independently of each other. I think the results can fairly be described as chaotic: the Army planning, for example, was based primarily on a long war of attrition, while the Air Force planning was based, largely, on a short war of nuclear bombardment. Consequently, the Army was stating a requirement for stocking months of fighting supplies against the event of a sizable conventional conflict, while the Air Force stock requirements for such a war had to be measured in days, and not very many days at that. Either approach, consistently followed, might make some sense. The two combined could not possibly make sense. What we needed was a coordinated strategy seeking objectives actually attainable with the military resources available.

We are moving with all reasonable speed towards a properly balanced force structure. I say with all reasonable speed because there would be enormous practical difficulties in trying to get this job done overnight. But we are moving as fast as we sensibly can to balance men against supplies; deployable divisions against sea and airlift capability to handle those divisions; ground combat units against tactical air squadrons to support those units.

· · · · · · · · · · · · · · · · ·

The new form of budget for the first time grouped together for planning purposes units which must fight together in the event of war. The Navy strategic force, the POLARIS submarines, are considered together with the Air Force Strategic Air Command; Navy general purpose forces are considered together with the Army and Marine divisions and the Air Force Tactical Air Command. This kind of reform provides substantial improvement in the effectiveness of our military establishment. Even where it does not lead directly to lower expenditures, it is economical in the true sense of the word; that is, it gives us the maximum national security obtainable from the dollars we do spend. We can imagine many different kinds of wars the United States must be prepared to fight, but a war in which the Army fights independently of the Navy, or the Navy independently of the Air Force, is not one of them. Quite obviously, the coordination of the planning of the four Services makes eminently good sense on the narrowest military grounds.

So I would repeat: it is a mistake to equate our efforts towards improving effectiveness and efficiency solely with a desire to save money. That is very important. But military effectiveness is even more important. Money savings are what is easiest to talk about: for it is easy to explain something in terms of saving X hundreds of millions of dollars, and complicated to get into the details of planning and logistics, and the like. But the fact is that the total effort is aimed *both* at saving money and improving military effectiveness. And it is the latter, improving the effectiveness of our military establishment, which is the first priority, for it is the latter which directly affects national security.

Where the situation becomes more complicated is when decisions must be made on requested force level increases or development or procurement of new weapons.

The first thing to remember is that adding a weapon to our inventory is not necessarily synonymous with adding to our national security.

The second thing to remember is that even if we were to draft every scientist and engineer in the country into weapons development work, we could still develop only a fraction of the systems that are proposed. We must pick and choose very carefully among the proposals to get the ones on which we should actually proceed. This process of choice must begin with a requirement for solid indications that a proposed system would really add something to our national security. Even then, we still have to pick and choose, but we cannot even seriously consider going ahead with a full-scale weapons system development until that basic requirement has been met.

. . . .

HOW MUCH IS ENOUGH?

What I have been suggesting . . . is that the question of how to spend our defense dollars and how much to spend is a good deal more complicated than is often assumed. It cannot be assumed that a new weapon would really add to our national security, no matter how attractive the weapon can be made to seem, looked at by itself. Anyone who has been exposed to so-called "brochuremanship" knows that even the most outlandish notions can be dressed up to look superficially attractive. You have to consider a very wide range of issues—the missions our forces must be prepared to perform, the effects of a proposed system on the stability of the military situation in the world, the alternatives open to us for performing the missions required.

You cannot make decisions simply by asking yourself whether something might be nice to have. You have to make a judgment on how much is enough.

I emphasize judgment because you can't even be sure yourself, much less prove to others, that your decision was precisely right to the last dollar—even to the last billion dollars. But the decision has to be made.

There is an important difference between the way we make these tough decisions today, and the way they used to be made. Formerly, an arbitrary budget ceiling was fixed for national defense, and funds were then apportioned among the Services. Today we examine all our military needs, and then decide at what point our military strength is in balance with the requirements of our foreign policy.

There are, of course, sharp differences of opinion on where we should spend our marginal defense dollars. And here is where the responsibility most clearly falls on the Secretary of Defense, because here is where it must fall not only constitutionally but under any rational system. For these decisions can only be made from the point of view of the defense establishment as a whole, not from the point of view of the individual Services. Indeed the very biggest decisions—such as the basic kinds of forces we need, and the occasions on which we might want to commit those forces —must be made at an even higher level: for they involve basic questions of national policy which transcend the interest of the Defense Department, or the State Department, or indeed any part of the government, and must be made at the Presidential level.

Earlier, I described the chaotic situation that resulted from the individual Services deciding unilaterally what kind of defense preparations were most urgently needed. Each of the Services had a different concept of what kinds of wars we should be prepared to fight, with the result that the forces under the Army, Navy and Air Force simply did not fit together in the way they must to maximize their combat effectiveness. Now this same problem comes up when the Services recommend weapons systems. There is nothing wrong with that. It is inevitable. The Services properly fight hard for their viewpoints. This is probably the greatest single advantage of having separate Services, instead of one unified Service. But as a practical matter, although it is important to consider a variety of alternative policies, at the end we must have one defense policy, not three conflicting defense policies. And it is the job of the Secretary and his staff to make sure that this is the case, just as it is the job of the President to see that we have one national security policy, and not a series of conflicting policies in the State Department, the Treasury, the Defense Department, and so forth.

There is nothing innately desirable about centralization. But the fact remains that when national security decisions affect broad interests they must be made from a central point, not from subordinate points each specially concerned with one part of the forest—and not even by a committee made up of representatives of the different parts of the forest. For the nature of committees is to compromise their special interests, which is not the same as making the decision from the point of view of the national interest.

The Secretary of Defense—and I am talking about any Secretary of Defense—must make certain kinds of decisions, not because he presumes his judgment to be superior to his advisors, military or civilian, but because his position is the best place from which to make those decisions.

This same kind of argument applies when economic interests affected by defense decisions generate, as they inevitably will, political pressures on defense officials. Such pressures are an intrinsic and necessary part of a democratic political process. There are a good many advantages in forcing public officials to listen to people outside of their own staffs who do not share their views and assumptions. But it is the duty of government officials, representing the national interest rather than any smaller interest, to stand up to these pressures where what is asked cannot be reconciled with the national interest.

No single speech can do justice to the full complexity of defense decision-making. But at heart the problem comes down, always, to the same questions: What is really in our national interest? What will help this country to play the role we want it to play in this terribly critical period of the world's history? We are interested in saving money, in alleviating economic hardships from base closings and the like, in sound military-civilian relations, in the whole range of issues which tend to dominate the headlines. But the national interest towers above them all; and it is the national interest, above all, that we seek to serve.

3

THE FORMULATION OF POLITICAL OBJECTIVES AND THEIR IMPACT ON THE BUDGET*

By Robert S. McNamara

. . . .

Senator Jackson. Mr. Secretary . . . could you indicate to us how you go about formulating the defense budget? We have had guidelines in the past. I do not mean you should do this in great detail; I do not want to place that burden on you. But you might consider in general terms fiscal year 1963, just what the procedures are, whether you have budget ceilings, guidelines, and so on.

Secretary McNamara. Yes; we start with the political objective, the formulation of which is presented to us by the Secretary of State and upon which the President indicates his desires that we develop a military program that will support the political objective.

As you know, the President has stated that the defense budget is to be established without regard to arbitrary ceilings.

We determine the force levels which we believe are necessary to support the political objective and then act to fulfill the President's second direction to us. He has indicated that we are to attain the specific force levels necessary to support the political objective at the lowest cost.

Every effort is made to do that.

Now, further, I would say that the budget process in the full sense of the word will be a continuing one, that we expect to lay out a budget or an operating plan, operating military program, covering a sufficiently long period of time so that the period covered by the plan or the budget will equal or exceed the longest leadtime of the actions included in that budget.

This means that the plan must cover at least 5 years.

We then propose to maintain that plan or budget up to date with monthly revisions to it so that at any particular time when a budget for a special period, such as the fiscal year, is required,

*Excerpts from testimony before the Subcommittee on National Policy Machinery of the Committee on Government Operations, U.S. Senate, on 7 August 1961. *Hearings, Organizing for National Security: State, Defense, and the National Security Council,* Part IX (87th Cong., 1st Session; Washington: U.S. Government Printing Office, 1961), pp. 1193–1194, 1195, 1218-1219.

it can be abstracted from the continually modified and continually adjusted military program.

Senator Jackson. So that in your initial effort, which is to provide that force level sufficient to carry out the strategy set by the President in consultation with you and the Secretary of State, there is no arbitrary budget ceiling?

Secretary McNamara. There is not.

Senator Jackson. And the effort you are making is to achieve the forces necessary to implement our strategic objectives.

Secretary McNamara. And to achieve those at the lowest possible cost.

. . . .

Senator Jackson. Do you feel that the planning that you are now engaged in in the Department of Defense . . . can . . . be very helpful in avoiding waste and in putting you in a better position to assist the State Department and the National Security Council in achieving the long-range objectives that the President will set in the future?

Secretary McNamara. Yes. I think the planning ahead can lead, for example, to a much closer and more efficient relationship between our procurement programs and technological advances and technological changes thereby avoiding waste that might otherwise occur.

. . . .

Senator Jackson. What steps have you taken to insure that budget decisions will be properly related to policy decisions? In other words, if an agreed-upon policy is worked out at the NSC level, what followthrough is there to make sure that the Department of Defense will have the necessary ability to implement the decision?

Secretary McNamara. I consider the budget nothing more than and nothing less than the quantitative expression of a plan or a policy.

So in developing the budget I propose to start with the plan or the policy and translate it into quantitative terms, terms of benefit and cost. This you might contrast with a budget that starts without any specific policy or plan but is based on meeting a specific dollar ceiling.

We are not starting that way. We are starting with the policy or the plan as the case may be and developing a quantitative expression of that in terms of our military force levels and military requirements.

Senator Jackson. In other words, what you are trying to do is work out a long-range strategic plan and make sure that the budget decisions you make reflect the objectives in the plan.

Secretary McNamara. Yes; exactly so.

Senator Jackson. Do you feel that progress is being made in that direction?

Secretary McNamara. I do.

. . . .

4

THE FOUNDATION FOR DEFENSE PLANNING
AND BUDGETING*

By Robert S. McNamara

Secretary McNamara. . . .

Mr. Chairman, members of the committee, this is the third Defense program and budget it has been my privilege to present to this committee. Again, my prepared statement is arranged in the same manner in which the Defense program is developed; namely in terms of the principal missions of the Defense Establishment, rather than by organizational component or by budget category. Attached to each copy is a set of related tables which you may wish to follow as we proceed through the statement.

. . . .

By and large, we have projected our forces and programs through fiscal year 1969, 5 years beyond the current fiscal year. As I pointed out last year, the further into the future we project these programs the more provisional they should be considered. Changes will inevitably have to be made as we move along, and entirely new projects whose need we cannot now clearly foresee will have to be added. I have attempted in this statement to note the more important changes that have taken place since I appeared here last year and to explain the reasons why they were made.

Throughout the statement I will be discussing costs in terms of "total obligational authority" (TOA), that is, the full cost of an annual increment of a program regardless of the year in which the funds are authorized, appropriated, or expended. These costs will differ, in many cases, from the amounts requested for authorization and appropriation, especially in the procurement accounts where certain prior year funds are available to finance 1965 programs. Moreover, most of my discussion will deal with the total cost of a program, including the directly attributable costs of military personnel and operation and maintenance, as well as procurement, research and development, and military construction.

Throughout the preparation of the fiscal year 1965–69 program

---

*Excerpts from testimony before the House Appropriations Committee. *Hearings, Department of Defense Appropriations for 1965*, Part 4 (88th Cong., 2d Session; Washington: U.S. Government Printing Office, 1964), pp. 3-7, 304-306.

and the fiscal year 1965 budget, we have been guided by the same two general instructions given to me originally by President Kennedy and reemphasized so strongly by President Johnson; namely, to develop the force structure necessary to meet our military requirements without regard to arbitrary budget ceilings or predetermined financial limits, and to procure and operate this force at the lowest possible cost.

As I have pointed out in previous appearances before this committee, in adding to a Defense program as large as the one we now have, we soon encounter the law of diminishing returns, where each additional increment of resources used produces a proportionately smaller increment of overall defense capability. While the benefits to be gained from each additional increment cannot be measured with precision, careful cost/effectiveness analyses can greatly assist in eliminating those program proposals which clearly contribute little to our military strength in terms of the costs involved.

This principle is just as applicable to qualitative improvements in weapons systems as it is to quantitative increases in our forces. The relevant question is not only "Do we want the very best for our military force?", but also, "Is the additional capability truly required and, if so, is this the least costly way of attaining it?"

Let me give you one hypothetical example to illustrate the point. Suppose we have two tactical fighter aircraft which are identical in every important measure of performance, except one—aircraft A can fly 10 miles per hour faster than aircraft B. However, aircraft A costs $10,000 more per unit than aircraft B. Thus, if we need about 1,000 aircraft, the total additional cost would be $10 million.

If we approach this problem from the viewpoint of a given amount of resources, the additional combat effectiveness represented by the greater speed of aircraft A would have to be weighed against the additional combat effectiveness which the same $10 million could produce if applied to other defense purposes—more aircraft B, more or better aircraft munitions, or more ships, or even more military family housing. And if we approach the problem from the point of view of a given amount of combat capability, we would have to determine whether that given amount could be achieved at less cost by buying, for example, more of aircraft B or more aircraft munitions or better munitions, or perhaps surface-to-surface missiles. Thus, the fact that aircraft A flies 10 miles per hour faster than aircraft B is not conclusive, We still have to determine whether the greater speed is worth the greater cost. This kind of determination is the heart of the planning, programming, budgeting, or resources allocation problem within the Defense Department.

Through the rigorous application of these policies, principles and techniques and through the cost reduction program which I will discuss later, we were able in our program and budget reviews to reduce our fiscal year 1965 budget request, including military assistance, from about $61 billion proposed by the services and defense agencies to approximately $50.9 billion, a reduction of about $10 billion. . . .

. . . .

ASSESSMENT OF THE INTERNATIONAL SITUATION AS IT BEARS ON MILITARY POLICIES AND PROGRAMS

When I appeared before this committee 2 years ago, our attention was focused particularly on the Berlin crisis, which had been precipitated by the Soviet Union in the summer of 1961. Last year when I appeared here, the Nation and, indeed, the entire world had just experienced perhaps the gravest crisis in recent history, again precipitated by the Soviet Union, this time in Cuba. And, on the other side of the world, Communist China had created still another crisis with its attack on the northern frontiers of India.

This year, although the struggle for ideological, political, economic, and military advantage continues in many parts of the world, we have not been confronted with any new crisis provoked by the Soviet Union and no new armed aggression has been undertaken by Communist China. Indeed, as far as the Soviet Union is concerned, the Cuban crisis of October 1962 seems to have marked the crest of the latest in the series of crises cycles engendered by that country since the end of World War II. We now appear to be on the downward slope of this latest cycle and tensions in our relations with the Soviet Union are easing. Within the last 12 months, all of the Soviet combat units in Cuba have been removed, although several thousand training and technical personnel still remain there; after years of negotiation, agreement has finally been reached on a limited nuclear test ban; and just last December Chairman Khrushchev announced a 4-percent cut in the Soviet defense budget and hinted at reductions in military personnel. Far less tangible but perhaps just as significant is the change in the demeanor of Soviet diplomacy.

What do these developments presage for the future? Has there been a basic change in Soviet policy toward the United States and the free world, or do these developments simply reflect a change in tactics forced upon the Soviet Union by events beyond its control? The answers to these questions are of crucial importance not only to our foreign policy but to our military policies and programs as well.

I do not believe we can reasonably assume that these manifestations of a change in policy reflect a change in the ultimate objective of the Soviet leadership, which is to extend the sway of communism over the rest of the world. Their dispute with the leadership of Communist China is not over the ultimate objective but how it is to be achieved and who is to control the worldwide Communist movement. Expansionism is so deeply engrained in Communist doctrine that it would be naive for us to expect any Communist leader to repudiate it.

Much more likely, these apparent changes in policy were brought about by forces and pressures beyond the control of the Soviet leadership. What are some of these forces?

First and foremost among them, I would list the substantial buildup in our own military strength during the last 3 years, both for general and for limited war. . . .

Second, I would list our demonstrated willingness to risk using these forces in defense of our vital interests. . . .

Third, I would list our continuing efforts to assist other free nations in defending their sovereignty and in building a better future for their people. Our military and economic aid to such nations, particularly those on the periphery of the Communist bloc, has given them a more desirable alternative to communism and has made them less vulnerable to Communist penetration and subversion.

Fourth, I would list the economic difficulties being encountered by both the Soviet Union and Communist China, particularly the failure of their agricultural programs. The recently announced reduction in the Soviets' defense budget and the slowdown in their foreign aid and space programs are, no doubt, related directly to the recently announced massive investment in their chemical industry. As I pointed out last year, the resources and capabilities of the Soviet Union are by no means unlimited. The stress and strain imposed on the economy by their military and space programs, their efforts to raise the standard of living of the people and compete with the United States in foreign aid were becoming increasingly apparent even then. That is why we concluded a year ago—

* * * that the strain of so many competing claims on the Soviet economy will tend to limit the size and help determine the character of the Soviet military program at least over the next few years.

Finally, I would list our own policy of holding the door wide open to proposals for lessening world tensions, for reaching agreements on nuclear tests, and for bringing the armaments race to a halt. This policy has presented the Soviet Union an alternative to the cold war. How far the Soviet leadership will go in accepting it is still to be seen.

If this analysis is correct, then our future course is clear. We must continue to maintain powerful and ready military forces. We must continue to demonstrate our willingness to risk their use where our vital interests are at stake. We must continue to hold out a helping hand to those nations directly exposed to Communist aggression and to those nations which are striving to provide a better life for their people. And we must continue to keep open the door to peace.

As President Kennedy said at the time the limited test ban treaty was signed in Moscow:

> This treaty is not the millenium. It will not resolve all conflicts, or cause the Communists to forego their ambition, or eliminate the dangers of war. It will not reduce our need for arms, or allies, or programs of assistance to others.

Nothing has occurred in the intervening months to change that assessment. Notwithstanding the economic difficulties now being experienced within the Communist camp, as long as political and economic instability continues to exist in so many countries around the world, both the Soviet Union and the Chinese Communists will find many low-cost opportunities to carry on their assault on freedom and to spread the doctrine of communism. The fact that they are now competing with one another in trying to win the allegiance of uncommitted nations may actually increase our difficulties, since it may well stimulate them to even greater efforts in penetrating the more vulnerable areas of the world.

Thus, the struggle against communism is far from over and although the prospects for peace look somewhat more encouraging than they have for many years, this is not the time to relax our efforts and cut back our national security programs.

.   .   .   .

The basic objective of the management system we are introducing and trying to operate, is to establish a rational foundation as opposed to an emotional foundation for the decisions as to what size force and what type of force this country will maintain. This rational structure, this intellectual foundation for determining the military forces we should build and support is something that is laid out on paper. It is laid out first in the form of an analysis of the potential contingency war plans for a variety of situations and, then, a translation of those war plans into military forces. And finally, that force structure must be translated into programs and budgets. There is no reason in the world why this cannot be continued in the future. As matter of fact, I think it must be continued in the future, and I think, if the executive branch does not continue it, Congress itself can force a continuation of it.

Mr. Flood. Would you not consider that your greatest legacy rather than a line of hard decisions?

Secretary McNamara. I do not like to take credit.

Mr. Flood. The language is mine.

Secretary McNamara. Yes; I want to strike this out of the record.

Mr. Flood. It was a leading question. Leave it in.

Secretary McNamara. The answer is "Yes, indeed." The introduction of a rational foundation for military force planning, to be quite frank with you, is what we are trying to establish.

Mr. Flood. If you have a monument, you prefer it rather than striking out a series of programs.

Secretary McNamara. Once one has a rational foundation from which to begin, it is relatively easy to decide not to have a particular weapons system, the requirement for which cannot be found in the rationalization of the program.

Mr. Flood. I have always been concerned about this with you, that in your eagerness to do what you have done so well, that you are not Alexander the Great and break down and cry because there are no other hard decisions to make, if you know what I mean.

Secretary McNamara. There are a few left I can think of, not the least of which is the naval shipyard problem.

Mr. Laird. When you get into this area of decisionmaking, you are relying more and more on cost effectiveness studies?

Secretary McNamara. No; I think not. We are relying more and more upon sophisticated analyses of potential political-military conflicts and an appraisal of the advantage to the United States of alternative force sizes in relation to those contingencies, and the various applications of those forces in those contingencies. The cost effectiveness study as it would be narrowly defined—

Mr. Laird. On systems you sometimes get into this.

Secretary McNamara (continuing). As it would be narrowly defined comes into importance only in choosing between alternative means of satisfying an established force requirement.

Let me illustrate by this—

Mr. Laird. You had a good illustration in your statement between aircraft A and B.

Secretary McNamara. I think that is a very good illustration of the point.

The cost effectiveness study as it is narrowly thought of is applicable when we are trying to decide to buy aircraft A or aircraft B, one having a 10-mile-per-hour advantage over the other at a specific cost increase.

The basic question, first, is, Should we have either one of them, and to determine whether or not you should have either aircraft, and to determine whether you should have 100 or 200 or 1,000 of them, requires a rather sophisticated analysis of the potential threat, and our potential responses to it under a variety of circumstances. When I say we are trying to establish a rational foundation for our military forces, I am thinking of exactly that kind of analysis.

Mr. Laird. Mr. Secretary, the thing that bothers me and worries me, as you look to the future, we also must be sure that our opponent is making his decisions on that same type of basis.

Secretary McNamara. No. I would say we must try to anticipate what our opponent's forces will be, and how he will apply them. But it is not essential that he make his decisions on the same basis we do.

What is certainly desirable is that we be able to predict his decisions with a certain amount of accuracy, or if we feel we cannot predict them accurately, that we establish the proper range within which his decisions most likely will fall, and we plan for both the low end and the high end of that range of possible decisions.

Mr. Laird. You know what the 10-mile-an-hour lead the Jap Zero meant in the early stages of the war. If this, probably, would have been decided on a cost-effectiveness basis, the Japanese would not have cranked this 10-mile advantage into that plane.

Secretary McNamara. I think they would have, yes, indeed.

Mr. Laird. Would we now?

Secretary McNamara. Oh, yes. In that kind of a situation, absolutely. Every one of our decisions is based on the recognition of what I call a range of uncertainty. You saw it in our discussion of the adequacy of the strategic forces.

The strategic theory that stems from the "overkill" argument does not do this. It does not provide adequately for the range of uncertainty. We are not certain, and we know we will never be certain, as to the number or the exact type of Soviet missiles when we are predicting 2, 3, or 5 years ahead, so we estimate a range for these variable factors and build our forces, so that they would be effective even if the pessimistic factors included in that range of estimate turn out to be correct.

Mr. Laird. The question is the range?

Secretary McNamara. Yes.

Mr. Laird. The range factor here is all-important with your state of technology?

Secretary McNamara. Absolutely. We must consider the full range of uncertainties when making these important decisions.

Mr. Laird. You need 5 and probably 7 years, do you not?

Secretary McNamara. It depends on the specific decision. If you are talking about simply buying an additional number of MINUTEMEN ICBM's which are already designed—

Mr. Laird. That is a different problem.

Secretary McNamara (continuing). We need a leadtime of only 2 or 3 years. If you are talking about being prepared to face a potential Soviet technological development sometime in the future, then we probably will need 5 to 7 years, as you suggest. I think it puts a great premium, therefore, on the skill with which we predict their actions.

We spend a considerable amount of time looking into the possible actions they may take and insuring that the plans we have underway today adequately protect against those uncertainties. This is one reason we increased the research and development budget roughly 40 percent between fiscal years 1961 and 1963, excluding the research and development cost on systems approved for deployment. The roughly 40-percent increase I am talking about is simply on research and development for systems not yet approved for deployment. We did it simply because we wanted to protect ourselves against potential technological breakthroughs by the Soviets.

5

THE DEPARTMENT OF DEFENSE BUDGET AND THE NATIONAL ECONOMY*

By Charles J. Hitch

. . . .

The close relationship between foreign policy and Defense policy has long been widely recognized and this understanding can now be taken for granted. There are very few major Defense Department decisions today which do not also involve foreign policy and, obviously, foreign policy decisions frequently have great bearing on Defense programs and operations. Similarly, we all understand the important influence of science and technology on Defense policies and programs. But for the President, the harmonizing of economic-fiscal and Defense policies is one of the most important and difficult problems that must be faced.

And let me point out right at the outset that this is one of the most important and difficult problems with which the head of government in any major nation has to deal. The naive notion, which was prevalent in some quarters not many years ago, that the Communist governments did not have to cope with this problem should, by now, be completely dispelled by the growing awareness of the critical economic problems encountered by those governments in recent years. As long as we live in a world in which resources are limited in relation to wants, every government must make choices on how available resources are to be allocated among the nation's wants. Because Communist China and even the Soviet Union have far less resources at their disposal than we do, the problem of allocation is just that more intense for them. For example, the limited availability of resources in relation to needs sets very definite limits on the overall size of their military efforts. Although per capita gross national product in the Soviet Union is far greater than in Communist China, the Soviet leaders find themselves hard pressed to provide for the continued growth of the Soviet economy, the support of science and technology, the expansion of foreign aid, etc., while at the same time satisfying the growing expectations of the Soviet people for a better life and a higher standard of living. For Communist China, this

---

*Address before the joint assembly of the National War College and the Industrial College of the Armed Forces, Washington, D. C., 19 October 1964, with omissions.

problem is most acute. Their choice, at the moment, is between investment for economic growth and current consumption. They have been forced to reallocate available resources from the expansion of their productive facilities to current consumption, and the "great leap forward" has ended as a step backwards.

But even in the United States, with by far the highest per capita gross national product in the world, the Government is still hard pressed to meet all the demands made upon it—more defense, more welfare, more highways, etc.—*and* lower tax rates. At the same time, the Government is charged with the responsibility for maintaining full employment with a stable price level, as was explicitly set forth in the Employment Act of 1946. All of these competing demands must be brought into balance, year by year. But the problem of resources allocation at the national level does not end there. We have learned from hard experience during the last seven years that we must also maintain a balance in our financial transactions with the rest of the world. For many years no one worried about this problem except specialists in the field of international finance, since it seemed to concern only other countries. But, since 1958, we have all become acquainted with it. We have learned that the United States, too, can have balance of payments deficits and that, when they do occur and persist for a period of years, they come to influence the conduct of all our programs which involve expenditures in other countries—including defense.

DEFENSE EXPENDITURES AND THE BALANCE OF PAYMENTS

I am sure you are familiar with the many actions the Defense Department has taken in the last four or five years to help solve this national problem. We have reduced our dollar expenditures in other countries, and have also greatly increased our receipts from the sale of military goods and services to other countries. The net deficit in the balance of payments, on military account, has been cut from about $2.7 billion in CY 1960 to about $1.6 billion, estimated, for CY 1964.

This result was not easily achieved. We have had to review in detail all of our procurements overseas and divert to United States sources those which could be made here within a reasonable cost penalty. We have taken steps to reduce our employment of foreign nationals overseas and the manning levels of our own overseas headquarters. Wherever possible, without adversely affecting our combat potential, we have redeployed military units back to the United States and closed unneeded military installations overseas. And, finally, we have persuaded some of our Allies, notably Germany, to increase substantially their procurement of military materiel and services from the United States.

Defense spending overseas, of course, is by no means the only factor contributing to our balance of payments problem. Another major factor has been the flow of long-term U.S. capital abroad. It is ironic that even countries enjoying substantial surpluses in their balance of payments have also been borrowing in United States capital markets. They do so because long-term investment funds are cheaper in the United States and more readily available as a result of the more efficient organization of our money markets. It was for this reason that the Administration proposed and the Congress enacted an interest equalization tax on purchases of foreign securities by Americans from foreigners. Although this new tax was just recently enacted, the mere announcement that the Administration would request such a law had already greatly reduced long-term borrowing by foreigners in the United States.

To meet the related problem of short-term capital outflow, the Government has been maintaining short-term interest rates at a level competitive with money markets in other countries. For example, 90-day Treasury bills which yielded $2\frac{1}{2}$ percent in mid-1961 now yield nearly $3\frac{1}{2}$ percent.

As a result of all of the actions taken by the United States Government, the overall balance of payments deficit in 1964 should be reduced to about $2 billion compared with nearly $4 billion four years ago. The solution of the balance of payments problem is of special significance to the Defense Department because continuing large deficits could, over the long run, force a reconsideration of our basic overseas deployments and thereby adversely affect our entire military posture.

Over the long run, a fundamental improvement in our international payments position depends upon our ability to achieve greater industrial efficiency, to maintain price stability, and to utilize more of our savings at home. The first two are objectives which we would want to achieve in any event, and we have been fairly successful in doing so. We have not, however, in recent years, succeeded in achieving a still more important economic objective; namely, the full use of our economic potential. Although the Gross National Product, in constant prices, has been increasing at the rate of about 4 percent since 1960, unemployment, except for a very few months, has continued to exceed 5 percent of the civilian labor force. The President's Council of

Economic Advisers estimates that GNP would have to be $30 to $40 billion higher to reduce unemployment to about 4 percent of the labor force. Putting it another way, the reduction of unemployment to 4 percent would produce an increase in GNP of $30 to $40 billion.

It was to speed up the rate of economic growth, alleviate the problem of unemployment, increase the efficiency of the American economic system and make investment of capital in the United States more attractive that the Administration pressed the Congress to enact a tax cut. Of course a tax cut of the magnitude enacted this year will, initially, significantly reduce Federal revenue. But when there are substantial unemployed resources in an economy the stimulus to economic activity produced by a tax cut can, within a few years, create a tax base sufficiently larger to more than offset the revenue loss caused by the lower rates. Even under the new tax rates, the Federal Government's revenue is estimated to increase approximately $1.00 for each $4.00 rise in GNP. This, together with the normal growth in GNP, could produce a balanced budget within the near future— provided that no further *major* tax cuts are made and that the growth of Federal expenditures can be held in check. This constraint will be one of the most important connecting links between economic-fiscal policy and the military program in the years immediately ahead.

DEFENSE EXPENDITURES AND THE NATIONAL ECONOMY

This does not mean that military requirements will be subordinated to the requirements of economic and fiscal policy. But it does impose on the Federal Government, and, because of its size particularly on the Defense Department, a special responsibility for the utmost restraint in its demands for additional resources. Nor does it mean that this Administration subscribes to the theory of a balanced budget at all costs in each and every year. To try to achieve such a balance would contribute to making recessions worse and inflationary booms higher and would have a destabilizing effect on the national economy. But by the same token, it is also important to have a budget surplus or at least a balance in years of high economic activity and full employment when potential inflationary pressures are the greatest. Thus, the achievement of full employment and a balanced budget are still the twin objectives of this Administration. But the balanced budget is to be achieved by an increase in economic growth and not by a sharp reduction in Federal expenditures, which, under present conditions, would be self-defeating.

Not only is the Defense program influenced by economic and fiscal policies; the Defense program itself influences those policies. In the early years of the Kennedy Administration, Defense expenditures had to be increased substantially to strengthen our capabilities for limited war and to put in place more quickly those strategic retaliatory weapon systems which offered the best chances of surviving a surprise nuclear attack on the United States. To provide for these requirements, Defense expenditures, excluding military assistance, were increased from $41.2 billion in FY 1960 to nearly $50 billion in FY 1964. In order to overcome the Soviet Union's lead in space research and technology, expenditures for that purpose were increased from $.4 billion to $4.2 billion during the same period while total Federal expenditures were increasing from $76.5 billion to almost $98 billion. Thus, of the total increase in Federal expenditures of about $21 billion, defense and space accounted for nearly $13 billion or about three-fifths.

This major increase in Defense expenditures is now behind us. We have acquired for the most part the weapon systems and inventories of combat consumables we needed to place ourselves in a position to deal with both general and limited war. Indeed, assuming no change in the international situation and no active military conflicts, expenditures in the current fiscal year and perhaps over the next few years can be expected to decline a little, even though the costs of military and civilian personnel, retired pay and operation and maintenance may be expected to continue to increase by perhaps one-half to three-quarter billion dollars per year. This means that expenditures for procurement and to a lesser extent for research, development, test and evaluation (RDT&E) will tend to decline moderately over the next few years.

In the case of procurement, the expected decline simply reflects the fact that we have already substantially acquired the necessary inventories of weapons and equipment. The decline in RDT&E expenditures reflects, in large part, the completion of the development phase of a number of major systems and, for the remainder, a hardening of attitudes, particularly in the Congress, towards Federal research and development expenditures generally. It is worth noting that total Federal R&D expenditures have increased 4½ fold over the last eight or nine years, from about $3½ billion in FY 1956 to about $15 billion in FY 1964. This rapid increase has caused considerable concern in the Congress and questions are being raised as to the relative productivity of the increased expenditure levels of recent years. Even though our FY 1965 budget request for RDT&E was $225 million below the amount appropriated for FY 1964, the Congress reduced the amount by another $275 million, for the most part in a flat 3 percent cut across-the-board in all RDT&E appropriations. It is quite clear that the RDT&E appropriation request will have hard going on the Hill next year and we will have to have an extremely good case for whatever amount we request.

This leveling off, or slight decline, in total Defense expenditures was hardly unanticipated. We estimated when we had completed our review of the first Five Year Force Structure and Financial Program three years ago, that Defense expenditures would tend to level off at about $50 billion a year. Yet the leveling off of Defense expenditures has apparently come as a surprise to many people, particularly in industry. The difficulty is further compounded by the fact that the National Aeronautics and Space Administration (NASA) expenditures for space will also be leveling off after this year, having risen from about $400 million in FY 1960 to about $5 billion estimated for the current year.

I do not want to minimize the significance of these trends for the economy in general and for the aerospace industry in particular. The increase in Defense and space expenditures over the last several years has indeed been a stimulating influence in the national economic picture. Although it created pressures in certain limited areas such as scientific and technical personnel, this increased spending did not constitute an inflationary threat since we had ample unused capacity. At that particular time, therefore, requirements for higher military and space expenditures were in harmony with the Administration's economic policy, and in this case fiscal policy was accommodated to the needs of national security.

From the viewpoint of the economy as a whole, the prospect for a leveling out of NASA expenditures and a slight decline in Defense expenditures presents no particular problem since the tax cut and other economic measures taken by this Administration—the investment tax credit, the revision of depreciation schedules, etc.—have been successful, beyond the expectations of many, in stimulating strong, healthy economic growth. In the overall picture, the adjustments now taking place in the Defense program are hardly more severe than the kind of adjustments the economy normally has to make to changes in consumer demand, the effects of automation and so forth.

But the adverse impact of these changes on the aerospace and other defense related industries and on the communities near large military installations can be very serious indeed. The Ordnance industry and the Aircraft and Parts industry, for example, are almost wholly dependent on Government business, primarily Defense and NASA. Half or more of the employees in such industries as Communications Equipment, Electronic Components, and Shipbuilding are estimated to be engaged in defense production. Other industries heavily involved in defense work include those producing scientific instruments, primary metals, fabricated metal products, machinery, fuel and power, and transportation services. The Department of Labor has estimated that, including direct military and civilian employment, nearly one-tenth of all U.S. employees are engaged in national defense work.

Even a leveling off of Defense expenditures for procurement and RDT&E would have created an impact on these defense related industries since it takes more dollars each year to support one job. An actual decline, even of $1 billion a year, could have serious repercussions. Yet it has been the long established policy of the Government to avoid using the Defense program as a "prop" for industry. Indeed, the Defense Appropriation Act each year includes a provision expressly forbidding the Defense Department to pay a premium in order to alleviate economic dislocation. While we must, as a matter of national policy, maintain a strong Defense industry base, we have no obligation or intention to preserve any particular company or sustain employment in any particular community.

We have assumed the obligation of providing to industry advance information about their probable Defense markets. We have started during the last year a major effort to ascertain more precisely the character and location of Defense-related industry and to develop a system whereby we can translate our Five Year Force Structure and Financial Program into the kind of data needed to forecast the likely economic impact of changes in the Defense program on specific industries and geographic areas. Within the Defense Department, we have also assumed the obligation of providing a focal point known as the Office of Economic Adjustment for mobilizing the capabilities of all Federal Government agencies to provide all possible assistance to adversely affected industries and communities. The measures needed to mitigate the adverse effects of defense shifts are the same as those required for other kinds of economic dislocation. These could include expanded retraining programs, new redevelopment programs for distressed communities, measures to improve the mobility of labor and capital, changes in unemployment insurance, etc. The need for these and other measures is now being considered by a special Government-wide committee established by the President last January.

In the final analysis, however, a strong and growing economy still offers the best means for orderly adjustment to changes in the defense and space industries since it facilitates a shift of resources, particularly manpower, from one industry or location to another.

PART II

THE ORGANIZATIONAL FRAMEWORK

What organizations and agencies participate in formulating military plans and the budgets that support them? This question is the subject of the three selections that make up Part II. First, in selection 6, Mr. Hitch traces briefly the evolution of the Joint Chiefs of Staff and the Department of Defense. This account summarizes past attempts to solve through reorganization the problem of coordinating national plans and operations. Only changes in procedures and not changes in organization were required after 1961 in order to improve further the integration of policymaking and execution.

The roles of the military Services and of the Bureau of the Budget—the latter an arm of the President—were explored by the Jackson Committee with the Secretary of Defense; this interesting colloquy is included as selection 7. Of equal interest to the Congress is the special role of the Joint Chiefs of Staff. Secretary McNamara and General Maxwell D. Taylor, then Chairman of the Joint Chiefs of Staff, discussed with the House Appropriations Committee in 1963 the increasingly active participation of the Joint Chiefs in the Defense budgetary process. Their testimony appears as selection 8.

6

EVOLUTION OF THE DEPARTMENT OF DEFENSE*
Charles J. Hitch

. . . .

It was the Second World War, in which combined land/sea/air operations played such a vital role, that finally cracked the opposition to unification, at least with respect to planning and operations. The Joint Chiefs of Staff organization was born during that war, with broader purposes than the old Joint Board, and unified commands were established, although full legislative sanction for these changes had to await the National Security Act of 1947. (A unified command has a continuing mission, a single commander and consists of elements of two or more Services, e.g., the European Command, the North American Air Defense Command, etc.) The Army Air Corps was represented on the Joint Chiefs of Staff and joined with Army and Navy as a virtual equal in the formulation of joint plans. But the JCS could act only by unanimous consent, a procedure which often leads to compromises that are decidedly inferior to the views of any member. By 1943 the Army, led by General Marshall, had accepted the principle of a unified Defense establishment—although the Navy definitely had not.

After much study and discussion within the Executive Branch, President Truman, in December 1945, proposed to the Congress a single Department of National Defense, headed by a Secretary of Cabinet rank and supported by an Under Secretary and several Assistant Secretaries. The Department was to comprise three coordinate branches—land forces, naval forces, and air forces—each under an Assistant Secretary. Each branch was to have a military commander, and these three military commanders, together with the Chief of Staff of the Department of National Defense, were to constitute an advisory body to the Secretary of National Defense and to the President. President Truman's plan also provided for unified, centralized common service organizations under either civilian or military leadership in order to "ensure that real unification is ultimately obtained."

---

*Excerpts from the "H. Rowan Gaither Lectures in Systems Science" delivered at the University of California on 5–9 April 1965. Reprinted by permission from The Regents of the University of California, copyright owners, and published under the title *Decision-Making for Defense* (Berkeley and Los Angeles: University of California Press, 1965).

The central purpose of President Truman's proposal was to provide for "unified direction of the land, sea, and air forces at home as well as in all other parts of the world where our armed forces are serving." In order to achieve this purpose, he felt that "we should have integrated strategic plans and a unified military program and budget." In this connection he stressed a principle which I believe is only now being generally accepted in the Defense Department, namely, and I use his words, that "strategy, program, and budget are all aspects of the same basic decisions." His plan also stressed the economies that could be achieved through the unification of supply and service functions, the need for strong civilian control, and the requirement for unity of command in outlying bases.[1]

The President's plan was generally favored by the Army but opposed by the Navy.[2] The law which finally evolved after another year and a half of discussion was very different from the one President Truman had proposed. It provided for the creation of a National Military Establishment headed by a Secretary of Defense and comprising three separately organized and administered Executive Departments—Army, Navy, and Air Force—retaining in these Departments "all powers and duties relating to such Departments not specifically conferred upon the Secretary of Defense." The law also provided for the establishment of the Joint Chiefs of Staff, supported by a Joint Staff, and for various boards and committees. In effect, the National Security Act of 1947 established not a unified department or even a federation, but a confederation of three military departments presided over by a Secretary of Defense with carefully enumerated powers.[3]

It is an irony of history that one of the men who most vehemently and effectively opposed President Truman's proposals for a truly unified Department of Defense was destined to be the first to head the new National Military Establishment. Mr. Forrestal, an extremely able and experienced public servant, destroyed his health while trying to make this loose confederation of three military departments work. Within little more than a year, Secretary Forrestal (in his first annual report) was recommending that "the statutory authority of the Secretary of Defense should be materially strengthened . . . by making it clear that the

---

[1] "Special Message to the Congress Recommending the Establishment of a Department of National Defense, December 19, 1945," *Public Papers of the Presidents, Harry S. Truman, 1945* (Washington: U.S. Government Printing Office, 1961), p. 546.

[2] For reaction of official Army and Navy witnesses to various unification proposals, see *Hearings before the Committee on Military Affairs on S. 84*, U.S. Senate, 79th Congress, 1st Session (Washington: U.S. Government Printing Office, 1945), and *Hearings before the Committee on Naval Affairs on S. 2044*, U.S. Senate, 79th Cong., 2d Sess. (Washington: U.S. Government Printing Office, 1946).

[3] National Security Act of 1947, P.L. 253, 80th Cong., July 26, 1947 (61 Stat 495).

Secretary of Defense has the responsibility for exercising 'direction, authority, and control' over the departments and agencies of the National Military Establishment."[4] The 1947 Act had authorized the Secretary to establish only "general" policies and programs and to exercise "general" direction, authority and control. Secretary Forrestal also recommended that the Secretary of Defense be the only representative of the National Military Establishment to sit on the National Security Council. Under the 1947 Act, the Service Secretaries were not only members of the Council but were Heads of Executive Departments as well.

These and other recommendations from Secretary Forrestal, the Hoover Commission, and others, were incorporated in the 1949 Amendments to the National Security Act. The primacy of the Secretary of Defense as the principal assistant to the President on defense matters was stressed. The Army, the Navy, and the Air Force lost their status as Executive Departments and all that went with it. The Secretary of Defense was given a Deputy and three Assistant Secretaries, a Chairman was provided for the JCS, and the Joint Staff was increased from 100 to 210 officers. And, finally, Title IV was added to the Act creating the Office of the Assistant Secretary of Defense, Comptroller, and providing for uniform budget and fiscal procedures throughout the Department.[5]

On June 30, 1953, Defense's top management was again reorganized. The old statutory agencies, the Munitions Board and the Research and Development Board, were abolished and their functions transferred to the Secretary of Defense whose own office was expanded from three Assistant Secretaries to nine.[6] In transmitting this reorganization plan to the Congress, the President made it clear that *no* function was to be carried out independently of the Secretary of Defense and that the Secretaries of the military departments were to be his "operating managers" in addition to being heads of their own respective departments.[7]

The latest chapter in the history of Defense unification legislation was written after Sputnik, in 1958, when the Act was again amended to increase further the responsibilities and authority of the Secretary of Defense, especially with regard to the opera-

4 *First Report of the Secretary of Defense, 1948* (Washington: U.S. Government Printing Office, 1948), p. 3.

5 National Security Act Amendments of 1949, P.L. 216, 81st Cong., August 10, 1949 (63 Stat 578).

6 Reorganization Plan No. 6 of 1953 (67 Stat 638).

7 "Special Message to the Congress Transmitting Reorganization Plan 6 of 1953 Concerning the Department of Defense, April 30, 1953," *Public Papers of the Presidents, Dwight D. Eisenhower, 1953* (Washington: U.S. Government Printing Office, 1960), pp. 225-238.

tional direction of the armed forces and in the research and development area.[8] The three military departments were no longer to be "separately administered" and instead were only to be "separately organized." A new post of Director, Defense Research and Engineering was created, not only to "supervise" research and development activities, but to "direct and control" those activities needing centralized management. Also in the 1958 reorganization, the military departments which had been acting as executive agents in the operational control of the unified and specified commands were taken out of the command chain so that the line of command now runs from the President to the Secretary of Defense through the Joint Chiefs of Staff to the unified commands. And, finally, to enable it to carry out its enlarged functions, the Joint Staff was strengthened further from 210 to 400 officers.

As President Eisenhower pointed out at the time—

> . . . complete unity in our strategic planning and basic operational direction [is a vital necessity]. It is therefore mandatory that the initiative for this planning and direction rest not with the separate services but directly with the Secretary of Defense and his operational advisers, the Joint Chiefs of Staff, assisted by such staff organization as they deem necessary.
>
> No military task is of greater importance than the development of strategic plans which relate our revolutionary new weapons and force deployments to national security objectives. Genuine unity is indispensable at this starting point. No amount of subsequent coordination can eliminate duplication or doctrinal conflicts which are intruded into the first shaping of military programs.[9]

These changes greatly enhanced the authority of the Secretary of Defense as the true operating head of the Defense Department. But it was not until 1961 that the full powers of the Secretary of Defense to run the Department on a unified basis were actually used.

I imply no disrespect to the predecessors of the present Secretary of Defense when I say that although we have now had unification "in name" for almost 18 years, there was little unification "in fact" until 1961, except in three areas—

1. Unified commands had been created in all overseas theaters and for continental air defense—unified before the beginning of hostilities for the first time in history. But we still do not have a unified command for our strategic retaliatory forces.

---

[8] Department of Defense Reorganization Act of 1958, P.L. 85–599, 85th Cong., August 6, 1958 (72 Stat 514).

[9] "Special Message to the Congress in Reorganization of the Defense Establishment, April 3, 1958," *Public Papers of the Presidents, Dwight D. Eisenhower, 1958* (Washington: U.S. Government Printing Office, 1959), pp. 278–279.

2. Joint contingency plans for the use of existing forces had been prepared by the Joint Chiefs of Staff for many contingencies. This had been a strictly military function, with little participation by the civilian Secretaries, but the planning was joint. However, again, there was no joint plan for the targeting of our strategic retaliatory forces until Secretary Gates in 1959/1960 established the mechanism for achieving one. And the plan that was achieved, although joint, was originally a single plan with little in the way of options.

3. Finally, the civilian Secretaries had taken control of the over-all level of the defense budget and brought it into line with the fiscal policy of the administration. The primary method of so bringing the defense budget into line, used by all Secretaries before the present incumbent, was to divide a total defense budget ceiling among the three military departments, leaving to each department, by and large, the allocation of its ceiling among its own functions, units, and activities. The Defense Secretaries used this method because they lacked the management techniques needed to do it any other way.

In view of these shortcomings, President Kennedy before he took office was inclined to believe that some further changes in the organization of the Defense Department would be required to improve its effectiveness and make it more responsive to national security objectives and changes in technology. And his Committee on the Defense Establishment, chaired by Senator Symington and including such Old Defense hands as Thomas Finletter, Roswell Gilpatric and Marx Leva, did indeed propose such changes. The Committee's proposals, aimed at achieving unification in fact as well as form, would have replaced the three Service Secretaries with three Under Secretaries of Defense, vesting directly in the Secretary of Defense the administration of the Services. The Chairman of the Joint Chiefs of Staff would have replaced the Joint Chiefs in the chain of command and the Chiefs would have remained solely as heads of their respective Services, their advisory job being assumed by a Military Advisory Council under the Chairman.[10] But the management innovations introduced in the Department of Defense during 1961–62 made unnecessary so drastic an overhaul of the existing organizational structure. What they are and how they have been applied will be the subject of my next two lectures. (See below, pp. 64–85, 121–132).

---

[10] "Report to Senator Kennedy from the Committee on the Defense Establishment," *New York Times,* December 6, 1960, p. 30.

7

AGENCY RESPONSIBILITIES FOR PLANNING AND BUDGETING*
By Robert S. McNamara

. . . .

Senator Jackson. Would you say that the three departments, Army, Navy, and Air Force, are likely to play a different role in defense planning and organization than they have previously?

Secretary McNamara. I would say they are likely to play a fuller role. The Navy will participate in a discussion of the Air Force's strategic systems. The Air Force will participate in a discussion of the Navy's strategic systems. We held just exactly that kind of discussion with all of the chiefs and all of the secretaries participating last Friday afternoon.

Similarly, the Navy and Air Force and Army will join together in a consideration of the airlift, sealift, and ground requirements in a way that had not been done previously. So in a very real sense the military departments will more actively participate in the planning and budgeting process.

By the way, in my mind, I equate planning and budgeting and consider the terms almost synonymous, the budget being simply a quantitative expression of the operating plans.

Senator Jackson. This increased Service department participation should be a very healthy development. It would seem to me that it would expose the mistakes made by the Services—and they are bound to make mistakes—and also bring out new ideas and fresh approaches.

Secretary McNamara. Yes; and more importantly, it will assure that the programs of each department are in balance with the programs of the other departments which they affect. The airlift-sealift problem is an illustration of that.

Senator Jackson. You might discover some resources you do not know about.

Secretary McNamara. Or alternatively we might discover some gaps that exist that might not have been realized.

. . . .

*Excerpts from testimony before the Subcommittee on National Policy Machinery of the Committee on Government Operations, U.S. Senate, on 7 August 1961. *Hearings, Organizing for National Security: State, Defense, and the National Security Council,* Part IX (87th Cong., 1st Session; Washington: U.S. Government Printing Office, 1961), pp. 1196–1197, 1198–1199, 1221.

Senator Jackson. . . . Do you think the military officers of the three services will have a different role in planning under your leadership than they did formerly?

Secretary McNamara. Again it is difficult for me to speak with any authority of their operations in the past because I am not intimately acquainted with them and I would not wish to misstate the way in which they did operate.

But the development of the program concept and the manner in which we are planning to review the programs will require that each Service Secretary and each Service chief participate fully in those discussions and thereby he will be participating in the review of the proposals of the other Services to a much greater degree, I believe, than has been true in the past. That is the major change.

Senator Jackson. You would say that is a major change?

Secretary McNamara. Yes.

Senator Jackson. In other words, they will sort of play the role of "generalist" in that they are not merely advocates of their own individual service, but they have a responsibility to look upon the whole concept and make their comments known.

Secretary McNamara. Yes. That has, of course, been a responsibility of the chiefs in their capacity as members of the Joint Chiefs, but now we will not only recognize it formally, but also in practice by introducing them much more fully into the total planning and budgeting process.

. . . .

Senator Mundt. When you start out with your budget procedure at the beginning, do you get any indication at all from the Bureau of the Budget as to what your slice of the pie is to be or how much it is to be or do you just start out with an open-end program?

Secretary McNamara. At the beginning we start out with an open-end program. Unless that seems completely irresponsible, we proceed every step of the way to recognize the costs associated with a particular program of action and eventually pull the entire set of programs together in a total financial budget.

Senator Mundt. At that point, does the Bureau of the Budget have any impact on the Defense budget?

Secretary McNamara. The Budget Bureau works with us from the very beginning in analyzing the courses of action we propose to follow and in particular in analyzing the costs we ascribe to a particular course of action. For example, we propose to retain B-47 wings on active duty, wings that had been scheduled for deactivation.

For that we estimate a cost of X. The Budget Bureau will have been working with us during the review of our strategic forces. They will have participated in the discussions that led to our conclusions that we should retain those wings but they will play their strongest role at the point they say, "You believe it will cost X to obtain these things. We feel it will cost X minus Y because you estimated flying hours in excess of whatever is required to obtain readiness of the crews. You have planned to procure spare parts in this volume. We believe that in relation to past experience you would be able to support those forces with a lesser volume of spare parts usage. You propose to provide this amount of money for travel of these individuals. We think that, based on our records, you should be able to operate those particular forces with a lower level of travel expenditures."

The Budget Bureau is constantly at work with us on these particular aspects of our operations but they would play a lesser role in determining whether we should or should not retain those wings.

8

THE JOINT CHIEFS OF STAFF AND THE DEFENSE BUDGET*

By Robert S. McNamara

Mr. Laird. . . .
My question is, Mr. Secretary, what weight is given to the decisions of the Chiefs? Do you have a tabulation of programs considered by the Chiefs and their recommendations on these programs? I am interested specifically in determining how many of the Chiefs' recommendations were approved or disapproved by the Department. If you do not have the tabulation, would you please provide it for the record?

Secretary McNamara. Yes, Mr. Laird, I will provide such a tabulation.

(The tabulation is classified and will be separately provided to the committee.)

Secretary McNamara. It reminds me of the estimates some people make of the reliability of their predictions. They lump apples and eggs together. I would have to do the same thing in a tabulation of the kind you request. I will have one made up and inserted in the record. I think the important question, and I believe it is what you are driving at, is, "Do the Chiefs participate in the discussion of the military force requirements and the related financial budget?" The answer is "Yes." It has been my purpose in the Department to insure that they participate more fully than they ever have before. We endeavored to do that in the preparation of the amendments to the fiscal year 1962 budget. We did it in the 1963 budget, and we endeavored to accomplish the same objective in the fiscal year 1964 budget. I would like you to hear from General [Maxwell D.] Taylor, [Chairman, Joint Chiefs of Staff, 1962–64] on this and get his impression. He can report to you both his impression of this year's budget review and perhaps how it compared with some prior year reviews he participated in. I believe I am right in saying that the Chiefs held about 64 meetings on the subject of the 1964 force requirements and budget, and I participated in about 13 meetings with them, in addition to submitting to them and receiving back from them in

---

*Excerpts from testimonies of Secretary McNamara and General Maxwell D. Taylor before the Appropriations Committee, U.S. Congress, House. *Hearings on Department of Defense Appropriations for Fiscal Year 1964*, Part 1 (88th Cong., 1st Session; Washington: U.S. Government Printing Office, 1964), pp. 343–348.

writing their views on every one of the major issues in the budget. Perhaps General Taylor can expand on that.

General Taylor. Much of this occurred before I came in as Chairman on October 1. For my own interest I have had the record examined and I confirm the Secretary's statement. Certainly, based upon the record which I have brought up to date I would say the Joint Chiefs of Staff participated more in this budget than in any other budget I have been connected with in the past. I am speaking of the Joint Chiefs as a corporate body, not as individual chiefs of the Service, in which capacity, of course, they are very active in their own service submissions. It has always been something of a question as to what extent the Joint Chiefs should get into the budget. If we got into it to the same degree Mr. Hitch does, we would be able to do little else. So it is a question of common sense, really. I find we now can get into it just about as much as we want to. By the program change device, all the program changes are available to the Chiefs for comment. We select only those of major importance for consideration, comment, and recommendations to the Secretary of Defense.

With regard to the budget this year, after October 1 when I became Chairman, there were a series of very important meetings held to comment on the Secretary's proposed position on several of the most important subjects. For example we commented on the major force tabulations through the fiscal year 1967, the Service and DOD proposals for modifying force levels and procurement rates in the 5-year program, the military assistance program, the logistics guidance and then on some of the major weapons programs such as the SKYBOLT, RS–70 and NIKE-ZEUS. So I would say the Joint Chiefs participated very fully and probably up to the level of their capacity. If the Joint Chiefs took over fiscal matters in too much detail it would completely stalemate their other very important planning and operational functions.

Mr. Ford. Mr. Chairman, I think it would be very beneficial for the record if we could take the figure that the Secretary indicated that the Services had requested, $67 billion and the figure that we have before us of $53.7 billion and have an itemization of the reductions which were made. Included with this information it would be helpful I believe if we could show certainly the major areas involving this $13.3 billion where the Joint Chiefs took action and what their action was. Is this feasible, Mr. Secretary?

Secretary McNamara. Mr. Ford, it is feasible to detail the approximately $13 billion reduction. As a matter of fact, I have it here; it includes some 600-odd items.

It is not feasible, I think, to summarize specifically the portion of that list which represented the Joint Chiefs' recommendations versus mine. In some cases, the Chiefs were explicit and in other cases they did not consider the problem primarily from a financial point of view. They may have considered an alternative other than those I considered. I do not know quite how to answer that facet of your question.

Perhaps we should do the best we can to throw some light on it.

Mr. Ford. I think it is important we have an explanation of why this $13.3 billion figure was reduced below the Service levels as requested. Certainly in the major areas we ought to have the record show what the situation is as far as the Joint Chiefs were concerned.

Secretary McNamara. We will try to develop some reasonable answer to that question.

(The information requested is classified and has been separately provided to the committee.)

Mr. Ford. Let me say the problems you faced in reducing the total figure requested below that recommended by the various Services are not unique. Your predecessors as far back as Mr. Truman and his Secretaries had similar problems.

It is my recollection that Mr. Truman once said he had budget requests of $102 billion and he ended up recommending a figure of around $60-some-billion.

All of the Secretaries since that time and up to you certainly have had this annual problem. I am not saying that the Secretary of Defense and the President should not make these reductions. In fact, they should, but in the past we have had these figures included in the record. I think in 1964 we should follow the same pattern.

APPEAL RIGHTS OF CHIEFS OF STAFF

However, there is another aspect of this that I think ought to be explored at this time.

Under the law, as I understand it, the Chairman of the Joint Chiefs and each of the Chiefs has the opportunity, if they exercise their prerogatives, to go over the head of the Secretary of Defense, if the individual Chief or the Chairman so desires, and go to the President for a statement of his own policy or reclama from the action taken by the Secretary of Defense; is that correct?

Secretary McNamara. I think the Chiefs perhaps not explicitly by law, but certainly by practice and tradition—and in my case by policy—have the right to speak to the President individually or collectively on any matter they wish to at any time.

I believe perhaps the paragraph you are referring to in the law relates to the right of a Chief to appeal to Congress if he believes that the program for his Service is such as to endanger the security of our Nation. Those may not be the specific words but that is the intent, I believe of that particular paragraph.

Mr. Ford. I think it is Public Law 85–599 approved August 6, 1958.

This does give the Chief the right to go to Congress on his own initiative. I do not believe the law provides that a Chief can go to the President, although by practice or tradition this is certainly an accepted prerogative.

Secretary McNamara. In my case, it is an established policy. Perhaps General Taylor wishes to comment on that.

General Taylor. I would think the point is met by the provision in the law that makes the Joint Chiefs of Staff, as a body, advisors, not only to the Secretary of Defense, but also to the National Security Council and the President, which certainly makes it very clear that the body, as such, has the right to direct approach to the President.

Mr. Ford. I suspect that that is right. Certainly the practice has been in those cases where a Service chief had this strong feeling or belief he could, and in many cases did—go to the President. I know that General Taylor when he was Chief of Staff of the Army exercised this prerogative and went to President Eisenhower in some instances. I do not know how many times. It might be interesting for the record, General, if you would tell us how many times you went to the President.

General Taylor. I think two, actually, as a formal appeal. Of course, President Eisenhower, like President Kennedy, always had his door open to the Joint Chiefs. We talked to him many times but hardly within the context of a formal type of appeal.

Mr. Ford. Since you have been Chairman of the Joint Chiefs, have you ever exercised that procedure or tradition?

General Taylor. No sir; I have not.

Mr. Ford. There is nothing in this budget that you felt was worthwhile to so exercise that prerogative?

General Taylor. I had my opportunity to comment in the making up of the budget so that the President had my views on the budget. However, I never felt this was an appeal in the sense you are using the word now.

Mr. Ford. Appeal in the sense you exercised it in the two times you recall?

General Taylor. That is right, sir.

Mr. Ford. Under President Eisenhower?

Secretary McNamara. Perhaps I should add in response to Mr. Ford's question that it has been my practice when I submit my recommendations to the President, to state in the document in which I submit them, the contrary views of the Chiefs, if there are contrary views, and, as best I can, to explain why the Chiefs take a contrary view.

It is also my practice to submit such a document in draft form to the Chiefs for their review before I submit it to the President in order to insure that I am properly reflecting their views and the reasoning that lies behind them.

Moreover, it is also my practice in any case of disagreement between myself and the Chiefs on a major issue to insure that not only my views and theirs are submitted to the President in writing, but also to insure that there is proper oral discussion on the issue. I believe that generally we have followed those practices during the development of the fiscal year 1964 budget.

Mr. Ford. In the 2 years and several months you have been Secretary of Defense, Mr. McNamara, have any of the Chiefs who have served under you exercised this privilege or prerogative to go to the President?

Secretary McNamara. The President has arranged for meetings with the Chiefs at which time their views on matters in which their recommendations individually or collectively might have been different than mine have been expressed to him. So, I would say the answer to your question is yes. Views of the Chiefs contrary to mine have been expressed to the President during this 2-year period.

Mr. Ford. Were these meetings more or less joint meetings? Were you and the others present or were they instances where the individual Chiefs went to the President alone?

Secretary McNamara. Well, I would not want to comment on the latter because I really would have to check the record thoroughly. I do not believe there have been any instances where a Chief went to the President alone to express serious disagreement with some recommendation I was making with regard to a military force structure or budget. Perhaps the Chiefs themselves would be better authorities on this than I.

In any event, I do know to my own knowledge that the views of the Chiefs on major points on which they may have recommended differently than I, have been properly and fully expressed to the President.

Mr. Ford. I gather there is some difference in what you are describing and what General Taylor indicated he did on two occasions when he went to see former President Eisenhower. Am I assuming correctly or otherwise?

General Taylor. I think the difference is only in the sense of degree. As I say, a Service chief has many conversations with the President and I have never known a Chief reluctant to express his own views, even though different from that of the Secretary at the time. In the two cases I have in mind, there were very important issues involved. In at least one case, a whole shift in strategy was involved. It was a rather dramatic occasion when I went with Admiral [Arthur W.] Radford [Chairman, Joint Chiefs of Staff, 1953–57] to present our differing views.

Mr. Ford. In other words, you, as Chief of Staff for the Army in these two instances, felt to some extent a cause celebre in that you believed it was of major importance to your Service and to military policy, and as a consequence you took the matter to the President himself?

General Taylor. Actually, in the more important occasion, I represented not only the Army, but also the Navy and the Marine Corps.

Mr. Ford. With their concurrence?

General Taylor. Yes sir.

Mr. Ford. I gather from what you are saying then that in the two years plus that Mr. McNamara has been Secretary no Chief has had this strong feeling that you apparently had on these two previous occasions?

Secretary McNamara. I do not want to say that without qualification, Mr. Ford, because I think we ought to search the record to be sure of this. I think the question ought to be directed to the Chiefs. I do say that it was not necessary because the Chiefs had full opportunity to discuss their views with the President, in the meetings that he initiated with them.

Whether any Chief, in addition to those discussions, felt that he should expand on those views expressed at that time, I am not certain. We would have to examine the record to find out. I know it has not occurred often, if it occurred at all.

There was no need for it because of the system we have been using.

Mr. Ford. From what you have said, Mr. Secretary, you have very detailed information which had been submitted to the President over the last several years indicating those instances where your recommendations to the President were not fully concurred in by a Chief, or several Chiefs, or the Joint Chiefs as a corporate body.

With that kind of information available, I would gather that for fiscal 1964 the information could be made a part of the record involving this $13.3 billion reduction?

Secretary McNamara. Yes, on some portions of it. On the major part of the $13 billion reduction the Chiefs, as a group, cannot express their views. For example, I recall that $1 billion of the $13 billion represents reductions in proposed construction projects. The Chiefs, as General Taylor indicated, did not think it necessary as a group to review all elements of the budget. One of the elements they did not review as a group was the construction budgets of the individual services. On that part, they have not expressed a view. Similarly, the Chiefs, as a group, I believe, did not express their views on the procurement of administrative aircraft. There is about one-quarter of a billion dollars of the $13 billion represented by my action recommending against the administrative aircraft procurement proposed by the Services. Other instances of that kind would occur in the $13 billion.

What we will try to do is to indicate on major elements of the $13 billion the extent to which the Chiefs expressed their views.

REQUESTS OF FIELD COMMANDERS

Mr. Andrews. Would the gentleman yield?

Mr. Ford. Surely.

Mr. Andrews. Mr. Secretary, as I understand it, each commanding officer of each military installation sends in his request for the budget for his installation for the fiscal year; is that correct?

Secretary McNamara. Yes, sir; that is correct.

Mr. Andrews. Was this $67 billion the total of those requests sent in by military commanders throughout the world?

Secretary McNamara. No sir, Mr. Andrews, the budgets proposed by the individual military commanders went in to their Services through a series of reviews at successively higher echelons and at each such review the proposals were changed up or down.

Mr. Andrews. Do you know what the totals were of those letters to "Santa Claus?"

Secretary McNamara. No; I do not.

PART III

THE PROGRAMMING SYSTEM

A most important innovation in Defense budgeting occurred in 1961 with the introduction of a programming phase. Its purpose is to provide the means for translating military requirements into annual fiscal year budgets—in a department where requirements are established by long and medium range plans and expressed in terms of missions, forces, and weapons systems while budgets must deal with the inputs of resources—men, materiel, facilities, and the like. Under the new system, Defense activities —or programs—are grouped by major mission without regard to Service. Through programming, requirements are related to the total cost of meeting them during a five-year planning period. This phase of the budget cycle affords decision makers the opportunity to evaluate the costs and relative effectiveness of alternative ways to meet present and anticipated future needs.

Mr. Hitch in selection 9 discusses the problems that programming was designed to overcome and briefly describes the mission-related programs that have been established to encompass all Defense activities. As an example of how the system operates, the documentation for a hypothetical "program element" is presented in selection 10, along with a short account of how programs are subsequently converted to annual requests for appropriations. The objectives of the system were discussed by Mr. Hitch with the Jackson Committee in the summer of 1961, and some of his testimony is presented as selection 11. Nearly four years later Mr. Hitch reviewed the progress made through this new approach to budgeting and pointed out some of the remaining problems to be resolved to meet future management needs. His account appears as selection 12.

9

DEVELOPMENT AND SALIENT FEATURES OF THE PROGRAMMING SYSTEM*

By Charles J. Hitch

I noted toward the close of my first lecture (see above, pp. 51–52), that although unification had been achieved in form with the passage of the National Security Act in 1947, it was not until 1961 that the full powers of the Secretary of Defense to run the Department on a unified basis—spelled out by various amendments in the intervening years—were actually used. And I suggested that this situation existed principally because earlier Secretaries of Defense lacked the necessary tools to do so.

. . . From a modest beginning, limited to the protection of our land frontiers against the Indians and our neighbors in Florida and Canada, our national security objectives have expanded to involve us in an interlocking system of Free World military alliances with over forty sovereign nations. We now maintain for this purpose by far the largest peacetime establishment in our history. We have, today, a force of almost 2,700,000 military personnel on active duty, supported by about 900,000 civilians in the United States and about one-quarter of a million overseas, the latter mostly citizens of other countries. In addition, we have almost one million reserve personnel and about one-half million retired military personnel on our payrolls.

Pay alone accounts for more than $20 billion out of a total defense budget of $50 billion. The remaining $30 billion is used to procure a staggeringly large variety of goods and services from the private sector of the economy—aircraft, missiles, tanks, food, clothing, research and development, construction and utilities. We draw from virtually every segment of the American economy and utilize a very large share of the Nation's total research and development capacities. Because of the vast scope of our activities—on the land, on and under the seas, in the air and in space—and the great demands we make on our weapons and equipment, the Defense Department is vitally interested in virtually every field of scientific and technological knowledge. The value of our current inventory of equipment, weapons, and supplies is con-

---

*Excerpts from the "H. Rowan Gaither Lectures in Systems Science" delivered at the University of Cali'ornia on 5–9 April 1965. Reprinted by permission from The Regents of the University of California, copyright owners, and published under the title *Decision-Making for Defense* (Berkeley and Los Angeles: University of California Press, 1965).

servatively estimated at $135 billion. Our principal installations and facilities number in the thousands, and we control nearly 15,000 square miles of land. Our military operations extend around the world, and we spend almost $3 billion a year in other countries.

How, one might ask, can any one man or group of men ever hope to manage such a vast aggregation of men, equipment, installations, and activities spread all over the globe? And yet, . . . the defense effort, to be fully effective, must be managed on a unified basis, not only in the conduct of combat operations but also in the planning and execution of the programs. And, as President Eisenhower stressed in 1958: "It is . . . mandatory that the *initiative* for this planning and direction rest not with the separate services but directly with the Secretary of Defense and his operational advisors. . . ."[1]

The revolution in military technology since the end of World War II, alone, would make necessary the central planning and direction of the military program. The great technical complexity of modern day weapons, their lengthy period of development, their tremendous combat power and enormous cost have placed an extraordinary premium on sound choices of major weapon systems. These choices have become, for the top management of the Defense Department, the key decisions around which much else of the Defense program revolves. They cannot be made properly by any subordinate echelon of the Defense establishment. They must be directly related to our *national* security objectives. rather than simply to the tasks of just one of the military Services.

The revolution in military technology has not only changed the character of our military program, it has also, to a significant degree, blurred the lines of demarcation among the various Services. Is the missile an unmanned aircraft, as the Air Force likes to think, or extended-range artillery, which is the Army view? Most of our major military missions today require the participation of more than one of the military Services. Therefore, our principal concern now must be centered on what is required by the Defense establishment as a whole to perform a particular military mission—not on what is required of a particular Service to perform its part of that mission. This is not only true with regard to the planning of our military forces and programs, but also with respect to the development of new major weapon systems.

---

[1] "Special Message to the Congress on Reorganization of the Defense Establishment, April 3, 1958," *Public Papers of the Presidents, Dwight D. Eisenhower, 1958* (Washington: U.S. Government Printing Office, 1959), p. 278.

BUDGETING BEFORE 1961

I noted in my first lecture that because, prior to 1961, the Defense Secretaries lacked the tools to manage the overall effort on a truly unified basis, they had to resort (except in times of emergency, like Korea) to what might be described, generically, as the "budget ceiling" approach. The President would indicate the general level of Defense expenditures which he felt was appropriate to the international situation and his overall economic and fiscal policies.[2] The Secretary of Defense, by one means or another, would allocate this figure among the three military departments. Each military department would in turn prepare its basic budget submission, allocating its ceiling among its own functions, units, and activities, and present additional requests, which could not be accommodated within the ceiling, in what was variously called an "addendum" budget, "B" list, etc. Then all the budget submissions were reviewed together by the Office of the Secretary of Defense in an attempt to achieve balance.

Let me make quite clear the fact that this was indeed the traditional way of preparing the Defense budget. Frank Pace, then Director of the Bureau of the Budget, in testifying before a congressional committee in 1949 on how the Defense budget was prepared in the Truman Administration, described the process as follows:

> We [the Bureau of the Budget] would provide him [the President] with certain factual information as to where certain policies would lead. From that the President sets a ceiling on the armed services, which was last year, I think, generally known as $15 billion.
>
> However, I think it should be explained that under the ceiling process—and this is not solely for the armed forces but exists for every department of the Government—. . .
>
> There is also the proviso that if within that limitation it is impossible to include certain programs which the Secretary of Defense considers of imperative importance to the national defense, they shall be included in . . . what is termed the 'B' list. . . . The 'B' list is what cannot be included under the ceiling.[3]

It was recognized long ago that this was a rather inefficient way to go about preparing the Defense budget. Its consequences were precisely what could have been predicted. Each Service tended to exercise its own priorities, favoring its own unique missions to the detriment of joint missions, striving to lay the

---

[2] For an interesting example of this technique, see "Memorandum for the Secretary of the Army," June 9, 1960, signed by the Special Assistant to the Secretary of Defense. Mr. O. M. Gale, which outlines the budget guidelines set forth by President Eisenhower at a Cabinet meeting on June 3, 1960. Reprinted in the *Congressional Record*, June 30, 1960, vol. 106, part 11, pp. 15100–15101.

[3] *Hearings on S. 1269 and S. 1843*, U.S. Senate, Committee on Armed Services, 81st Cong., 1st Sess., April 6, 1949 (Washington: U.S. Government Printing Office, 1949), p. 79.

groundwork for an increased share of the budget in future years by concentrating on alluring new weapon systems, and protecting the overall size of its own forces even at the cost of readiness. These decisions were made by patriotic generals and admirals, and by dedicated civilian leaders as well, who were convinced that they were acting in the best interests of the Nation as well as their own Service—but the end result was not balanced effective military forces.

The Air Force, for example, gave overriding priority to the strategic retaliatory bombers and missiles, starving the tactical air units needed to support the Army ground operations and the airlift units needed to move our limited war forces quickly to far-off trouble spots. The Navy gave overriding priority to its own nuclear attack forces—notably the aircraft carriers—while its anti-submarine warfare capability was relatively neglected and its escort capability atrophied. The Army used its limited resources to preserve the number of its divisions, although this meant that they lacked equipment and supplies to fight for more than a few weeks.

Moreover, because attention was focused on only the next fiscal year, the Services had every incentive to propose large numbers of "new starts," the full cost dimensions of which would only become apparent in subsequent years. This is the "foot in the door" or "thin edge of the wedge" technique which the one-year-at-a-time approach to Defense budgeting greatly encouraged.

Another unsatisfactory aspect of this method of attempting to exercise control and direction of the Defense effort through the annual budget was the almost complete separation between budgeting and military planning (I speak here of medium and long-range planning, including weapon systems planning—not the contingency planning for the use of existing forces to which I referred in my first lecture).

1. These critically important functions were performed by two different groups of people—the planning by the military planners and the budgeting by the civilian Secretaries and the comptroller organizations.

2. Budget control was exercised by the Secretary of Defense but planning remained essentially in the Services. It was not until 1955–56 that the first Joint Strategic Objectives Plan (JSOP), projecting the requirements for major forces some four to five years into the future, was prepared by the Joint Chiefs of Staff organization, but the early JSOP was essentially a "pasting together" of unilaterally developed Service plans.

3. Whereas the planning horizon extended four or more years into the future, the budget was projected only one year ahead, although it was clear to all involved that the lead time from the start of a weapon development to the equipping of the forces ranged from five to ten years, depending on the character of the particular development effort.

4. Planning was performed in terms of missions, weapon systems, and military units or forces—the "outputs" of the Defense Department; budgeting, on the other hand, was done in terms of such "inputs" or intermediate products as personnel, operation and maintenance, procurement, construction, etc.; and there was little or no machinery for translating one into the other.

5. Budgeting, however crudely, faced up to fiscal realities. The planning was fiscally unrealistic and, therefore, of little help to the decision-maker. The total implicit budget costs of the unilateral Service plans or of the Joint Strategic Objectives Plan always far exceeded any budget that any Secretary of Defense or administration was willing to request of the Congress.

6. Military requirements tended to be stated in absolute terms, without reference to their costs. But the military effectiveness or military worth of any given weapon system cannot logically be considered in isolation. It must be considered in relation to its cost—and in a world in which resources are limited, to the alternative uses to which the resources can be put. Military requirements are meaningful only in terms of benefits to be gained in relation to their cost. Accordingly, resource costs and military worth have to be scrutinized together.

As a consequence, the Secretary each year found himself in a position where he had, at least implicitly, to make major decisions on forces and programs without adequate information and all within the few weeks allocated to his budget review. Moreover, every year the plans and programs of each of the Services had to be cut back severely to fit the budget ceiling, by program cancellations, stretch-outs, or postponements—but only for that year. Beyond the budget year, unrealistic plans continued to burgeon— perhaps next year the ceiling would be higher.

These deficiencies did not go unnoticed in the Congress. Representative George Mahon, then Chairman of the House Defense Appropriations Subcommittee and now also Chairman of the full Committee, addressed two letters to the Secretary of Defense

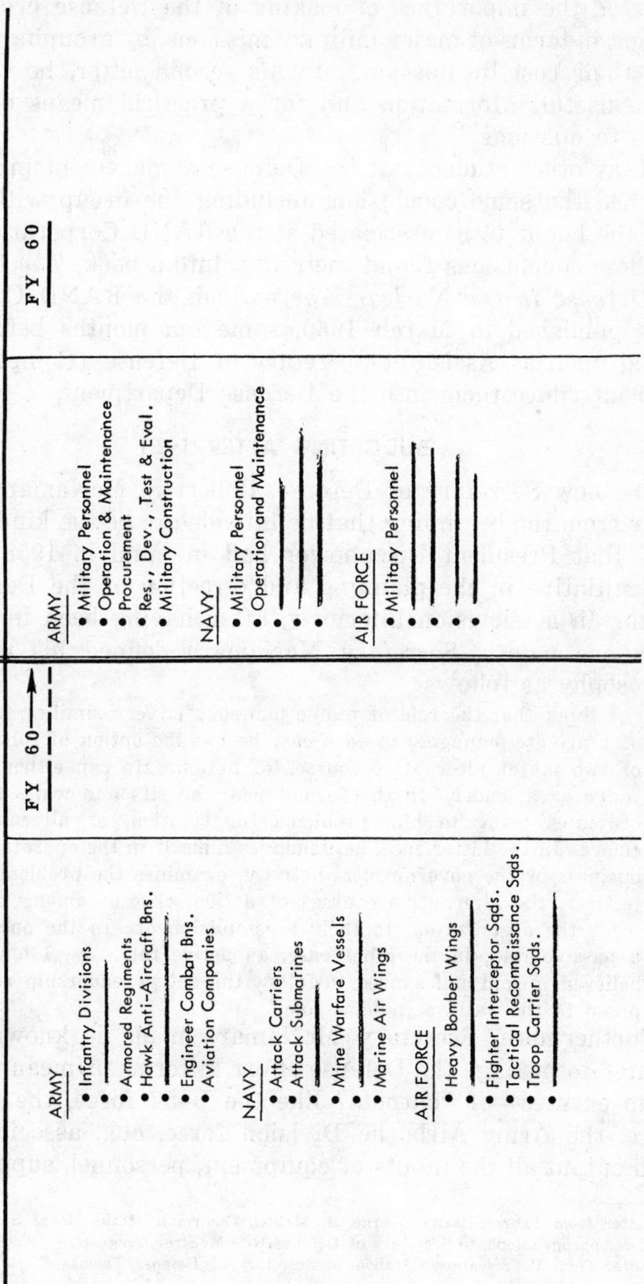

MILITARY PLANNING

FY 60 →

ARMY
- Infantry Divisions
- Armored Regiments
- Hawk Anti-Aircraft Bns.
- Engineer Combat Bns.
- Aviation Companies

NAVY
- Attack Carriers
- Attack Submarines
- Mine Warfare Vessels
- Marine Air Wings

AIR FORCE
- Heavy Bomber Wings
- Fighter Interceptor Sqds.
- Tactical Reconnaissance Sqds.
- Troop Carrier Sqds.

BUDGETING

FY 60

ARMY
- Military Personnel
- Operation & Maintenance
- Procurement
- Res., Dev., Test & Eval.
- Military Construction

NAVY
- Military Personnel
- Operation and Maintenance

AIR FORCE
- Military Personnel

Figure 1

in the summer of 1959 and fall of 1960. In his first letter he stressed the importance of looking at the Defense program and budget in terms of major military missions, by grouping programs and their cost by mission.[4] In his second letter, he called "for more useful information and for a practical means of relating costs to missions."[5]

Many other students of the Defense management problem had reached the same conclusion, including the group with which I had the honor to be associated at the RAND Corporation. Many of these conclusions found their way into a book, *The Economics of Defense in the Nuclear Age*,[6] which the RAND Corporation first published in March 1960, some ten months before I was called upon as Assistant Secretary of Defense (Comptroller) to help introduce them into the Defense Department.

BUDGETING AFTER 1961

The new Secretary of Defense, Robert S. McNamara, made it clear from the beginning that he intended to be the kind of Secretary that President Eisenhower had in mind in 1958 and take the initiative in the planning and direction of the Defense program. In a television interview, after having been in office less than one month, Secretary McNamara defined his managerial philosophy as follows:

> I think that the role of public manager is very similiar to the role of a private manager; in each case he has the option of following one of two major alternative courses of action. He can either act as a judge or a leader. In the former case, he sits and waits until subordinates bring to him problems for solution, or alternatives for choice. In the latter case, he immerses himself in the operations of the business or the governmental activity, examines the problems, the objectives, the alternative courses of action, chooses among them, and leads the organization to their accomplishment. In the one case it's a passive role; in the other case, an active role. . . . I have always believed in and endeavored to follow the active leadership role as opposed to the passive judicial role.[7]

Furthermore, Secretary McNamara made it known that he wanted to manage the Defense effort in terms of meaningful program entities—of "outputs" like the B–52 force, the POLARIS force, the Army Airborne Division force, etc., associating with each output all the inputs of equipment, personnel, supplies, facil-

4 Letter from Representative George H. Mahon, Chairman of the House Subcommittee on Defense Appropriations, to Secretary of Defense Neil McElroy, August 18, 1959 (unpublished).

5 Letter from Representative Mahon to Secretary of Defense Thomas S. Gates, September 6, 1960 (unpublished).

6 Charles J. Hitch and Roland N. McKean, *The Economics of Defense in the Nuclear Age* (Cambridge, Mass.: Harvard University Press, 1960).

7 Extract from the transcript of an interview with Secretary of Defense Robert S. McNamara on the National Broadcasting Company program, "Today," February 17, 1961.

ities, and funds, regardless of the appropriation account in which financed. He wanted to know and, indeed, would have to know in order to optimize the allocation of resources, the cost of, for example, a B–52 wing—not only the cost of equipping the wing but also the cost of manning and operating it for its lifetime or at least for a reasonable period of years in the future. Only then would he be in a position to assess the cost and effectiveness of a B–52 wing as compared with other systems designed to perform the same or similar tasks.

Moreover, he wanted to know the total costs of the forces assigned to each of the major missions—the costs of the strategic offensive forces, the continental defense forces, the general purpose forces, etc. As General Maxwell Taylor had pointed out to a congressional committee in 1960:

> . . . If we are called upon to fight, we will not be interested in the services as such. We will be interested rather in task forces, those combinations of Army, Navy, and Air Force which are functional in nature, such as the atomic retaliatory forces, overseas deployments, continental air defense forces, limited war expeditionary forces, and the like. But the point is that we do not keep our budget in these terms. Hence it is not an exaggeration to say that we do not know what kind and how much defense we are buying with any specific budget.[8]

These views closely coincided with my own. The Secretary and I both realized that the financial management system of the Defense Department must serve many purposes. It must produce a budget in a form acceptable to the Congress. It must account for the funds in the same manner in which they were appropriated. It must provide the managers at all levels in the Defense establishment the financial information they need to do their particular jobs in an effective and economical manner. It must produce the financial information required by other agencies of the government—the Bureau of the Budget, the Treasury, and the General Accounting Office.

But we both were convinced that the financial management system must also provide the data needed by top Defense management to make the really crucial decisions, particularly on the major forces and weapons systems needed to carry out the principal missions of the Defense establishment. And we were well aware that the financial management system, as it had evolved over the years, could not directly produce the required data in the form desired. It was clear that a new function, which we call

---

[8] Statement of Gen. Maxwell D. Taylor, *Hearings on Organizing for National Security,* Subcommittee on National Policy Machinery, Committee on Government Operations, U.S. Senate, 86th Cong., 2d Sess., June 14, 1960 (Washington: U.S. Government Printing Office, 1960), p. 769.

programming, would have to be incorporated in the financial management system. I had hoped that I would have at least a year to smooth the way for the introduction of this new function. I recall outlining the proposed programming system to Secretary McNamara in the spring of 1961 and recommending that we spend 18 months developing and installing it, beginning in the first year with a limited number of trial programs, with a view to expanding the system to include all programs during 1962. The Secretary approved the proposed system but shortened my timetable from 18 months to 6. Somehow we developed and installed it, Department-wide, in time to use it as a basis for the FY 1963 Defense budget. Submitted to Congress in January 1962, this was, of course, the first budget to be prepared wholly under the new Administration.

Since the military planning function and the budget function were already well established, the role of programming was to provide a bridge between the two. It was, of course, theoretically possible to recast both the planning and budget structures in terms of major programs related to missions. In fact, the military planning operation was later adapted to the program structure, and I once thought that the budget structure should be similarly realigned. You will find on page 56 of *The Economics of Defense in the Nuclear Age* a format for such a program budget.

But the existing budget structure serves some very useful purposes. It is organized, essentially, in terms of resource categories: (1) Military Personnel; (2) Operation and Maintenance; (3) Procurement; (4) Research, Development, Test and Evaluation; and (5) Military Construction.

This type of structure lends itself ideally to the manner in which the Defense Department actually manages its resources. While military planning and the formulation of programs should logically be done in terms of missions and forces, the Department must be managed not only in those terms but also in terms of resources. For example, we have to manage the acquisition, training, and careers of military personnel; the operation of bases and facilities; the procurement of aircraft, missiles, ships, and tanks; the research and development program; and the construction of airfields, missile sites, quarters, and other additions to our existing physical plant. The present budget structure facilitates the estimation of resource costs as well as the execution of the resource programs.

This division of the budget by broad input or resource categories also provides needed flexibility for the adjustments in the program that are inevitably required in the course of the budget year. Program priorities and requirements always change in unanticipated ways even in the course of a single year as a result of international developments, technological breakthroughs (or disappointments), and all sorts of other events. It is important not to freeze programs in appropriation bills.

Finally, the Congress, and particularly the Appropriations Committees, prefer the existing arrangement of the Defense budget.[9] They have been working with it for more than a decade and have established an historical basis for forming judgments on the validity of the budget requests. It is much easier for an Appropriations Committee, for example, to review a budget request of $4.3 billion for pay and allowances for 960,000 active duty Army personnel than, say, a request of $18 or $19 billion for the major program "General Purpose Forces," or even a request of $700 million for the program element "Army Infantry Divisions." Although the President, under the Budget and Accounting Act of 1921, can propose his budget in any form he pleases, it is the Congress that determines how the funds will be appropriated and this, in turn, determines how the funds will be accounted for. I now feel that the advantages of the existing budget structure far outweigh the disadvantages, which are principally mechanical, namely, the need to translate program categories into budget categories and vice versa. This is the sort of disadvantage that modern high speed computers are well designed to overcome.

Accordingly, we decided to leave the budget structure undisturbed and to span the gap between planning and budgeting with the new programming function. This resulted in a three phase operation: planning-programming-budgeting.

PLANNING PHASE

The first phase—military planning and requirements determination—we envisioned as a continuing year around operation involving the participation of all appropriate elements of the Defense Department in their respective areas of responsibility. We anticipated that the Joint Chiefs of Staff organization and the planners in the military departments would play a particularly important role in this phase. What we were looking for here were not just requirement studies in the traditional sense, but military-economic studies which compared alternative ways of accomplishing national security objectives and which tried to

---

9 For example, see House of Representatives Report No. 1607, 87th Cong., 2d Sess., (House Committee on Appropriations Report on the Department of Defense Budget for Fiscal Year 1963), April 13, 1962, pp. 4-7.

determine the one that contributes the most for a given cost or achieves a given objective at the least cost. These are what we call "cost-effectiveness studies" or systems analyses, and are the subject of my third lecture. (See below, pp. 121–132).

I had originally thought that once an approved five-year program had been developed, the Joint Chiefs of Staff organization and the military planners in the departments would concentrate their attention on specific segments of the program which might require change, and that they would propose such changes whenever the need became apparent any time during the year. When these change proposals were approved, the five-year program would be modified accordingly, thereby providing an up-to-date long range plan at all times. But I had given too little weight to the need to review and analyze, at least once a year, the entire long range program in all of its interrelated parts, rather than in bits and pieces during the course of the entire year. I must confess that the Joint Chiefs of Staff saw this need more clearly than I did. They wanted to make a comprehensive program review each year to take account of the latest changes in military technology and in the international situation; so did each of the military departments; and so did the Secretary.

Accordingly, the planning-programming-budgeting process now starts with the Joint Strategic Objectives Plan prepared by the Joint Chiefs of Staff organization with the help of the military planners in the Services. As I noted earlier, the format of this plan has been modified to bring it into harmony with the new program structure. Thus, the Joint Chiefs of Staff have the opportunity each year to recommend to the Secretary of Defense on a comprehensive basis the military forces and major programs which they believe should be supported over the next five to eight years. The Secretary of Defense in the spring of each year reviews these recommended forces and programs, makes preliminary decisions, and provides to the military departments what is called "tentative force guidance" to serve as a basis for the preparation of their formal change proposals to the official five-year program. The principal "cost-effectiveness" studies are scheduled for completion at about the same time in order to provide the Secretary and his principal advisors with information in depth on the most critical and difficult requirement problems.

I recall that the first list of these requirements projects was developed by Secretary McNamara and were known at the time as "McNamara's 100 trombones". These projects were assigned to the Joint Chiefs of Staff, the military departments, and various elements of the Office of the Secretary of Defense. One, for example, dealt with the question of how many strategic bombers and missiles we would need during the next decade to destroy priority targets. Another involved an examination of requirements for airlift and sealift to meet various contingency war plans and the most economical means of providing that lift. Still another dealt with the comparative advantages and cost of: (a) refurbishing existing items of ground equipment, (b) replacing them with new equipment off the assembly lines, and (c) expediting the development of still better equipment. The Secretary of Defense still originates many of these requirements studies. Others are originated by the Joint Chiefs of Staff, the military departments, and various elements of the Secretary's staff.

PROGRAMMING PHASE

The initial development of the programming system, the second phase, was an enormous undertaking, considering the short time allowed and the fact that we had to handle simultaneously three amendments to the fiscal year 1962 budget originally prepared by the preceding Administration. The problem here was to sort out all of the myriad programs and activities of the Defense establishment and regroup them into meaningful program elements, i.e., integrated combinations of men, equipment, and installations whose effectiveness could be related to our national security objectives. These are the basic building blocks as well as the decision-making levels of the programming process. As I noted earlier, the B–52 bomber force, together with all the supplies, weapons, and manpower needed to make it militarily effective, is one such program element. Other examples are Attack Carriers, F–4 Fighter Wings, the Manned Orbiting Laboratory development project, and Recruit Training. Wherever possible, program elements are measured in physical terms such as numbers of aircraft per wing, numbers of operational missiles on launchers, numbers of active ships, and so forth as well as in financial terms, thus including both "input" and "output"—costs and benefits. Of course, such program elements as research projects can only be measured in terms of inputs.

Costs are measured in terms of what we call "total obligational authority"—the amount required to finance the program element in a given year, regardless of when the funds are appropriated by the Congress, obligated, placed on contract, or spent. Now, admittedly, this is something of a compromise.[10]   It would be

---

[10] For further discussion of program element costs as well as a description of the Defense programming system in 1962, see *Programming System for the Office of the Secretary of Defense, 25 June 1962* (Washington: U.S. Government Printing Office, 1963).

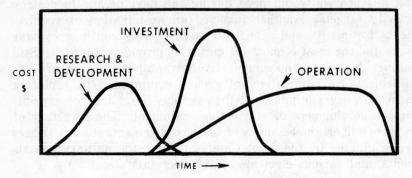

COST CATEGORIES

RESEARCH & DEVELOPMENT	DEVELOPMENT OF A NEW CAPABILITY TO THE POINT OF INTRODUCTION INTO OPERATIONAL USE
INVESTMENT	COSTS REQUIRED BEYOND THE DEVELOPMENT PHASE TO EQUIP FORCES WITH NEW CAPABILITY
OPERATION	RECURRING COSTS REQUIRED TO OPERATE AND MAINTAIN THE CAPABILITY

Figure 2

preferable to cost the program in terms of expenditures, or ideally in terms of resources consumed. However, the accounting difficulties appeared so great that we did not attempt that approach. Moreover, as long as the budget is in terms of obligational authority, the program must be, for the program has to be firmly anchored to the budget. We do not even find it necessary to cost individual program elements in terms of cash expenditures. We have a much better idea of the full cost of 100 MINUTEMAN missiles, for example, than of the phasing of the actual expenditures year by year. And from the point of view of planning and decision-making we are far more interested in the full cost of a program—in "cost to complete"—than in the precise phasing of the costs.

To tie in with the "branch points" at which critical decisions must be made, we subdivide program costs into three categories: development costs, investment costs, and operating costs. Because of the great expense involved in just developing a new weapon system to the point where it could be produced and deployed, a determination to go ahead with full scale development is, in itself, a major decision. There are few major weapon system developments today that can be accomplished for less than $1 billion.

For example, we will have spent $1.5 billion making two proto-
types of the B–70. We have already spent $1.5 billion developing
the NIKE-ZEUS antiballistic missile system and are now spending a comparable amount on the NIKE X. We spent $2.3 billion
developing the ATLAS ICBM, $2.6 billion on TITAN, $2.5 billion
on POLARIS, and $2.1 billion on MINUTEMAN I. Even the de-
velopment of a new torpedo can cost as much as $75 million.
Therefore, we need to know in advance the likely cost of complet-
ing any major weapon development.

Obviously, before we go ahead with the next phase, production
and deployment, we need to know the investment cost of providing
initial equipment for the proposed forces. And, finally, we need
to know the cost of operating the proposed forces each year. In
many cases, for example a B–52 wing, the five-year operating
costs are about equal to the initial equipment costs, and in some
few cases, for example an infantry division, the operating costs
for just one year are actually greater than the initial investment
costs.

To facilitate the conversion of program costs to the budget and
vice versa, we also had to break down the costs of each program
element by the various budget appropriation accounts in which
it is financed. Operating costs typically are financed in the "Military Personnel" and "Operation and Maintenance" appropriations
and, where operating spares are involved, in the "Procurement"
accounts as well. Initial investment costs typically are financed
in the "Procurement" and "Military Construction" appropriations.

We have nearly 1,000 program elements. Where military forces
are involved, they are projected eight years ahead in order to
provide the necessary lead time for the determination of the
procurement programs. All other program data, both physical
and financial, are projected five years ahead. For purposes of
continuity, all program data are shown for each year beginning
in fiscal year 1962; thus, our present Five-year Force Structure
and Financial Program extends from fiscal year 1962 through
fiscal year 1970, with forces projected through fiscal year 1973.
The entire program is subject to continual change and is, therefore, updated every other month. Whenever a change is made in
the cost of a program element in the current fiscal year, it must
also be reflected in the budget for the same year and vice versa.
Considering the vast quantities of data involved in the planning-
programming-budgeting system, the only practical solution was
to computerize the entire operation. This we have now accomplished.

The next task was to relate the program elements to the major missions of the Defense Department. The objective here was to assemble related groups of program elements that, for decision purposes, should be considered together either because they supported one another or because they were close substitutes. The unifying principle underlying each major program is a common mission or set of purposes for the elements involved. We now have nine major programs—

    I. Strategic Retaliatory Forces.
    II. Continental Defense Forces.
    III. General Purpose Forces.
    IV. Airlift and Sealift.
    V. Reserve and Guard.
    VI. Research and Development.
    VII. General Support.
    VIII. Retired Pay.
    IX. Military Assistance.

STRATEGIC RETALIATORY FORCES

AIRCRAFT FORCES

- B-47
- RB/B-47
- B-52
- B-58
- KC-97
- KC-135
- RC-135

MISSILE FORCES

LAND-BASED
- ATLAS
- TITAN
- MINUTEMAN

SEA-BASED
- FLEET BALLISTIC MISSILE SYSTEM (POLARIS)
- REGULUS MISSILE SYSTEM

COMMAND CONTROL, COMMUNICATION & SUPPORT

- SAC CONTROL SYSTEM
- POST-ATTACK COMMAND & COMMUNICATIONS SYSTEM
- BASE OPERATING SUPPORT
- ADVANCE FLYING AND MISSILE TRAINING
- HEADQUARTERS AND COMMAND SUPPORT

Figure 3

The Strategic Retaliatory Forces program includes the manned bomber forces, the land-based missile forces, the sea-based missile forces, and related headquarters and command support activities. Within the aircraft forces are the B–52 long range bombers together with their air-to-ground HOUND DOG missiles and QUAIL decoy missiles, the B–58 and B–47 medium bombers, and the refueling tankers. Within the missile forces are the ATLAS, TITAN, and MINUTEMAN ICBM's and the POLARIS submarine-launched missiles. Also included in the Strategic Retaliatory Forces are the SR–71 and other strategic reconnaissance aircraft and the special communication links and control systems, such as the Post Attack Command and Control System aircraft, which are required for the effective direction of these forces.

The Continental Defense Forces, which might be called the strategic defensive forces, include the North American surveillance, warning, and control network, consisting of land-based, sea-based, and air-borne radars and control centers; the manned interceptors; the surface-to-air missiles; the ballistic missile warning systems; the anti-satellite defense systems; and the civil defense program.

GENERAL PURPOSE FORCES ARMY
COMBATANT FORCES

DIVISIONS	**Missile Commands**
by type	
Brigades	**S S Missile Battalions**
by type	by type - Sep/Org.
Maneuver Battalions	**Air Defense Batteries**
by type - Sep/Org.	by type - Sep/Org.
Artillery Battalions	**Aviation Companies**
by type - Sep/Org.	Sep/Org.
Other Combat Battalions	**Other Combat Forces**
by type - Sep/Org.	
Special Forces Groups	**Combat Support Units**
Armored Cavalry Rgmnts.	**Provisional Air Mobile Units**

Command & Support Forces

Logistic and Support Forces	Support to Non-Army Agencies
Command and Admin. Forces	PACOM & EUCOM Elint. Centers

Base Support

Figure 4

All of the forces in these two major programs would come into play in a general nuclear war. And, as a matter of interest, we have, during the last year, broadened our analyses to treat all of these forces simultaneously in the context of a general nuclear war. This is important because the strategic offensive forces also make a contribution to the "damage limiting" mission, which is the principal purpose of the Continental Defense Forces. A portion of our strategic offensive forces can be applied against an enemy's strategic offensive forces, thus reducing under certain circumstances the potential weight of his attack.

The third, and the largest, major program is that for the General Purpose Forces. These are the forces designed to fight local or limited wars and to engage in theater operations in general war. This major program is organized broadly along Service lines. Within the Service breakdowns, the basic identifiable combat units form the program elements. Army General Purpose Forces include almost all of the regular combat units and command support elements. They range from the four basic kinds of divisions—infantry, armor, mechanized, and airborne—through the missile commands to artillery battalions, air defense units for the field army, and aviation companies.

GENERAL PURPOSE FORCES - NAVY

ATTACK CARRIER STRIKE FORCES
  Attack Carriers (By Type)
  Attack Carrier Air Groups

SURV. & OCEAN CONTROL FORCES
  ASW Aircraft Carriers
  Carrier ASW Air Groups
  Submarines
  Escort Ships
  Small Patrol Ships
  Patrol Aircraft (Sqdns)

MINE WARFARE FORCES

AMPHIBIOUS ASSAULT FORCES

MULTI-PURPOSE COMBAT FORCES
  Cruisers
  Frigates
  Destroyers

SPECIAL COMBAT SUPPORT FORCES

LOGISTIC & OPER. SUPPORT FORCES

COMD. COMMUN. & COMD. SUPPORT

MARINE CORPS DIV. WING TEAMS
  Marine Divisions
  Tank Battalions
  Light Anti-Aircraft Msle. Bns.
  Honest John Bns.
  Amphib. Tractor Bns.
  Other Combat Support Forces
  Marine Air Wings
  Air Sta. & Air Facil.
  Hq. Fleet Marine Forces

RESERVE FLEET FORCES

FLEET SUPPORT BASES, STA. & ACTIV.

Figure 5

The Navy's list is even longer, embracing all of the combatant ships and support vessels except for the strategic missile firing submarines, the radar warning picket ships, and the Military Sea Transportation Service ships. All of the Fleet's various aircraft units are also included except, of course, those assigned to airborne early warning as part of the continental defense system. Components of Navy General Purpose Forces include the carrier task forces and antisubmarine warfare forces.

All Marine Corps units are listed under General Purpose Forces, including the Marine aircraft wings.

The Air Force General Purpose Forces consist principally of those units assigned to the Tactical Air Command in the United States and to the theater commands overseas. The tactical fighters and bombers, tactical reconnaissance aircraft, and the MACE missiles, and their associated command and control systems and headquarters, all fall within this category.

The fourth major program is that for Airlift and Sealift. The troop carrier wings of the Air Force, including theater airlift, the Military Air Transport Service aircraft, and the Military Sea Transportation Service ships, make up the essential components of this group.

The fifth major program is composed of the Reserve and National Guard Forces. The program elements are arranged by Service and by the major mission each element or unit supports. Actually, Reserve and National Guard program elements are reviewed as parts of the appropriate mission packages—Continental Defense Forces, General Purpose Forces, Airlift and Sealift

GENERAL PURPOSE FORCES - AIR FORCE

TACTICAL AIRCRAFT FORCES		SURFACE-TO-SURFACE MISSILE FORCES
F - 84	B - 57	MACE
F— 100	B - 66	COUNTERINSURGENCY FORCES
F - 101	RF - 101	COMMAND CONTROL COMM. & SUPPORT
F - 104	RF - 4	Air Weapon Control System
F - 105	RF - 111	PACOM & EUCOM ELINT Centers
F - 4C	RB - 66	Other Communications
F - 111	KB - 50	Base Operating Support
INTERCEPTOR AIRCRAFT FORCES		Advanced Flying Training
F - 102		Hq. & Command Support

Figure 6

Forces, and so forth, as well as in the context of the reserve components themselves. This is a case where for decision purposes we want visability both ways—as reserve components and as parts of mission forces.

The sixth major program, Research and Development, includes all of the R&D projects which are not directly associated with program elements in other major programs. The R&D program elements are grouped into several categories, ranging from pencil pushing to operational hardware—

1. Research—the effort directed toward the expansion of knowledge of natural phenomena and our environment and the solution of problems in the physical, biological, medical, behavioral, social, and engineering sciences.

2. Exploratory Developments—the effort directed toward the expansion of technological knowledge and the development of materials, components, devices, and sub-systems which it is hoped will have some useful application to new military weapons and equipment. Here the emphasis is on exploring the feasibility of new ideas, up to the point of demonstration with "breadboard" devices and proto-type components and sub-systems.

3. Advanced Developments—the effort directed toward the development of experimental hardware for technical or operational testing of its suitability for military purposes, prior to the determination of whether the item should be designed or engineered for actual Service use. Here is where we begin to identify each project with a specific military application or technique, and we begin to question in depth its potential military utility. During this phase we also begin to explore the costs of the most likely applications in order to determine whether the potential operational benefit would be worth the cost of development, production, and deployment.

4. Engineering Developments—the effort directed toward the development of a particular system engineered for Service use and for operational employment, but which has not as yet been approved for production and deployment. It is at this point that large commitments of resources must be made to single projects. Accordingly, before full-scale development is initiated, the specific operational requirements and the cost-effectiveness of the system must be confirmed, and goals, milestones, and time schedules must be established.

5. Operational Systems Developments—the effort directed toward the continued development, test, evaluation, and design improvement of projects which have already entered (or have been approved for) the production-deployment stage—are included in other major programs as integral parts of the appropriate program elements. For example, the continuing development of MINUTE-MAN II is included in the program element "MINUTE-MAN II" under the major program "Strategic Retaliatory Forces."*

The seventh major program, General Support, is the "all other" program containing all of the activities not readily allocable to mission forces or weapons systems. Some of its major sub-categories are: individual training and education including recruit training, technical training, flight training, and Service academies; communications between higher headquarters and Unified Commands; most intelligence collection; medical services; support of higher headquarters; and so forth. In dollar value this is a large category accounting for almost 30% of the total Defense budget. It is essentially the "overhead" of the Defense Department, although much of it, like training, is "variable" overhead.

The eighth major program, Retired Pay, has been separately identified because it represents costs beyond our direct control. The terms of retirement and the rates of pay are established by law. Expenditures for this purpose will amount to $1.5 billion in the next fiscal year and are increasing rapidly as World War II veterans join the retired ranks.

The last major program, Military Assistance, includes the military equipment and training being provided to some 59 foreign nations. For administrative purposes, we have found it best to retain this activity as a separate program.[11]

All of the program data, together with the description of the forces, their tasks and missions, procurement lists, facility lists and so forth, constitute, collectively, what we term "The Five-Year Force Structure and Financial Program." Since the data are machine processed, they can be summarized in different ways. For the use of top management in the Defense Department we

[11] For another, fuller description of the Defense programming system, see presentation and testimony of Assistant Secretary Hitch, *Hearings on Systems Development and Management*, Subcommittee of the Committee on Government Operations, House of Representatives, 87th Cong., 2d Sess. (Washington: U.S. Government Printing Office, 1962), pp. 513-547.

* The Armed Services Procurement Regulation, Rev. 8, 1 Nov. 1964, also lists a sixth category, *Management and Support*. This category includes all effort directed toward support of installations or operations required for general research and development use.

prepare and update at regular intervals a special summary volume which displays in tabular form the forces, financial, manpower, and procurement programs. The Five-Year Force Structure and Financial Program is formally approved by the Secretary of Defense and is binding for programming purposes on all components of the Department.

We recognized from the beginning that the Defense program is extremely dynamic and that changes would be required at various times during the year. Accordingly, we established a formal program change control system. The basic elements of this system involve the submission of program change proposals by any major component of the Defense Department, their review by all interested components, the Secretary's decision on each proposal, and finally, the assignment of responsibility for carrying out this particular decision to the appropriate military department or agency. Hundreds of program change proposals are submitted each year requesting changes involving billions of dollars.

BUDGETING PHASE

This brings us to the third phase of the planning-programming-budgeting process. It may be worth emphasizing at this point that the programming review is not intended as a substitute for the annual budget review. Rather, it is designed to provide a Defense Department-approved program to serve as a basis for the preparation of the annual budget as well as guidance for future planning. In the budget review we go into greater detail, for the next year of the Five-Year Program, on procurement lists, production schedules, lead times, prices, status of funds, and all the other facets involved in the preparation of an annual budget. And, as I pointed out earlier, we still manage our funds in terms of the appropriation accounts as well as in terms of the program structure. Essentially, the annual budget now represents a detailed analysis of the financial requirements of the first annual increment of the approved Five-Year Program.

Thus, we have provided for the Secretary of Defense and his principal military and civilian advisors a system which brings together at one place and at one time all of the relevant information which they need to make sound decisions on the forward program and to control the execution of that program. And we have provided the necessary flexibility in the form of a program change control system. Now, for the first time the largest business in the world has a comprehensive Defense Department-wide plan that extends more than one year into the future. And it is a realistic and responsible one—programming not only the forces, but also the men, equipment, supplies, installations, and budget dollars required to support them. Budgets are in balance with programs, programs with force requirements, force requirements with military missions, and military missions with national security objectives. And the total budget dollars required by the plan for future years do not exceed the Secretary's responsible opinion of what is necessary and feasible.

With this management tool at his command, the Secretary of Defense is now in a position to carry out the responsibilities assigned to him by the National Security Act, namely, to exercise "direction, authority, and control over the Department of Defense"—and without another major reorganization of the Defense establishment.

10

PROGRAMMING AND BUDGETING IN THE DEPARTMENT OF DEFENSE*

By Alain C. Enthoven

PROGRAM ELEMENT SUMMARY DATA

A "program element" is defined as an integrated force or activity—a combination of men, equipment, and facilities, to which we must relate their costs, projected over a five-year period. All of these data for each "program element" are assembled on what we call a "Program Element Summary Data" sheet.

The figure on page 87 is a "Program Element Summary Data" sheet for a hypothetical U.S. Air Force program element—F–202, a tactical fighter.

The first section (the figure on p. 88) shows the military forces which are the "product" or "output" of the Defense program— that is, the numbers of F–202 wings, squadrons, and unit equipment (U.E.) aircraft programmed for operational deployment through fiscal year 1971.

The last line of figures in this section represents the number of GAM–99 air-to-ground missiles programmed for this force on the basis of 25 Unit Equipment (U.E.) missiles per squadron of aircraft.

The forces are projected eight years beyond the current year, three years more than the rest of the program element data. This is to allow for the leadtime required between the ordering of equipment and its availability for operational deployment.

The data presented in subsequent sections of this form will be more meaningful if the reader keeps in mind that in this hypothetical case the force increases from zero squadrons in 1966 to 18 squadrons by 1970.

---

*Editor's note: The following description of programming and budgeting was drawn from briefing materials developed by the Office of the Assistant Secretary of Defense (Comptroller). This account of DOD procedures has been presented several times by Messrs. Hitch and Enthoven to Defense officials and military officers of the North Atlantic Treaty Organization, its member governments, and other friendly nations. The version of the briefing that appears here is based on Mr. Enthoven's remarks before the representatives of the Government of India and the National Defense College in New Delhi, March 1-6, 1965. Some revisions were made, however, to incorporate information about the latest developments in the system and to adapt the text for a printed presentation, as contrasted to an oral one.

HYPOTHETICAL ELEMENT

PROGRAM ELEMENT SUMMARY DATA		IMPLEMENTING DOD COMPONENT Dept. Of The Air Force		PROGRAM CHANGE NO. 3.88.77.01.4-2				
PROGRAM ELEMENT F-202					CODE 3.88.77.01.4			

APPROVED PROGRAM - BY FISCAL YEAR

FORCES	CFY 63	FY 64	FY 65	FY 66	FY 67	FY 68	FY 69	FY 70	FY 71
U.E.									
Wings						1	2	6	6
Squadrons 20					1	3	6	18	18
Total U.E.					20	60	120	360	360
GAM. 99 (non-add)									
Squadron (ea.) 25									
Total U.E					25	75	150	450	450

TOTAL OBLIGATIONAL AUTHORITY (In millions of dollars)

	CFY 63	FY 64	FY 65	FY 66	FY 67	FY 68	FY 69	FY 70	FY 71
RESEARCH AND DEVELOPMENT: RDT & E	100	200	300	200	50				
MILITARY CONSTRUCTION									
TOTAL RESEARCH & DEV.	100	200	300	200	50				
INVESTMENT: Aircraft Proc.			150	500	900	750			
Missile Proc.			15	20	25	25			
Other Proc.					1	1			
MILITARY CONSTRUCTION									
TOTAL INVESTMENT			165	520	926	776			
OPERATING: O & M				1	2	3			
Aircraft Proc.			1	3	5	7			
Missile Proc.						1			
Other Proc.					1	5			
MILITARY PERSONNEL									
TOTAL OPERATING			1	4	8	16			
TOTAL OBLIGATIONAL AUTH.	100	200	466	724	984	792			

MANPOWER (in thousands)

	CFY 63	FY 64	FY 65	FY 66	FY 67	FY 68	FY 69	FY 70	FY 71
MILITARY OFFICER					.1	.3			
ENLISTED					.3	1.5			
CIVILIAN DIRECT HIRE									
CONTRACT FOREIGN NAT'L									

NET CHANGE SINCE LAST SUBMISSION OF 1 April 1963 (date)

	CFY 63	FY 64	FY 65	FY 66	FY 67	FY 68	FY 69	FY 70	FY 71
FORCES (Squadrons)								+6	+6
TOTAL OBLIGATIONAL AUTH.					+450	+400			
MANPOWER MILITARY									
CIVILIAN									

BASIS FOR CHANGES

Authorized increase in forces - Program Change, 1 May 1963

DATE 15 May 1963 | IMPLEMENTING DOD COMPONENT (Signature)

FORMAT C

Figure 7

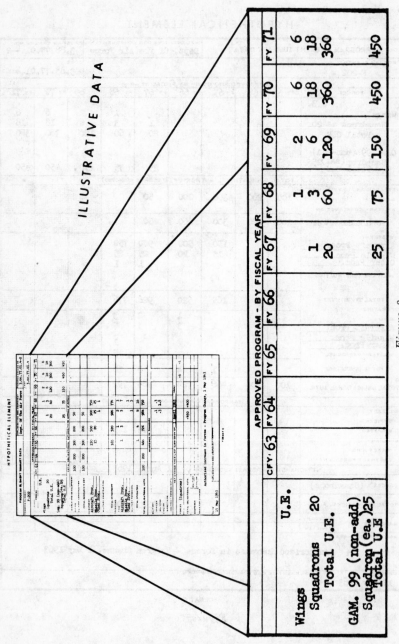

Figure 8

The next section (the figure on p. 90) shows the programmed costs of this force through the next five years. These are the resource "inputs" to the program. We use the term "total obligational authority" to describe the full cost of an annual increment of the program, regardless of when the money is appropriated by the U.S. Congress or when it is actually spent by the Defense Department. In this way the Defense managers are able to see the program elements in relation to their costs—"outputs" related to "inputs."

The costs are first broken down into the three broad categories: Research and Development; Investment; and Operating. Under each of these costs categories are listed the budget "appropriation accounts" from which this program element is financed.

For example, under the "Research and Development" category, two appropriation accounts are listed: "Research, Development, Test and Evaluation, Air Force," and "Military Construction, Air Force." In our hypothetical example, we would have included in our 1963 budget for "RDT&E, Air Force," $100 million for this "program element." The Congress actually appropriated more than $3.6 billion for "RDT&E, Air Force," in fiscal year 1963. The relation between the program and the budget will be treated in greater detail a little later. In this hypothetical example, no funds are required for the construction of R&D facilities.

Under the "Investment" category, we provide lines for the different procurement appropriation accounts used by each of the military departments. In the case of the Air Force, there are three such accounts: "Aircraft Procurement, Air Force," "Missile Procurement, Air Force," and "Other Procurement, Air Force."

The rising level of investment funds required over the fiscal year 1965–1967 period reflects the leadtime required between the ordering of the aircraft and missiles and their availability for operational deployment beginning in fiscal year 1967. The reader will note that no funds are required in the "Other Procurement" account until 1967, reflecting the shorter leadtimes of equipment such as standard ground support equipment. Since these aircraft would use existing facilities or inherited assets, no funds are needed for "Military Construction."

Under the "Operating" category, we have the "Operations and Maintenance" appropriation from which we would pay the day-to-day costs of operating the forces; the "Aircraft Procurement" and "Other Procurement" accounts to pay for the spare parts

ILLUSTRATIVE DATA

	CFY 63	FY 64	FY 65	FY 66	FY 67	FY 68
TOTAL OBLIGATIONAL AUTHORITY (In millions of dollars)						
RESEARCH AND DEVELOPMENT:						
RDT&E	100	200	300	200	50	
MILITARY CONSTRUCTION						
TOTAL RESEARCH & DEV.	100	200	300	200	50	
INVESTMENT:						
Aircraft Proc.			150	500	900	750
Missile Proc.			15	20	25	25
Other Proc.					1	1
MILITARY CONSTRUCTION						
TOTAL INVESTMENT			165	520	926	776
OPERATING:						
O&M			1	1	2	3
Aircraft Proc.				3	5	7
Missile Proc.					1	1
Other Proc.						5
MILITARY PERSONNEL						
TOTAL OPERATING			1	4	8	16
TOTAL OBLIGATIONAL AUTH.	100	200	466	724	984	792

Figure 9

consumed; and the "Military Personnel" account for the pay and allowances of military personnel.

The still small but increasing amounts programmed for Operating costs reflect the initial stages of the force build-up projected for fiscal years 1967-70. These costs would rise very quickly in subsequent years.

The next section of the "Data" sheet (the figure below) shows the numbers of military personnel, both officer and enlisted, required to man this force in each of the fiscal years shown. The

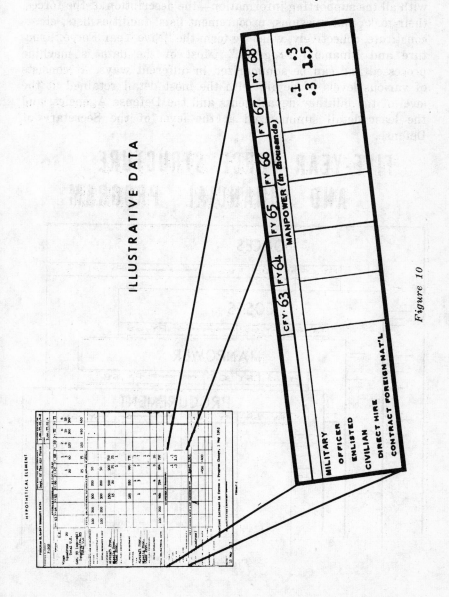

Figure 10

approximately 100 officers and 300 enlisted men shown in 1967 reflect the initial manning of the first squadron that year. Again, as in the case of other types of operating cost, which vary with the size of the force, these numbers would increase rapidly in later years. If there were any civilian personnel directly associated with this program element, they too would be shown here.

THE FIVE-YEAR FORCE STRUCTURE AND FINANCIAL PROGRAM

All of the "Program Element Summary Data" sheets, together with all the supporting information—the description of the forces, their tasks and missions, procurement lists, facilities lists, etc.— constitute, collectively, what we term the "Five-Year Force Structure and Financial Program." Most of the data is machine processed and can be summarized in different ways. It consists of various levels of detail, with the most detail retained at the level of the military departments and the Defense Agencies, and the least detail summarized at the level of the Secretary of Defense.

FIVE-YEAR FORCE STRUCTURE
AND FINANCIAL PROGRAM

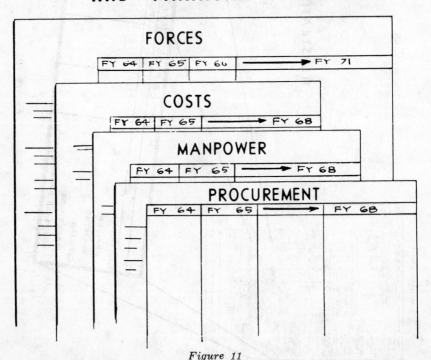

Figure 11

For the Secretary's own use, we put together a book containing a large number of summary tables, showing forces, dollars, manpower, procurement, construction, equipment inventory, and balance-of-payments data. The forces are projected ahead eight years and the rest of the data five years. Also we prepare for the Secretary's book matrix tables containing the nine programs in the column headings and the traditional budget categories in the stub. This ability to translate the Five-Year Program into budget terms and vice versa is an essential ingredient of the programming system.

The Five-Year Force Structure and Financial Program is formally approved by the Secretary of Defense and is binding for programming purposes on all components of the Department.

Changes in the program are made as necessary, at any time during the year. However, the majority of the important changes are concentrated in the three-month period—April, May, June—following the completion of the annual Joint Strategic Objectives Plan by the Joint Chiefs of Staff and the Secretary's force guidance on April 1. Proposals for changes in programs are processed in the succeeding months and the Secretary makes his decisions by the end of August so that the military departments can be furnished an approved program for the next five fiscal years upon which to base their budget estimates for the next fiscal year.

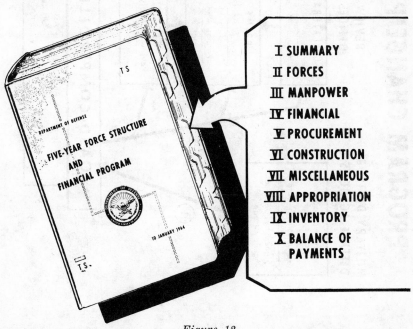

Figure 12

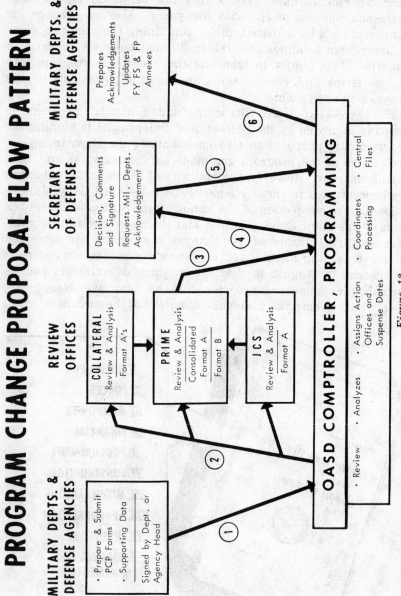

PROGRAM CHANGE PROPOSAL FLOW PATTERN

MILITARY DEPTS. & DEFENSE AGENCIES

- Prepare & Submit PCP Forms
- Supporting Data

  Signed by Dept. or Agency Head

REVIEW OFFICES

COLLATERAL
Review & Analysis
Format A's

PRIME
Review & Analysis
Consolidated
Format A
Format B

JCS
Review & Analysis
Format A

SECRETARY OF DEFENSE

Decision, Comments and Signature
Requests Mil. Depts. Acknowledgement

MILITARY DEPTS. & DEFENSE AGENCIES

Prepares Acknowledgements
Updates
FY FS & FP
Annexes

OASD COMPTROLLER, PROGRAMMING

- Review
- Analyzes
- Assigns Action Offices and Suspense Dates
- Coordinates Processing
- Central Files

Figure 13

The specific administrative procedure for making these changes is known as the "Program Change Control Procedure." The basic elements of this procedure involve the submission of program change proposals (PCP's) by any major component of the Department of Defense, their review by all interested components, the Secretary's decision and finally, the assignment of responsibility for carrying out this decision to completion.

In summary, this formalized program change procedure helps to ensure—

(1) that there is only one channel for major decision-making;

(2) that proposed changes receive a rapid, but complete, review by all parties concerned;

(3) that program decisions are made on the basis of the best information available, including a validation of their long-range cost implications;

(4) that all major changes are made only after approval by the Secretary of Defense; and

(5) that there is always available an up-to-date, approved five-year program for U.S. defense activities.

BUDGETING PHASE

The third phase of the planning-programming-budgeting system is the preparation of the annual budget estimates. The budget phase, by its nature, is an annual operation which must mesh with the preparation of the Federal Government budget as a whole. However, this requirement in no way interferes with the programming process or with our continuing consideration of the longer-range problems of Defense since we simply use the next one-year increment of the approved five-year program as the basis for the budget request, thereby, in effect, financing the program one year at a time.

The budget is prepared in terms of functional (or resource) categories, i.e., military personnel; operation and maintenance; procurement; research, development, test, and evaluation; and military construction. The military departments submit their budget estimates for the up-coming fiscal year early in October. These estimates are reviewed in the Office of the Secretary of Defense where such things as production schedules, prices, lead-times, activity rates, personnel plans, training requirements, funding problems, etc., are very closely scrutinized. Detailed shopping lists for missiles, aircraft, guns, and all of the thousands of individual items of equipment and supplies which are requested for funding in the next fiscal year are given a final review and approval.

In practice, the Military Departments submit their annual budget estimates in two parts, a basic budget and an addendum budget. The basic budget reflects the latest approved program for the first year of the Five Year Program, incorporating all of the PCP decisions up until the time the estimates are prepared. The addendum budget covers additional requests beyond the approved program, including PCP's that were still in process but had not been resolved when the estimates were submitted. It should be noted that one of our ground rules for including an item in the addendum budget is the submission of a PCP. Decisions on both basic budget and addendum budget items are made by the Secretary of Defense in the budget review. This detailed budget review, which is conducted by the Office of the Secretary of Defense, terminates in the preparation of the Department of Defense budget by approximately mid-December. Although it is true that program decisions are the basis for the Departmental budget submission, it is nevertheless necessary that decisions in the budget review, which sometimes modify earlier program decisions, be reflected back into the Five Year Program. A revised Five Year Program is published in January to reflect the budget decisions, to up-date the base for programming and budgeting actions during the rest of the calendar year, and to provide information for the Secretary's statement to Congress in support of the President's Budget.

The chart on page 97 shows, in a very truncated form, the distribution of the FY 1964 Defense budget plan as it was submitted to the Congress. The complete table showing all the major programs and all the appropriation accounts is too voluminous to put on a table or slide.

Across the top of the chart are the major programs: Strategic Retaliatory Forces, Continental Air and Missile Defense Forces, etc. The third from the last column shows the Total Obligational Authority (TOA) for all of the programs. The second from the last column shows, primarily, the amounts in each appropriation account which are available for application to the next year's program. Predominantly, these are funds appropriated in prior years which are no longer needed for the originally intended purpose because of program cancellations, administrative economies, etc.

The last column, therefore, is the amount of new obligational authority, that is, appropriations, required to finance the 1964 program increment, and these are the amounts we requested from the Congress.

Department of Defense
FY 1964 BUDGET PROGRAMS AND NEW OBLIGATIONAL AUTHORITY
By Appropriation Title
(Millions of Dollars)

Appropriation Title	Strategic Retaliatory Forces	Continental Air and Missile Defense Forces	General Purpose Forces	Total Programs (TOA)	Financing Adjustments	New Obligational Authority (Appropriation)
MILITARY PERSONNEL:						
Military Personnel, Army		92.6	2,626.0	4,035.0	-150.0	3,885.0
Military Personnel, Navy	56.2	48.9	1,569.6	2,796.0	-120.0	2,676.0
Military Personnel, Marine Corps	0.2	0.6	487.1	678.6	-	678.6
Military Personnel, Air Force	1,132.4	485.4	620.0	4,178.0	-30.0	4,148.0
Reserve Personnel, Army	-	-	-	210.1	-	210.1
TOTAL - Military Personnel	1,188.8	627.5	5,302.7	14,435.2	-300.0	14,135.2
PROCUREMENT						
Procurement of Equipment and Missiles, Army		75.6	2,711.5		-114.0	3,202.0
Procurement of Aircraft and Missiles, Navy	672.5	3.9	2,323.4	3,111.0	-45.0	3,066.0
Shipbuilding and Conversion, Navy	702.3	99.4	1,629.0	2,381.3	-71.3	2,310.0
Other Procurement, Navy	133.4		748.4	1,231.5	-23.5	1,208.0
Procurement, Marine Corps			176.1	221.6	-13.9	207.7
Aircraft Procurement, Air Force	641.4	103.9	1,395.1	3,956.5	-397.5	3,559.0
Missile Procurement, Air Force	1,974.4	17.3	206.3	2,405.0	-228.0	2,177.0
Other Procurement, Air Force	142.7	191.9	253.0	1,006.3	-54.8	951.5
Procurement, Defense Agencies	-	-	-	43.6	-	43.6
TOTAL - Procurement	4,266.7	492.0	9,442.8	17,672.8	-948.0	16,724.8
GRAND TOTAL - MILITARY FUNCTIONS	7,284.8	1,977.0	19,100.0	55,183.5	-1,522.9	53,660.6

Figure 14

We, of course, also estimate obligations and expenditures not only for the next fiscal year, but for the entire five-year period, but this is not done in terms of programs but rather in terms of appropriation accounts, the same as all the other departments and agencies of the United States Government.

Along the left hand side of the chart are the appropriation titles. We show here only a few selected accounts. There are many more shown in the printed tables.

In this way the Defense planning-programming-budgeting process is accommodated to the traditional functioning of the rest of the U.S. Government, including particularly the Legislative Branch. The fact that funds are appropriated for only one year at a time, and in a form quite different from the way in which we plan and program, does not offer an insurmountable obstacle. We can and do accommodate ourselves to this institutional environment, although it does complicate the accounting problem to some extent.

It should be noted that the Five-Year Force Structure and Financial Plan is an internal Defense Department tool and does not represent an approved program of the U.S. Government. The Congress of the United States reserves unto itself the right to authorize and appropriate funds, year by year, against this proposed program, and even the President of the United States is not unalterably committed to the five-year program in detail. It is essentially a planning tool—a road map, if you please, of where we hope to move over the next five years.

In summary, the Programming System has been a success. Our Congressional leaders like it because it provides them with valuable information on the shape of the Defense programs. Our military leaders have accepted it also and they recognize in it a number of important advantages from their point of view: for one, it gives them the same financial information as is available to the Secretary of Defense and it enables them to see the cost implications of the force levels they are considering; for another, operating within the rules of the Programming System, it would be difficult for the Secretary of Defense to say to the Army, "cut your budget by $1 billion, but do not cut the forces." As one general put it, "if he wants to make a cut, the Secretary has to name the units that will be dropped." This brings the point of view of our top military and civilian leaders much closer together than would otherwise be the case, and this improved understanding results in better decision making.

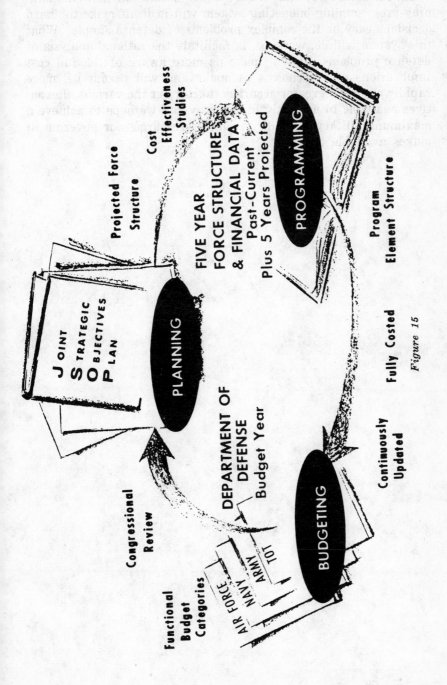

Figure 15

Let me assure you that we are under no illusion that our planning-programming-budgeting system will in itself make the hard decisions easy or the complex problems of defense simple. What this system will do, we hope, is facilitate the rational analysis of defense problems. It will make us more aware of the full cost implications of the choices we make and will permit us, more rapidly and with greater accuracy, to cost out the various alternatives available to us. Only in this way can we hope to achieve a maximum military capability from the resources our government makes available to us.

11

PROGRAM PACKAGES*

By Charles J. Hitch

.   .   .   .

Senator Jackson. Mr. Hitch, in order to clarify the procedure in your new program package system, let us consider POLARIS as an illustration. Who would be charged with the responsibility of making the POLARIS presentation, for instance, for the central offensive force package?

Mr. Hitch. The Navy Department.

Senator Jackson. Then from there would it be handled by the Joint Chiefs, or by the Secretary of Defense? What would be the procedure?

Mr. Hitch. The decision about the program would be made by the Secretary of Defense. He would, of course, get military advice from the Joint Chiefs. He would undoubtedly in a case like this also want the advice of the Director of Defense Research and Engineering on the technical aspects of the problem and the advice of the Assistant Secretary of Defense, Installations and Logistics, on the production problems and production schedules. As Comptroller, I would provide the cost analysis, and under our new procedure, the Programming Office would assemble and present all of the data.

The decision would have to be Secretary McNamara's. There is no one else who can make these decisions that influence so profoundly the allocation of resources among the Services.

Senator Jackson. What troubles me is that if, on this first go-round, under the program package approach, the service finds that with the big increase occurring—in this case in the strategic striking force— other items are cut back, maybe they would be reluctant to push the newer and more costly programs that would tend to offset the so-called balance of forces within their own department.

Mr. Hitch. All I can say is that it seems to me that under the program package procedures there is less chance of those cutbacks

---

*Excerpts from testimony before the Subcommittee on National Policy Machinery of the Committee on Government Operations, U.S. Senate, on 24 July 1961. *Hearings, Organizing for National Security: The Budget and the Policy Process,* Part VIII (87th Congress, 1st Session; Washington: U.S. Government Printing Office, 1961), pp. 1018–1021, 1032.

affecting programs in the same Service, so that the tendency to hold back for this reason should be considerably less.

Senator Jackson. Now, you will come to Congress, as you said you would, with the conventional budget, but would you also come with the program packages?

Mr. Hitch. Yes, sir. Our present plan is to present the budget in both ways. The Secretary wants to present it and justify it by programs.

We also, of course, have to present it by appropriation title. That is the manner in which we expect the Congress to appropriate the funds.

Senator Jackson. Now, who will defend the package, or packages?

Mr. Hitch. This will be the primary responsibility of the Secretary. He will have the help of all of us, including, we hope, some of the people in the Services.

Senator Jackson. That is what I am leading into, the question of the role of the commanders of the unified and specified commands in presenting the packages.

Now, if for example, you are dealing with the strategic striking forces, the organization is divided at the present time.

My questions, I want to assure you, are merely questions; they are not judgments on my part. I am just trying to bring out the full implications of your plan.

If the organization of the program packages along these lines makes sense for reasons of budget and decision-making, is it not possible that they make sense for the actual organization of the forces?

Or perhaps this does not necessarily follow. In other words, you may do it for purposes of budgeting, you may not do it for purposes of organization.

It would still seem to me that a single program package—in this case, the offensive striking forces—would be best advocated and defended by one overall commander.

I presume at the outset you are going to have this package defended by the people who are responsible for the separate elements.

Mr. Hitch. Yes, sir; each element of a program package will be defended in detail by the people who are responsible for that element.

Senator Jackson. So there would be no change organizationally?

Mr. Hitch. There will be no change. I am not saying there will be no organizational changes in the future, but we don't at present envision any change in this respect.

Certainly, ideally, the way you program and budget should parallel the way you are organized; they are interrelated. But the two do not have to mesh perfectly.

You can program and prepare your budget in one way while you are organized in a somewhat different way.

Senator Jackson. Then, I assume, in the case of our strategic offensive forces, you would have the commander of SAC defend most of the budget and the Chief of Naval Operations would handle it from the standpoint of the submarine-launched missiles.

Mr. Hitch. At present the commanders of the unified and specified commands do have an input to this programing. They make their submissions through the Joint Chiefs organization. They submit their requirements as they see them to the Joint Chiefs and it is the Joint Chiefs who directly advise the Secretary.

Senator Jackson. I want to turn again to the question of the program packages themselves. This, in general, is what General Taylor was advocating in connection with his functional budget approach, was it not?

Mr. Hitch. Yes; as I understand what General Taylor said, we are talking about the same things.

Senator Jackson. You have made certain refinements, but the approach is essentially the same.

Mr. Hitch. Yes.

Senator Jackson. You generally agree with his approach to this problem?

Mr. Hitch. To this problem; yes sir.

Senator Jackson. In what way will the preparation of a budget estimate for a program package differ from previous practice so far as the roles of the Services, the individual military departments, and the Joint Chiefs of Staff are concerned?

In other words, is the central war offensive package merely a compilation of figures which have been prepared by the individual Services, or is it a package in the sense that the balance between its various elements has been debated and agreed by the Joint Chiefs or some other appropriate joint body?

Mr. Hitch. The elements proposed for inclusion in a program package will each be prepared by some Service. Each of the elements is a Service element and the responsible Service will prepare the cost estimates associated with that particular element.

The decisions about the balance of the package as a whole, that is, which elements you will approve, and how large each of these elements should be, will be made by the Secretary on the basis of advice that he gets from, among others, the Joint Chiefs.

Senator Jackson. In other words, the Services provide the elements. Those elements are known.

Mr. Hitch. Those are known to everyone. Yes sir.

Senator Jackson. The Secretary of Defense will have the ultimate responsibility.

Mr. Hitch. I am sure that the sum total of the costs of all the elements proposed by the Services will add up to considerably more than the Secretary of Defense or the President or the Congress will approve.

So there will be, as usual, the necessity of review and of reduction in the proposals.

Senator Jackson. I mentioned earlier the question of long-range authority. We do have that provision for certain cases involving contracts in previous appropriation bills which have been passed.

Is this not helpful, especially in research and development projects, so that you could have some assurance that the projects could be seen through to completion?

Mr. Hitch. Yes, sir; I think it is desirable. In a good many research and development projects we now have what is called longevity funding. While there is a considerable amount of this now, it still is a very small proportion of the total research and development program.

In addition to longevity funding for some research and development programs there is what is called full funding for a number of procurement programs, particularly naval vessels. Naval vessels are now fully funded at the time Congress first approves going ahead with a particular naval shipbuilding program.

. . . .

Mr. Tufts. May I turn to the question of Defense relations with the Budget Bureau?

As I understand it, in the past, mainly for reasons of the technical complexity of the defense budget and the length of time required for its preparation, representatives of the Bureau have cooperated rather closely with your Office in the preparation of the defense budget?

Mr. Hitch. That is correct.

Mr. Tufts. Has that been changed in any way?

Mr. Hitch. No, we expect to continue this joint review with the Bureau of the Budget.

Mr. Tufts. In your judgment, does this practice, which is continuing, have any bearing on the independence of the Bureau's view, on its ability to advise the President, to help inform the President about the factors which he should bear in mind in his review of the defense budget?

As I understand it, the notion has been that the Bureau should preserve an arm's length relationship to the departments and agencies in the executive branch. One wonders whether there is quite this arm's length relationship between the Bureau and the Defense because of the close involvement of the Bureau personnel in the defense budget preparation.

Does this interfere in any way with the Bureau's responsibility at present?

Mr. Hitch. In theory, I suppose it might. I would say from my limited experience that the BOB seems to be able to maintain an independent point of view. I expect that ideally it would be better to have successive budget reviews, first within the Department, then by the Bureau. However, the amount of business to be done, and quantity of review that is required, is such that we just do not see how we can carry out completely separate reviews and fit the budget cycle into an annual timetable without adding a couple more months to the year.

Mr. Tufts. Do the Bureau people participate in all of the three phases of your program: requirement phase, programming phase, and budget?

Mr. Hitch. No, sir, I am referring to the budget phase.

Mr. Tufts. They do not participate in the first two.

Mr. Hitch. They are interested and we keep them informed, of course, but I do not anticipate that they will be regularly involved in the review during the requirements and program phase.

Mr. Tufts. Insofar as you have succeeded in clearly separating these phases, the Bureau's participation will be limited to the final phase, the budgetary phase?

Mr. Hitch. Yes, sir, it will. Of course, as I have pointed out, after this year we envisage the requirements and programming phases as being continuous year-round operations. They will not be concentrated in any particular month or two of the year.

12

RETROSPECT AND PROSPECT*

By Charles J. Hitch

In the course of the . . . preceding lectures, I have sketched the evolution of the Defense management problem over the years and discussed . . . major management innovations made since 1961. But while I have focused my attention on the central management system—the planning-programming-budget process—the Defense establishment is organized and managed in many different ways to perform its many different functions.

The principal operating subdivisions of the Defense Department are still the three military departments reporting directly to the Secretary of Defense. Most of the combat forces are organized in unified and specified commands, such as the Air Defense Command or the European Command, reporting to the Secretary of Defense through the Joint Chiefs of Staff. For certain services common to more than one of the military departments, there have been established over the years a number of what we now call "Defense agencies" reporting to the Secretary of Defense either directly or through the Joint Chiefs of Staff. These include the Defense Atomic Support Agency, which conducts joint research and technical operations in the nuclear field; the Defense Communications Agency, which handles the overall management of the long lines of communication; the Defense Intelligence Agency, which is responsible for military intelligence at the seat of the Government; the Defense Contract Audit Agency, which performs both pre-contract and post-contract audits; and the Defense Supply Agency, which provides logistics support involving common supplies and services for the entire Defense establishment.

The last three organizations have been created since 1961, although the initial studies looking to the establishment of the Defense Intelligence Agency were completed under the previous Administration. The Defense Supply Agency was established in 1961 by putting together under one head a number of separate organizations handling particular categories of common supplies

*Excerpts from the "H. Rowan Gaither Lectures in Systems Science" delivered at the University of California on 5-9 April 1965. Reprinted by permission from The Regents of the University of California, copyright owners, and published under the title *Decision-Making for Defense* (Berkeley and Los Angeles: University of California Press, 1965).

such as food, clothing and textiles, medical supplies, and so forth. This particular "Defense agency," like the Defense Contract Audit Agency, reports directly to the Secretary of Defense rather than through the Joint Chiefs of Staff because of the essentially "non-military" character of its activities.

The Secretary of Defense's own office is organized by fields of specialization—Research and Engineering, Installations and Logistics, Manpower, International Security Affairs, Comptroller, and so forth. His principal military advisors are the Joint Chiefs of Staff and the principal military planners are in the Joint Staff organization of the JCS and in the military departments.

I pointed out in my second lecture that, even at the Secretary's level, we cannot manage all of the Department's activities solely in terms of programming. The pay, allowances, and other benefits of military personnel are prescribed by law, generally not with reference to particular assignments but, rather, in terms of an over-all career development pattern. Accordingly, we have to manage our military manpower in the aggregate, by grade, skill, etc. as well as in terms of program elements, such as B–52 wings or Army divisions.

There are many other areas, such as procurement policies and procedures, which cannot be effectively managed in terms of program elements. Still another management tool introduced in the last few years is the Department-wide Cost Reduction Program, a highly structured program with its own detailed goals, reporting channels, and post-audit system.

Finally, we must appreciate that the management tools needed by the Secretary of Defense may not necessarily suit the needs of management at the lower levels. For example, the financial data required by the commander of a military base to carry out his mission differ markedly from that required by the Secretary.

But all of these diverse organizations and functions must be harnessed together into a single effort directed toward a single over-riding objective—the defense of the Nation, and this is the purpose of the planning-programming-budgeting system.

PROBLEMS REMAINING

Looking back over the last four years, I believe it is fair to say that the planning-programming-budgeting system is now well established and is working smoothly. Admittedly, there are still difficult problems to be surmounted. One of these is the calendar. Although planning and programming have been designed as continuous activities, permitting changes to be proposed, considered, and decided at any time during the year, the third phase, budgeting, is still tied to the calendar. As large as it is, Defense's budget is only a part of the total United States Government budget which has long been presented to the Congress on an annual basis. And, indeed, the submission of the annual budget by the President is required by law. There has been much talk over the years about two-year, three-year, or five-year budgets, but the Congress has made it plain, and for good and sufficient reasons, that it prefers to appropriate money annually, and I see no evidence that the Congress is about to change its mind on this point. But as I indicated earlier, an annual budget, in itself, offers no particular obstacle—we simply take the first-year increment of the five-year program as the base for determining the financial requirements for that year.

The annual budget development cycle, however, does have an impact on the rest of the planning-programming-budgeting system. Because the President must submit the budget to the Congress in January, we require all components of the Defense Department to submit their budget requests to the Office of the Secretary of Defense early in October. This means that the comprehensive program review must be completed by middle or late August at the latest, and this, in turn, means that the proposed military plans and projected forces in the Joint Strategic Objectives Plan, prepared annually by the Joint Chiefs of Staff, and related requirement studies must be reviewed in the spring of the year. And thus, we find the entire planning-programming-budgeting system back on an annual cycle.

An annual cycle, in itself, should offer no particular problem if the entire review operation could be held to a strict schedule. Unfortunately, we have yet to achieve that ideal. As a result, the program and budget reviews have up until now tended to overlap in an undesirable way, making it difficult to reflect properly some of the force structure decisions in the support programs in time to assist in making budget decisions. But there is always another annual cycle, and we are hopeful that the schedule we have devised for this year's review will solve the problem, or come close to it. (I admit that we thought the same thing this time last year and were wrong.) There will always, inevitably, for good reasons as well as bad, be some program decisions that get postponed to the last possible moment—i.e., to the budget review.

In addition, we are making an effort to schedule the completion of the various detailed military requirement studies and other analytical efforts so as to maximize their value as information inputs into the force structure and program reviews. This is not easy. Scheduling the completion of cost-effectiveness studies is a little like scheduling the completion of Ph.D. theses. But to serve their purpose, these cost-effectiveness decisions must be an integral part of the entire planning-programming-budgeting process. Worthwhile analysis is not likely to be performed in a vacuum for very long. Where the information generated is not visibly used in the actual decision-making process, the capability to perform such analysis will wither. So the programming system has been designed to ensure through the program change procedures that the fruits of cost-effectiveness studies in the form of proposals for program changes will receive a timely and complete review.

The other less-than-satisfactory aspect of the programming system is our machinery for measuring and estimating costs. We have made improvements and progress during the past four years, but much more remains to be done.

There is first the problem of estimating the development and production costs of new weapon systems. The record of the Department over the past fifteen years in such estimating has been spectacularly bad. We and our contractors have typically underestimated costs by factors of two to ten. (Not two to ten percent, but 100 to 900 percent.) An important cause has been our system of awarding contracts, in particular, the sequential awarding of development and procurement contracts, which places a premium on "optimistic" estimates by the contractor in the early bidding. We are trying, wherever feasible, to get away from the "cost plus" type of contract and the sequential letting of contracts. But we must also develop a much more adequate and sophisticated capability to make independent cost estimates— i.e., independent of contractor estimates.

We have had some promising successes in estimating aircraft and missile costs with multiple correlation techniques, developing estimating equations from past experience based on various physical and performance parameters. Errors of estimate are larger than we would like, but smaller than contractors' errors, and not biased as they are. To improve this technique we need many more trained people in the military departments and my office, and a large data bank, which does not now exist, of past cost experience reported on a uniform basis. We are introducing a new organization and reporting system known as the Cost and Economic Information System to provide the analysts and the data. It is just getting off the ground.

There is secondly the unsatisfactory state of operating costs in many areas. Our appropriation accounting systems do not directly yield operating costs by program element—e.g., by aircraft type. Many of the alleged "actual" operating costs of elements in the Five-Year Program are obtained by an arbitrary allocation of budget categories. Since these "actuals" constitute the base for projecting future operating costs, some parts of the financial program are not too meaningful. For example, we do not really know whether the Army's present cost projections accurately reflect the growing operation and maintenance requirements of its expanding fleet of aircraft. Improvements in the Department's cost estimating systems in the operation and maintenance area must definitely be placed high on our future agenda.

CRITICISMS AND REBUTTALS

Because all major Defense programs are now projected at least five years ahead, some early critics of the new system feared that it would tend to stifle change and place the defense effort in a straitjacket. I can assure you that their fears are unfounded. The Five-Year Program has proved to be quite amenable to change. Each year we consider three or four hundred program change proposals which, if they were all to be approved, would cause gross shifts in individual program amounts of $25 to $30 billion over the five-year planning period. Actually, the total gross value of changes, both plus and minus, which are approved each year, amount to somewhat less than half of this sum. I think we can safely conclude that constant change is likely to remain a characteristic of the Five-Year Force Structure and Financial Program.

However, the high volume and value of changes to the forward program do not lessen its worth to us as a management device. Indeed, one of the important purposes of any future plan is to indicate the areas where change may be desirable while there is still time to study, consider, and make such changes. In this respect, I think it is important to appreciate the role of the present leadership in instigating change. In developing the program, Secretary McNamara has chosen not simply to make decisions, but also deliberately to create opportunities to make decisions. He is constantly asking questions, requesting studies, goading the Services and his staff to propose new alternatives, better alternatives to programs currently incorporated in the Five-Year Program. The criticism that the Secretary's management techniques stifle initiative and the development of ideas at the middle and lower levels of the Department seems to me to be the exact reverse of the truth.

Another criticism of both the programming system and the increased reliance on systematic quantitative analysis is that they have acted to "downgrade" the role of military judgment. I do not think they have. There is nothing inherent in the programming system or in systems analysis that calls for downgrading military judgment or for relying on computers for anything other than computation. In fact, I would say that the uniformed military planners have in recent years been given a greater opportunity to influence the Department's programs than they ever had previously. When planning and budgeting were separate, the planners, both in the JCS organization and the Services, proceeded on their own, with little or no civilian control. But the plans they produced, because they were divorced from budget realities, were largely ignored in the actual decision-making process which determined the Defense program. As I have mentioned before, prior to very recent years the Joint Strategic Objectives Plan was duly noted and filed, and the effective "real-world" decisions were made by the Secretary of Defense in the budget process, with no systematic participation by the military planners.[1]

This has completely changed. The Joint Chiefs of Staff, through the JSOP, now initiate the major proposals for changes in the approved Five-Year Force Structure. Moreover, their advice is solicited on every other program change proposal. In every way, the entire JCS organization is enmeshed in the planning-programming-budgeting system to a far greater extent than ever before. And with respect to the differences of opinion which inevitably arise, the truth is that on practically every serious issue affecting the Defense program there are military and civilian partisans on both sides.

Criticism of the programming system is sometimes coupled with criticism of an alleged over-centralization of Defense managment generally. It is true, of course, that the institution of unified Defense Department-wide programming has provided the conceptual framework, the administrative mechanism, and much of the data needed to facilitate top-level decision-making. But these top-level decisions have always been made—if not explicitly, then implicitly by the imposition of ceilings. As I noted earlier, priorities among major program objectives can be rationally determined only in the context of the total program, and balance among all elements of the Defense effort can be achieved only at the Department of Defense level. The proper size of the MINUTE-MAN force cannot be determined simply in terms of our ICBM requirements, or even in the context of the entire Air Force

---

[1] An interesting account of the budget-making process as seen by a former member of the Joint Chiefs of Staff can be found in General Maxwell D. Taylor's book, *The Uncertain Trumpet* (New York: Harper and Brothers, 1959).

program. Being simply one element of the Strategic Retaliatory Forces, the MINUTEMAN program must be considered together with all of the other elements including the Navy's POLARIS force and, indeed, with all aspects of the general nuclear war problem. Similarly, the requirement for airlift/aircraft operated by the Air Force could hardly be established independently of the requirement for sealift, and neither, independently of the requirement for lifting Army ground forces. This kind of centralized planning and decision-making is essential if soundly balanced military programs are to be pursued, and I think that few in the Department would now disagree.

In fact, the need was recognized with the creation of the National Military Establishment in 1947, when, for the first time since 1798, all of our armed forces were brought together again under one civilian head, and, for the first time, a consolidated budget was prepared for the entire Defense organization.[2] It was Secretary Forrestal's hope that the Joint Chiefs of Staff would produce a unified military plan which could serve as a basis for the annual budget, and it is interesting to note how he visualized the planning-budgeting process at that time—

> "First," he said, "the National Security Council must periodically evaluate the international situation . . . to assess and appraise the objectives, commitments, and risks of the United States in relation to our actual and potential military power. . . .
>
> "Second, the Joint Chiefs of Staff must, based on the evaluation . . . bring up to date the long-range strategic plans and prepare a correlated annual operating plan. . . . In the first instance this plan should be prepared on military considerations alone."[3]

He then described the role of the Research and Development Board and the Munitions Board and pointed out that on the basis of the over-all plans prepared by the Joint Chiefs of Staff and these two Boards, the military departments would develop their subsidiary plans. He then went on to say:

> The next step is the preliminary pricing of these more detailed plans in order to get a picture of the cost . . . based on military considerations alone. If the aggregate of the price tags . . . is in excess of the amounts deemed by the President and his advisors to be allocable for defense purposes, the JCS must develop plans involving a lesser total strength, outlining the composition of such forces, a comparative

---

[2] After remarks of Secretary of Defense James Forrestal on a radio interview, American Broadcasting Company network, December 28, 1948.

[3] Statement of Secretary of Defense Forrestal before Eberstadt Committee on the Hoover Commission. October 6, 1948 (unpublished). A close paraphrase of this quotation can be found in the *First Report of the Secretary of Defense* (Washington: U.S. Government Printing Office, 1948), p. 41.

necessity of programs, and the relative readiness to be achieved by each of the Services. This revised program must be developed within fiscal limitations.

. . . .

> The next step is the preparation by the JCS of a statement . . . which will clearly show the implications of lessened military effectiveness resulting from fiscal limitations. It is the duty of the Secretary of Defense, after assuring himself of their correctness, to make a presentation of the implications of lessened military effectiveness to the National Security Council in order that the risks may be evaluated and a decision reached as to the type and character of the military establishment which will best meet the international situation.

> When the overall plans have been adjusted to fit within the fiscal limitations, or after the further adjustment as a result of the National Security Council action, there must follow the preparation of final subsidiary plans within the Department.

> The next step is the detailed pricing of these subsidiary plans. After internal scrutiny and review, the budgets will be ready for submission to the Secretary of Defense for final analysis and review . . .[4]

Thus, the major burden of preparing a "correlated" plan was to be placed on the Joint Chiefs of Staff. It never worked out that way. The JCS did eventually accomplish the first step, a plan prepared on the basis of military considerations alone (whatever that may mean), but they were never able to come up with a "revised program . . . developed within fiscal limitations." That task fell to the Secretary and his Comptroller, and that is how the dichotomy between military planning and budgeting, which I discussed earlier, developed.

The new National Military Establishment also created a need for an integrated, or at least a consolidated, Defense budget, which, in turn, immediately raised the problem of uniformity in budget procedures and structures. The two entirely separate military departments, over the course of some 150 years, had each developed in its own way and each had its own pattern of organization, budgeting, and administration. Even within each of the Departments there was no particular logic to the budget structure and systems of accounts. Although the major appropriations, in general, paralleled the organization of each of the two military departments, they did not follow any particular functional pattern. Furthermore, there were a great many appropriation accounts for minor and often obscure purposes, the original justifications for which had long since been lost in 150 years of history.

---

4 *Ibid.*

The Navy Department, for example, as late as fiscal year 1948 was still managing its affairs through some 130-odd separate appropriation accounts, and the Congress for that fiscal year had actually appropriated new funds for 87 of them.[5] These appropriation accounts ranged in size from fifty dollars for the payment of certain claims to $1,294 million for pay and subsistence of Navy personnel. There was even a separate appropriation of ten dollars for the U.S. Naval Academy Museum Fund in 1947. The situation in the War Department was no better.

When it is realized that each of these appropriation accounts has to be separately administered and accounted for, and that no funds may be transferred from one account to another unless specifically authorized by law, the problem which confronted the first Secretary of Defense is immediately apparent. It would have been virtually impossible for him to manage the Defense establishment as a single enterprise, especially when another and different set of appropriation accounts was created for the new Department of the Air Force. Accordingly, Secretary Forrestal and his chief financial assistant, W. J. McNeil, decided to develop an entirely new, uniform budget structure for each of the three military departments. From their efforts there evolved the five major groupings of appropriation accounts which still exist today and which I have described in an earlier lecture.

The establishment of a uniform budget structure throughout the new military establishment was as revolutionary for its time as the establishment of the programming system was in 1961. As a matter of fact, it took about ten years to refine the system to its present form, and this was not accomplished without considerable agony throughout the Department. Indeed, it has been my observation that it is much easier to change policy than to change procedures. Perhaps the reason is that policy involves a relatively small group of people at the very top of the Defense organization whereas procedures involve literally tens of thousands, if not hundreds of thousands, throughout the entire establishment and the way in which they have been doing things day after day, year after year. So it is not surprising that the installation of the new programming system since 1961 has caused considerable anguish for much of the Defense Department.

Yet it seems to me that the programming function was the next logical step in the evolution of the Defense management system. In fact, some efforts had already been made along pro-

---

[5] *The Budget of the United States Government for the Fiscal Year Ending June 30, 1948* (Washington: U.S. Government Printing Office, 1947), pp. A97-A89. Navy Appropriation Act for 1948, P.L. 202, 80th Cong., 1st Sess. (61 Stat 382).

gramming lines on a unilateral Service basis and without any official approval by the top management. The need was recognized and sooner or later some Secretary of Defense would have adopted some variation of it as a principal management tool. I feel confident that programming is here to stay. No doubt refinements and changes will be made; we have made quite a few ourselves over the last four years. But the basic scheme of things will survive until the next major advance in management techniques, whatever that may be.

However, there still exists, within the Pentagon, some scepticism as to the permanence of this particular management innovation, predicated on the proposition "that it takes a McNamara to make it work." Often, of course, this is intended not as a serious indictment of programming, but simply as a kind of back-handed compliment to the talents of the Secretary. Yet some—remembering the relatively passive decision-making roles played by some other Defense Secretaries—are convinced that, under a significantly different style of leadership, the programming system and the data it generates would tend to go unused, and that the system itself would eventually atrophy and be discarded.

I will readily admit that to push through the development of the programming system in so short a time and make it work required a Secretary as strong and decisive as Robert S. McNamara. But I believe that the programming system can be adapted without too much difficulty to almost any style of leadership we are likely to have in the future. Every Secretary will have his own style—his own manner of approaching and making decisions—and management techniques must be adapted to the Secretary. I can easily imagine that some future Secretary, for example, will not want to get involved in as much program detail as Mr. McNamara. I see no particular problem in modifying the programming system to accommodate such a preference—without doing violence to any of the principal objectives of the system. We have "thresholds" in the system now, below which program changes can be made by the Secretaries of the military departments or at lower echelons.[6] There is nothing sacrosanct about the level at which such thresholds are established. But I cannot imagine a Defense Secretary who would willingly forego the assurance, provided by the new planning-programming-budgeting system, that his military plans are in proper balance and that the budgets he proposes are both fiscally responsible and actually

---

6 For example, changes in the investment costs of a program element of less than $10 million in the first year and $25 million in total; or in the operating costs of a program element of less than $20 million in the first year and $50 million in total. Department of Defense Directive 7045.1, October 30, 1964.

provide the capabilities that his military planners are counting on. As President Truman pointed out at the end of World War II in his Message to the Congress proposing a single Department of Defense:

> . . . strategy, program and budget are all aspects of the same basic decisions.[7]

to which I would like to add, if I may be permitted to quote myself:

> That the job of economizing, which some would delegate to the budgeteers and comptrollers, cannot be distinguished from the whole task of making military decisions.[8]

. . . .

CONCLUSIONS

There is a sort of inevitability about the trend toward unified Defense management ever since the end of World War II—here and in the military establishments of other major powers. It stems from the increasing complexity and unprecedented destructiveness of modern warfare and the need to achieve an optimum balance among all the elements of the military establishment. The Federal Republic of Germany rebuilt its military establishment after World War II within a strong, single Ministry of Defense. More recently, the British have reorganized their Defense establishment within a single Defense Ministry and the Canadians are moving even more rapidly in the same direction.

On the other side of the Iron Curtain, all of the armed forces of the Soviet Union are under a Ministry of Defense. All components report to the Minister of Defense through the equivalent of a single Chief of Staff. Interestingly enough, one of these components is called the Strategic Rocket Troops. Unity of planning and operations appears to be a well-established concept in the Soviet Union. Marshal Sokolovsky, writing on "the art of war in the nuclear age" last August, laid down the principle that—

> . . . armed conflict . . . will consist of coordinated operations by all of the branches of the armed forces, according to a single plan and under a single strategic leadership, aimed at fulfilling the immediate military-political and strategic tasks.[9]

---

[7] "Special Message to the Congress Recommending the Establishment of a Department of Defense, December 19, 1945," *Public Papers of the Presidents of the United States, Harry S. Truman, 1945* (Washington: U.S. Government Printing Office, 1961), p. 551.

[8] Hitch and McKean, *op. cit.*, p. 3.

[9] V. Sokolovsky and M. Chedrednichenko, "The Art of War at the New Stage," *The Current Digest of the Soviet Press,* vol. XVI, no. 38, p. 15.

In the Western World, some of our allies, notably the British, Canadians, and Germans, are also introducing programming and systems analysis into the management of their defense establishments. Although their problems are somewhat different from our own because of the nature of their national security objectives and the size and composition of their military forces, they believe that these techniques can contribute to the more effective management of their respective defense efforts.

The objectives, the organization, and the management techniques of national defense are all interrelated. Organization and procedures must be adapted to our changing national policies and objectives as well as to changes in the character of our resources and technologies. It will take all our ingenuity and skill to continue to make these necessary adaptations so that we can continue to provide unified management of so great an enterprise as our present military establishment. At the beginning of our Constitutional history, the building of three frigates and the management of a few companies to fight Indians were deemed too great a task for the War Department alone.

PART IV

SYSTEMS ANALYSIS

The new discipline of systems analysis serves as a "partner in arms" with programming in the attack on the problems of national security policy. While there is a large and growing literature dealing with systems analysis and operations research, many of the publications in these fields discuss methods and techniques rather than their practical application. It is this latter concern, as well as definitions, general objectives, and present limitations, to which the selections in Part IV are directed.

In selection 13, Mr. Hitch discusses in general terms the need for "cost-effectiveness" studies that compare alternative ways of accomplishing military objectives, and he cites some contributions that such studies have made to Defense management. In a speech to the Naval War College in June 1963 (selection 14), Mr. Alain C. Enthoven, then Mr. Hitch's deputy and now Assistant Secretary of Defense (Systems Analysis), points out the constantly increasing requirement for careful analysis in the choice of weapon systems. He shows how the scientific method and economic concepts employed in systems analysis can assist both in posing the relevant questions and in suggesting the most likely pathways to solutions. Mr. Enthoven stresses that the techniques used by the analyst assist rather than supersede judgment and experience.

Mr. Enthoven discusses in selections 15, 16 and 17, the application of systems analysis to various Defense problems, and illustrates more concretely the content and limitations of this new discipline. The first of these three selections deals with our posture for thermonuclear war including questions about the "mix" of weapon systems, defensive as well as retaliatory, and about possible alternative strategies. The second selection treats in some detail the economic problems of concern to systems analysts, and draws on some problems that have arisen in the choice of naval weapon systems as examples of the issues facing decision-makers. The final selection in this part discusses techniques for evaluating the effectiveness of U.S. and Soviet Army divisions, and emphasizes the importance of a capability for such analyses.

Supplementing these more general discussions of the principles and objectives of systems analysis, Appendix II, pages 215–248, presents a case study of the manner in which these techniques might be applied in evaluating the cost-effectiveness of two different weapon systems for a particular tactical role.

13

COST EFFECTIVENESS*
By Charles J. Hitch

Midway in my second lecture I alluded, in connection with the first phase of the planning-programming-budgeting process, to the need for military-economic studies which compare alternative ways of accomplishing national security objectives and which try to determine the way that contributes the most for a given cost or achieves a given objective for the least cost. The extensive and comprehensive use of these "cost-effectiveness" studies or systems analyses was the second major innovation introduced into the decision-making process of the Defense Department.

While the introduction of the programming function was generally well received, considerable controversy arose over this extensive use of cost-effectiveness studies in the decision-making process, and some of this controversy continues. Why this is so is something of a mystery to me. We have made repeated efforts to explain the essential nature of these studies and the contribution that they make to the achievement of greater military effectiveness as well as economy in the Defense establishment. But the suspicion still persists in some influential quarters that somehow or other cost-effectiveness studies put "dollars before national security," or will result in our going to war with "cut-rate, cut-quality, cheapest-to-buy weapons."[1] Virtually every attempt we have made to explain the inexorable logic of relating cost to military effectiveness seems to shatter itself on the argument—"Nothing but the best will do for our boys." And the "best" usually refers to some particular characteristic of physical performance, such as speed, altitude, or firepower, or even unit cost!

Implicit in this challenge is the deeply rooted feeling that national defense is far too important a matter to be inhibited by cost. If one weapon system performs better than another, then we should buy the higher performance system, regardless of cost; the country can afford it. Indeed, the people who hold this view

*Excerpts from the "H. Rowan Gaither Lectures in Systems Science" delivered at the University of California on 5–9 April 1965. Reprinted by permission from The Regents of the University of California, copyright owners, and published under the title *Decision-Making for Defense* (Berkeley and Los Angeles: University of California Press, 1965).

[1] "Cost Effectiveness Vs. Defense Effectiveness," *Army-Navy-Air Force Journal and Register*, vol. 101, no. 27 (March 7, 1964), p. 11.

feel that it is somehow sinful, or at least unpatriotic, to try to relate performance or military effectiveness to costs; that considerations of military effectiveness and cost are antithetical.

To any one trained in economics, this is a most puzzling attitude. We know that the very act of making a choice—and that is all we are doing when we choose weapons—involves weighing the utility or benefit to be gained against the cost which must be incurred. Why is that so? It is so because benefits *cost* resources and we live in a world in which resources are limited. If we use more for one purpose, less remains for other purposes— even in as rich a nation as the United States.

Certainly, most of us are continuously being forced to make such choices in our personal lives. While explicit calculations may be rare in these personal choices, they are common, if not quite universal, in business affairs. Indeed, the weighing of benefits against costs is one of the imperatives of any good business decision. The fact that one machine can produce twice as much or twice as fast as another must obviously be weighed against its additional cost in order to determine which is the more profitable. The principle is exactly the same in Defense, except that in private business the manager is guided by the profit goal and the market prices of what he buys and sells; whereas in government the decision-maker, since he is not selling in a market, must determine the worth of his "product," e.g., of added performance, by careful analysis and the application of experienced judgment. In this respect, cost-effectiveness analysis is more difficult in Defense than in a private firm operating in a market economy, and even more important.

Contrary to the suspicion in some quarters, the scarcity of resources and the consequent necessity for economic choice is not the invention of economists or Defense comptrollers, or even of the Democratic administration. The Hoover Commission in its report of June 1955 pointed out that—

> The question of 'quantity' cannot be considered except in conjunction with that of 'cost.' Just as in a business, one cannot make a decision to buy material or equipment without simultaneous consideration of price, so the Government cannot intelligently consider the wisdom of embarking on any program without a similar consideration of its cost. A decision to increase or decrease the number of air wings is intimately connected with consideration of the cost at which an air wing can be equipped and operated.[2]

---

[2] Commission on Organization of the Executive Branch of the Government, *Task Force Report on Budgeting and Accounting in the United States Government* (Washington: U.S. Government Printing Office, 1955), pp. 11-12.

The role of the cost-effectiveness study is to assist management in making just decisions by bringing into clearer focus the impact on over-all military effectiveness of an increase or decrease in the number of air wings and the specific cost implications of such changes.

I was somewhat startled about a year ago to read a statement by a leading member of the Congress—

> There is no hard evidence that the Soviet Union is applying cost-effectiveness criteria in its planning for future weapons systems. In fact, many knowledgeable students of Soviet thinking believe that the opposite is quite probably the case.[3]

It reminds me of a statement made some years earlier by Hanson Baldwin to the effect that—

> In the Western World—though not in Russia—costs are a more decisive factor in shaping defense than is military logic.[4]

The idea that the Soviets pay little attention to cost is a very common misconception in this country. At the risk of opening up a new controversy on the "cost-effectiveness gap," let me assure you that the Soviet leaders are most sensitive to the need for applying cost-effectiveness principles in all of their economic planning and there is no reason to doubt that they follow the same approach in the military area. For example, here is a statement from the program adopted by the 22nd Congress of the Communist Party of the Soviet Union in 1961:

> Chief attention in all links of planning and economic management must be focused on the most rational and effective use of material, labor, financial and natural resources and on the elimination of excessive expenditures and losses. It is an immutable law of economic construction to achieve, in the interests of society, the greatest results at the lowest cost.[5]

The formulation is not elegant, or even accurate, but the sense of it shines through.

That military expenditures were not excluded from this consideration was made evident by Mr. Khrushchev's explanation of the cutback in the Soviet military forces announced in January 1960. At that time he said—

> The elimination of non-productive expenditures and the search for additional possibilities for economic development are tasks that constantly confront not only us but any state. I repeat that this matter

---

3 Statement of Representative Melvin Laird, April 21, 1964, *Congressional Record*, vol. 110. part 7, p. 8551.

4 "Arms and the Atom—1," *New York Times*, May 14, 1957, p. 21.

5 "Program of the Communist Party of the Soviet Union," *The Current Digest of the Soviet Press*, vol. XIII, no. 46, p. 8.

is always urgent and will always attract unflagging attention.. . . The proposal to reduce the Soviet Armed Forces . . . will yield an annual saving of approximately 16,000,000,000 to 17,000,000,000 rubles [old rubles]. This will be a very tangible saving for our people and our country. It represents a powerful reinforcement for fulfilling and over-fulfilling our economic plans.[6]

And as further evidence, the U.S.S.R. has now translated *The Economics of Defense in the Nuclear Age* into Russian, with a first printing of 10,000 copies (but no royalties!).

Thus it seems plain that the Soviets, too, realize that they are not immune to the laws of economics, that they are not exempt from having to choose among the various alternative claims on the limited resources available to them. Nor do they appear reluctant to make use of the most modern methods and techniques to assist their managers in making these choices. Clearly, the Soviets have also realized that the modern world is far too complex to rely solely on intuitive judgment and that their decision-makers must be supported by quantitative analysis.

But opposition to cost-effectiveness studies stems not only from a suspicion of quantitative analysis but also from the conviction—completely unsubstantiated but nevertheless firmly held—that these studies inevitably lead to decisions favoring the cheapest weapon. Nothing could be farther from the truth. Cost-effectiveness analysis is completely neutral with respect to the unit cost of a weapon. What it is concerned with is: Which strategy (or force, or weapon system) offers the greatest amount of military effectiveness for a given outlay? Or looking at the problem from another direction: How can a given level of military effectiveness be achieved at least cost?

In some cases the most "economical" weapon may be the one with the highest unit cost; in other cases, it may be the one with the lowest unit cost—it will depend on the relative military worth of quality and quantity in the particular circumstances. Unit cost, by itself, is simply an index—an inverse index—of quantity. There have been many cases in history where the cheaper and technically less efficient weapon proved to be the "best," simply because its lower cost permitted it to be acquired in much greater numbers.

. . . .

It should always be our policy to spend whatever is necessary for defense, but to spend whatever is spent in such a way as to

---

6 N. S. Khrushchev, "Speech to the Supreme Soviet, January 15, 1960," *ibid., vol.* XII, no. 2, p. 13.

achieve the greatest possible military capability—not to buy quality when the same amount spent on quantity will purchase greater effectiveness, and *vice versa*. Sometimes a weapon system with less than the maximum unit cost and effectiveness does win out as in the case of the new Navy attack aircraft, the A-7, which is far slower than many other aircraft now in the forces—and also much cheaper. The A-7 promises to be not only satisfactory for the missions it is intended to perform, but superior in those missions to alternatives which cost more per aircraft. As a Marine Colonel pointed out in an article last year—"Speed is not necessarily progress. . . . If . . . targets cannot be found and accurately hit, the effort is wasted."[7]

But sometimes it is just the other way round—cost-effectiveness studies lead us in the direction of higher quality, higher performance, higher unit cost. For example, during the past three years we have vastly increased the procurement of such relatively complex air-to-ground weapons as the radio-controlled BULLPUP close support missile, the SHRIKE anti-radar missile, and other quality modern ordnance. They are far more expensive per unit than the older "free fall" bombs they displaced, but also far more effective. Our cost-effectiveness studies have shown that we get a more economical defense from these weapons than from bombs —even if the bombs are inherited and therefore almost cost free.

MARGINAL UTILITY OF WEAPON SYSTEMS

Cost-effectiveness studies or systems analyses are needed in the Defense decision-making process for yet another purpose. This purpose might be labeled "how much is enough?" . . . Military requirements in the Department of Defense tend to be stated in absolute terms. The traditional military requirements study was typically a calculation of the forces required to achieve a single hypothesized objective.

To give an oversimplified example, suppose the objective were to achieve an expectation of destroying 97 percent of 100 targets, using missiles having a 50 percent single-shot "kill" capability. The traditional requirements study would conclude that 500 missiles were needed because 100 missiles would achieve an expectancy of 50 kills, 200 missiles—75 kills, 300 missiles—87 kills, 400 missiles—94 kills, and 500 missiles—97 kills. This, of course, merely reflects the operation of the familiar law of diminishing returns. But the significant point is that the last 100 missiles would increase the "kill" expectation by only three extra targets,

---

[7] Col. J. H. Reinburg, USMC, "Low Altitude, Close Air Support," *Army*, vol. XIV, No. 8, (March 1964), pp. 29-30.

from 94 to 97. Thus, we should not only ask the question, "Do we need a capability to destroy 97 percent of the 100 targets?"; we should also ask the question, "Is the capability to raise expected target destruction from 94 to 97 percent worth the cost of 100 extra missiles?" In other words, we must not only examine total costs and total products, but also marginal costs and marginal products.

Of course, when dealing with Defense problems, data on marginal costs and marginal products do not, in themselves, imply mathematically what the number should be, i.e., the number we should buy. Since we do not operate in the market place, we cannot usually calculate the point where, in the business world, marginal cost equals marginal revenue. The Defense decision-maker must exercise his own judgment as to whether the last three percent of kill capability is worth the cost of another 100 missiles. But data of this kind can contribute a great deal to making that judgment an informed one.

The example I used is a relatively simple problem. At a much higher level of difficulty are such questions as whether an air defense system capable of destroying say 95 percent of all the bombers an enemy could possibly launch against us is a desirable military objective. This depends not only on the cost of the air defense system itself but also on the relative costs and effectiveness of *other ways* of limiting damage to the United States, such as producing and deploying an anti-ballistic missile defense system, increasing our civil defense program, or adding to our strategic offensive forces. Thus, what are military objectives when viewed from one level, are simply means to a still higher objective when viewed from another level; and any given objective is likely to be only one of a number of alternative ways to achieving a still broader objective—in this case, limiting damage to the United States. The tradeoffs or substitution possibilities among them depend upon questions of cost and effectiveness, which in turn depend upon technology.

Although our national security objectives, in the highest sense of the word, reflect essentially the composite value judgments of the American people, the choice of a particular military strategy or military objective cannot be divorced from the cost of achieving it. Systems analysis at the national level, therefore, involves a continuous cycle of defining military objectives, designing alternative systems to achieve these objectives, evaluating these alternatives in terms of their effectiveness and cost, questioning the objectives and other assumptions underlying the analysis, opening new alternatives and establishing new military objectives, and so on indefinitely.

Thus, the problem of allocating resources within the Department of Defense itself involves the choosing of doctrines, weapons, equipment, and so forth, so as to get the most defense out of any given level of available resources or, to what is logically equivalent, achieve a given level of defense at the least cost. Approaching the problem from the first point of view—getting the most defense from a given level of resources—we work in terms of marginal rates of transformation and substitution. Approaching the problem from the second point of view—achieving a given level of defense at the least cost, which is the way Secretary McNamara prefers to look at the problem—we work in terms of marginal products and marginal costs in order to help the top decision-maker choose the appropriate level of resources.

Regardless of which approach we use in allocating resources within the Defense establishment, we must recognize that, at the highest level of government, there remains the problem of optimizing the allocation of resources across the entire spectrum of our national needs, and this means exercising choice among many desirable objectives. This in itself imposes certain constraints on the size of the Defense budget at any particular time and under any particular set of circumstances. Certainly, if the international situation were to worsen, the value of an additional increment to the Defense budget would be relatively greater than before, compared with other needs and concerns of the U.S. Government. Conversely, if the international situation were to improve markedly, then the value of the last increment of the Defense budget would be relatively smaller than before compared with our other needs. This problem of national choices is not unique to the United States. It is one with which the government of every nation has to cope, even, as we have seen, the Soviet Union.

But let me hasten to say that systems analysis or cost-effectiveness studies are by no means a panacea for all the problems of defense. Costs in general can be measured quantitatively, although not always with the degree of precision we would like. Measuring effectiveness or military worth poses a much more difficult problem. Reliable quantitative data are often not available. And even when such data are available, there is usually no common standard of measurement. This is particularly true with regard to systems analyses involving complex new technologies. Here, even reliable cost data are seldom available. Accordingly, the preferred alternative can rarely, if ever, be determined simply by applying a formula.

It has long been my contention—

> that economic choice is *a way of looking at problems* and does not necessarily depend upon the use of any analytic aids or computational devices. Some analytic aids (mathematical models) and computing machinery are quite likely to be useful in analyzing complex military problems, but there are many military problems in which they have not proved particularly useful where, nevertheless, it is rewarding to array the alternatives and think through their implications in terms of objectives and costs. Where mathematical models and computations are useful, they are in no sense alternatives to or rivals of good intuitive judgment; they supplement and complement it. Judgment is always of critical importance in designing the analysis, choosing the alternatives to be compared, and selecting the criterion. Except where there is a completely satisfactory one-dimensional measurable objective (a rare circumstance), judgment must supplement the quantitative analysis before a choice can be recommended.[8]

I am the last to believe that an "optimal strategy" can be calculated on slide rules or even high speed computers. Nothing could be farther from the truth. Systems analysis is simply a method to get before the decision-maker the relevant data, organized in a way most useful to him. It is no substitute for sound and experienced military judgment and it is but one of the many kinds of information needed by the decision-maker.

CONTRIBUTIONS BY ANALYSTS

It is my experience that the hardest problems for the systems analyst are not those of analytic techniques. In fact, the techniques we use in the Office of the Secretary of Defense are usually rather simple and old fashioned. What distinguishes the useful and productive analyst is his ability to formulate (or design) the problem; to choose appropriate objectives; to define the relevant, important environments or situations in which to test the alternatives; to judge the reliability of his cost and other data; and finally, and not least, his ingenuity in inventing new systems or alternatives to evaluate. My friend and former colleague, Albert Wohlstetter, used to insist that the systems analyst could contribute much more by inventing new systems than by comparing proposed systems: his own inventions are eloquent testimony to the validity of this view.

The analysis of rapid deployment of forces to trouble spots around the world illustrates many of these points. Early analyses (you may find one in *The Economics of Defense in the Nuclear*

---

8 Hitch and McKean, *op. cit.*, p. 120.

Age) concentrated on the question: what is the most economical type of aircraft to procure for the purpose? Sealift was regarded as much too slow to be a competitor. From an early date, extensive pre-positioning of men and equipment, or of equipment only, was recognized as an alternative, or a partial alternative, and included in the analysis.

Then a systems analyst made an invention. A great problem with prepositioning is the difficulty of acquiring real estate for the purpose in foreign countries, and the likelihood that the real estate, if acquired, and the pre-positioned stocks will turn out to be in the wrong country (or even the wrong continent) when hostilities actually threaten or break out. So this analyst thought: why not pre-position on ships? A pregnant thought. We now have many "forward floating depots"— Victory ships stocked with Army equipment—in the Western Pacific, ready to steam to any threatened area and substantially augmenting our airlift rapid deployment capability.

At about the same time a more straightforward design development or "invention" produced the Roll-on/Roll-off, or "Ro-Ro," ship which can rapidly load and unload Army vehicular equipment at even primitive ports.

Then a third invention was made by an ingenious systems analyst, who simply combined the characteristics of the forward floating depot and the Ro-Ro ship and developed an appropriate operational concept for the combination. This definitely made sealift competitive with airlift for rapid deployment in many situations, and we . . . asked Congress in the 1966 budget for four specially designed Ro-Ro's to be used as forward floating depots.

Meanwhile some design inventions stimulated by airlift analyses promise us much more efficient airlift aircraft. The most important permits us to combine the marked economies of a very large aircraft with a landing gear and power plant which permit operations from short, primitive forward air bases. This combination promises to reduce or even eliminate the ground line of communication in the combat theater, with substantial savings in time, troops, and equipment. We are starting full-scale development of such an aircraft—the C–5A—this year.

Our analytic problem now is to determine the best mix of this better sealift and this better airlift. In many situations (e.g., close to the shore in SE Asia and Korea), the ships can win handily on cost-effectiveness criteria. In other hypothetical situations (e.g., farther inland) the C–5A wins handily. Each system has capabilities the other has not. And problems the other has not. And different and difficult-to-analyze vulnerabilities to enemy action. No computer will automatically provide the answer to this problem of optimum mix, although a carefully formulated computer program can, under specified conditions, give valuable insights about break-even points and regions of sensitivity.

Typically in major systems comparisons this is the situation. There are multiple objectives or payoffs—not just one which is well defined and clearcut. There are multiple circumstances in which the system may be called upon to function. And there are usually great uncertainties about costs, enemy intentions and capabilities, and other factors. This kind of systems analysis makes great demands on the analyst's ingenuity, his experience, and above all his judgment and common sense. When Ellis Johnson called it "quantified common sense," he was not far off the mark.

Finally, we must recognize that if the objectives or the costs or the measurements of military effectiveness are wrong, the answers will also be wrong. The SKYBOLT air-to-ground missile is a case in point. A gross under-estimate of costs in 1961 led to a decision to carry that project into the production stage. When the full dimensions of the ultimate cost later became apparent, the decision was made to drop the project since it was not worth the increased cost in the light of the other alternatives available, namely, expanding the MINUTEMAN force and retaining more of the HOUND DOG air-to-ground missiles which were already in the inventory. You may recall that this decision led to some very painful moments with our British colleagues as the United Kingdom had also planned to use the SKYBOLT missile with its bombers. Our decision to drop the project created some very difficult problems for the British Government at the time and led to a meeting at Nassau between President Kennedy and Prime Minister Macmillan. Yet, no responsible military or civilian official in our Defense Department or, I believe, in the British Defense Ministry, would argue in favor of the SKYBOLT today.

But notwithstanding all of these dangers I have mentioned, the need for systematic quantitative analysis in Defense is much more important than in the private sector of the economy. Almost never do we find one person who has an intuitive grasp of all the fields of knowledge that are relevant to a major Defense problem. We may be able to assemble a group of experts, each of whom has a good intuitive grasp of the factors relevant for answering one of the many sub-questions and after discussion emerge with a fairly unequivocal answer. But in general, and especially when the choice is not between two but among many alternatives, systematic analysis is essential.

Moreover, in contrast to the private sector where competition provides an incentive for efficiency, efficiency in government depends on the conscious and deliberate selection of techniques and policies. And wherever the relevant factors are diverse and complex, as they usually are in Defense problems, unaided intuition is incapable of weighing them and reaching a sound decision.

The need for systems analysis exists not only in the Office of the Secretary of Defense, the Joint Chiefs of Staff, and the headquarters of the military departments, but also at the other levels of the management structure in the Defense establishment. After all, the purpose of this function is to help reduce the uncertainties involved in making choices among alternatives, and such choices have to be made at many different echelons. The areas of interest, the problems, and the subject matter will be different at these different levels, but the general approach—the way of looking at a problem—and the techniques will be basically the same.

Our objective, therefore, has been to build an integrated and mutually supporting structure of systems analysis throughout the Defense establishment, with the broadest kind of exchange of information and techniques at and between various levels. This arrangement provides the checks and balances so essential to minimizing parochial viewpoints and organizational bias. The systems analyst, like any other scientist, must always be prepared to submit his work to critical scrutiny, and not just by other systems analysts. This is one of the great merits of the scientific method—it is an open, explicit, verifiable, and self-correcting process.

In addition to its "in house" capability, the Defense Department also supports a number of outside groups such as the Air Force's RAND Corporation, the Army's Research Analysis Corporation, the Navy's Center for Naval Analysis, and the Defense Department's Institute for Defense Analyses. Whereas the "in house" systems analysis organizations can more easily achieve a close working relationship with the military experts, these outside supporting groups do have the advantage of greater detachment, of being better able to look at a problem with a fresh and relatively unbiased point of view. There is no question but that the systems analysis groups working within the Defense establishment tend to take on the philosophical coloration of their sponsoring organizations, if for no other reason than that they are exposed to the same environment and same influences. Thus, there is a need both for an "in house" and an "outside" systems analysis capability.

In my own office I have a Deputy for Systems Analysis with a staff whose functions are to raise the quality of analysis throughout the Department, to see that studies requested by the Secretary are responsive to his needs, to review studies for the Secretary, and where necessary to do or re-do studies.[9]

From a small beginning, systems analysis has now become a vital and integral part of the Defense Department decision-making process. The new programming function provides the link between planning and budgeting, relating both the forces and their resource costs to major military missions. Systems analysis provides the analytical foundation for the making of sound objective choices among the alternative means of carrying out these missions. Thus, the Secretary of Defense now has the tools he needs to take the initiative in the planning and direction of the entire Defense effort on a truly unified basis.

---

[9] President Johnson announced on 5 July 1965, that because of their importance, the functions formerly performed by the Deputy Assistant Secretary of Defense (Systems Analysis) in the Office of the Assistant Secretary of Defense (Comptroller) would be transferred to the newly established position of the Assistant Secretary of Defense (Systems Analysis).

14

CHOOSING STRATEGIES AND SELECTING WEAPON SYSTEMS*
By Alain C. Enthoven

It is both a privilege and a pleasure for me to be here today, to have an opportunity to join with you in discussion of some of the fundamental problems concerning the future character of our Armed Forces and the formation of national security policy. This spring I have had the pleasure of visiting the Naval Academy and the Naval Postgraduate School at Monterey, so that this visit completes my brief tour of higher education for Naval officers. In visiting these institutions, one cannot help being impressed by the heavy demands that a career in the Navy makes on its officers, by the scope and complexity of the problems with which you must be able to deal effectively, and by the great strides that these institutions are taking to keep up with the ever-increasing requirements for better trained officers.

Were it not for my respect for the gravity of our mutual responsibilities and the seriousness of your purpose, I would have been sorely tempted, in preparing my talk, to limit myself to a rather technical discussion of systems analysis and "cost-effectiveness," the workings of the Programming System, the importance of reliable cost estimates, and, to ramble on in a non-controversial way about the various innovations that have been made in the past two years in the Comptroller's Office. Such a course would minimize the risk of adverse criticism and leave everyone content, if somewhat bored.

However, you have been very kind in asking me to come here to speak, and I am sure that the technicalities of financial management are not really what is on your minds. I would like, therefore, to return your favor by discussing very frankly a question of great concern to all of us, which is: How are the fundamental choices of weapon systems and strategies to be made? What kind of information is needed to make those choices? On what basis should they be made? And, what are the roles of the military advisors and the civilian staff of the Secretary of Defense who, with the President, must make the final and critical decisions?

---

*From address before the Naval War College, Newport, R.I., 6 June 1963.

These problems are important. They affect the expenditure of tens of billions of dollars each year. But, far more important, the way in which these questions are answered is sure to affect profoundly the security of the United States and the prospects for freedom around the world.

It would not be possible to cover all of this subject in a brief talk. There is certainly no need to waste your time by defending the need for civilian control in the Department of Defense. In spite of the comments of a few journalists who like to fish in troubled waters, I am sure that there is no disagreement with the principle of civilian control among American military men. Admittedly, we in the Department of Defense may have our disagreements as to the extent to which that control should be centralized and I do want to say, just to keep the record straight, that I am convinced that the Secretary of Defense sits in the best place from which to make the final decisions about our basic strategies and our major weapon systems. However, rather than discuss these organizational questions, I would like to explore with you the character of the intellectual process that generates the assumptions, the questions, and the answers underlying defense planning.

THE PROBLEMS OF CHOICE TODAY

The problems of selecting strategies and choosing weapon systems today are quite unlike anything that existed before the Second World War. Although the change has been gradual, the Second World War seems as good a place as any to locate the watershed. Before that time military technology changed relatively slowly in relation to the average length of a military or political career. Both soldiers and statesmen could learn most of what they needed to know about military power and the relationship of weapon systems and forces to national security from their own direct experience and by reading history books. The direct personal experience of both military and civilian leaders, combined with the collective experience accumulated over centuries of warfare was sufficiently relevant to contemporary affairs that the problem of interpreting their experience by the careful rules of scientific method had not become a major one. Of course, this is not to say that there were no important failures to adapt to new military technology. History is full of examples of military successes and failures attributable to successful innovation, or to a lack of adaptation, and the beginnings of both World Wars were full of surprises on this account alone.

But something new has been happening in the past twenty years. Science and technology have gone through a "take-off" and they are now in a period of rapid, accelerating, and apparently self-sustaining growth. Nuclear weapons, nuclear power, computers, large-scale rockets, and space flight are but the most spectacular examples of a revolution which has been led by both military men and civilian scientists. Before World War II, we did not plan on technological change, we merely adjusted to it. Now we are planning on it. We are debating whether inventions can be scheduled, and we have weapon systems that are being called obsolescent while still in production.

This new development has two important implications for the problem at hand. First, rampant technological change is producing not only better weapons of familiar kinds, it is also producing for us the possibility of many new kinds of weapons. Consider long-range bombardment. The progression from the B–17 to the B–29 to the B–36 was straightforward and apparently obvious. But now we have the possibility before us of literally dozens of distinctly different strategic nuclear delivery systems, not to mention the endless array of other kinds of weapon systems and forces. And the number of possibilities is expanding almost daily. There are air breathing vehicles and ballistic vehicles that can be based and launched from fixed land bases, mobile land bases, platforms on the surface of the sea, under the sea, and in the air. There are missiles launched from aircraft, aircraft launched from missiles, missiles launched from submarines, and so on in endless progression. Although we have not tried to develop all of these possibilities, we have tried to develop many of them. In fact, within the past several years, the United States has had in development or production more than a dozen different long-range strategic nuclear delivery systems, including three different bombers (the B–52, the B–58, and the B–70), four different ICBM's (ATLAS, TITAN, FIXED MINUTEMAN, and MOBILE MINUTEMAN), three IRBM's (THOR, JUPITER, and POLARIS), two air-breathing intercontinental missiles (SNARK and NAVAHO), and three air-launched missiles (HOUND DOG, SKYBOLT, and RASCAL). A similar development is taking place in almost every kind of warfare.

But in the face of the expanding number of systems that we could buy, we have not escaped the ancient necessity for choice arising out of the scarcity of available resources. Whether we like it or not, in the United States today, we have only a limited amount of goods and services available at any one time. Our gross national product, though large, is limited. We have only a finite number of manhours available for all forms of productive activity. If we attempted to develop and procure a dozen or more distinctly different strategic nuclear delivery systems, not to mention the three or four dozens that one might be able to conjure up in an evening's discussion, we doubtless would end up squandering our resources and not doing a good job on any of them. Therefore, we have to choose.

I emphasize the inescapability of the scarcity of resources and the necessity for choice because many people seem to believe that the scarcity of resources and the resulting limits in our Defense budgets are really the invention of the Bureau of the Budget, the Comptroller's Office, or the Appropriations Committees. They are not. The limitation on our national resources is a fact of life, like the laws of physics or aerodynamics. There are other needs and demands for those resources besides the demands of defense and of expanding science and technology. There are such needs as feeding. clothing and housing our population, educating our children, and fighting disease, in almost endless number. Therefore, only a limited amount of resources are available for defense. And it is our responsibility, both yours and mine, military and civilians working together, to get the most out of our limited resources by facing up to the hard choices and helping those who must make the decisions to make the rights ones.

Another implication of the rapid pace of technological change is that today's weapons differ more and more from the weapons many of you used in World War II and in Korea. Although it is difficult to know exactly how and to what extent, this does mean that some aspects of earlier experience in combat are probably out of date. And peacetime experience with military operations, however valuable, does not completely make up for this. The wars of the future will differ in some important details from the wars of the past. If, therefore, we are to prepare for the next war rather than the last one, we must address these changes in a systematic way and do all we can to understand their implications for the choice of weapon systems and strategy. As I remarked earlier, this problem is not unprecedented. The machine gun reduced some of the tactical planning preceding the first World War to irrelevance. Armored warfare made a mockery of some of the assumptions on which the Maginot Line was based. The development of naval aviation dealt the battleships such a decisive blow that the defenders of battleships have become the symbol of adherence to outmoded thinking. But the problem is of greater proportions today than ever before.

To deal with it, the Office of the Secretary of Defense is trying to encourage, stimulate, and contribute to the development of a new analytical approach or discipline for synthesizing many of the factors that go into defense planning. It is clear that both the Secretary of Defense and our senior military leaders are being forced by present circumstances to place increasing reliance on such analysis rather than placing exclusive reliance on their experience and judgment. This development has become controversial. It has been described by some as "downgrading the military" or "excessive reliance on young and temporary civilians" and other such epithets. But such a characterization misses the point. It is not a matter of upgrading some people and downgrading others. That is neither the intent nor is it a necessary consequence of the development and reliance on improved methods of analysis. Rather, the problem is one of making a sensible adjustment in our ways of thought to deal with rapid changes in technology and in international circumstances, an adjustment that is appropriate for both military and civilian leaders.

To the extent that there is controversy, I do not think that it is constructive or accurate to describe it as military versus civilian, though unfortunately some may find it to their partisan advantage to do so. One can find both military and civilians on all sides of this issue. Rather, it is a conflict between new and old ways of thinking about national security problems. In fact, the reforms now taking place have their roots in many places, both military and civilian. They are not purely a civilian invention. All of the Services make extensive use of operations analysis. It was the Navy that created the Operations Evaluation Group, and the first important applications of operations analysis included Anti-Submarine Warfare. The Air Force sponsored the RAND Corporation. General Maxwell Taylor, in his book, called for the development of explicit quantitative standards of adequacy, something we are working hard to do now. But it is appropriate that the broader application of the analytical approach be led by the Secretary of Defense because an important part of his job is to stimulate innovation and reform.

WHAT IS SYSTEMS ANALYSIS?

What is this new approach all about? How far advanced is it? And what are its essential characteristics? I believe that the art of weapon systems analysis, and it is an art, is still in its embryonic stage. It is, in part, an outgrowth of military operations research which really had its start, as a systematic discipline, in World War II. It was not until after that war that economic analysis began to be applied to the problem of choice of weapon systems. And it is only in very recent years that it has been taken seriously by top-level decision-makers. I think that it is fair to say that one can find some good, thorough, reliable analyses that deserve to serve as a guide to serious decision-making.[1] Unfortunately, however, one can also find many bad ones. My general impression is that the art of systems analysis is in about the same stage now as medicine during the latter half of the 19th Century; that is, it has just reached the point at which it can do more good than harm, on the average. Of course, it would be no more sensible to conclude from this that we should not develop and use systems analysis now than it would have been to conclude that we should not use medicine then.

There is now a growing literature on methods of weapon systems analysis.[2] Therefore, I do not believe that a useful purpose would be served by my reviewing techniques or detailed methods. Rather, I would like to try to outline for you some of the broader aspects of this emerging discipline.

The problem of choosing strategies and weapon systems is a unique problem requiring a method of its own. It is obviously not Physics or Engineering or Mathematics or Psychology or Diplomacy or Economics, nor is it entirely a problem in military operations though it involves elements of all of the above. Because it involves a synthesis of the above-mentioned disciplines and others, it requires the cooperation of experts in all of these professions and many others. It is a not infrequent error, made by civilians and military alike, to identify defense planning uniquely with one of the above professions or disciplines.

Beyond its uniqueness and eclecticism, I would like to say that the art of weapon systems analysis, like the art of medicine, should be based on scientific method, using that term in its broadest sense. But one hesitates to say "scientific" for several reasons. First, there are many follies that have been advertised as scientific. I can appreciate that it would be tiresome to say the least for an experienced military man to be told that we need a "scientific" approach to war or to amphibious forces. Warfare is, after all, more an art than a science, combining such critical but intangible factors as training, morale, and leadership. Second, one risks suggesting that scientists are therefore the leading experts.

---

[1] One good example, now ten years old and therefore out of date, is Wohlstetter, Rowen, Hoffman, and Lutz, *Selection and Use of Strategic Air Bases*, the RAND Corporation, R–266, 1954.

[2] Among the best examples are: *The Economics of Defense in the Nuclear Age*, by C. J. Hitch and R. N. McKean; the methodological sections of *On Thermonuclear War*, by Herman Kahn; and *Analysis for Military Decisions*, E. S. Quade, editor (RAND Corporation, Report R-387-PR; Santa Monica, Calif.: The RAND Corporation, 1964).

One sees nuclear physicists advertised as experts on thermonuclear war despite the fact that they have never done any empirical study of war and know nothing about it, and this must also be tiresome to a military man. But the point is not the authority of science or of scientists. Rather, it is the *method* of science.

What are the relevant characteristics of scientific method as applied to the problem of choosing strategies and selecting weapon systems? There are several. First, the method of science is an open, explicit, verifiable self-correcting process. It combines logic and empirical evidence. The method and tradition of science require that scientific results be openly arrived at in such a way that any other scientist can retrace the same steps and get the same result. Applying this to weapon systems and to strategy would require that all calculations, assumptions, empirical data, and judgments be described in the analysis in such a way that they can be subjected to checking, testing, criticism, debate, discussion, and possible refutation. Of course, neither science nor systems analysis is infallible. Chemists used to believe in the phlogiston theory of combustion. Some biologists still claim to believe in the inheritance of acquired traits. And I have seen many systems analyses containing equally questionable conclusions. But infallibility is not being claimed; it would be worse than unscientific to do so. However, scientific method does have a self-correcting character that helps to guard science from persistence in error in the long run.

Second, scientific method is objective. Although personalities doubtless play an important part in the life of the physics profession, the science itself does not depend upon personalities or vested interests. The truth of a scientific proposition is established by logical and empirical methods common to the profession as a whole. The young and inexperienced scientist can challenge the results of an older and more experienced one, or an obscure scientist can challenge the findings of a Nobel Prize winner, and the profession will evaluate the results on the basis of methods quite independent of the authority of the contenders, and will establish what is the correct conclusion. In other words, the result is established on the objective quality of the physics and not on the reputations of the persons involved. Of course, doubtless, on such occasions, some will scoff at the challenger, and the odds favor the Nobel Prize winners. But the physics profession is not likely to go about harboring incorrect hypotheses for very long because of the authority of the originators.

Of course, let me emphasize that I say this with respect to the problem of selection of weapon systems and strategies and not with respect to military operational command which is a very different matter. In the latter case we have no sensible alternative to reliance on experience and reputation.

Third, in scientific method in the broadest sense, each hypothesis is tested and verified by methods appropriate to the hypothesis in question. Some are tested and verified logically, some experimentally, some historically, *et cetera*. Some sciences, of course, can reproduce experiments cheaply and they tend to emphasize experiment. This is notably the case with the physical sciences. In others, particularly some branches of medicine and the social sciences, one cannot experiment readily, if at all, and the detailed analysis of available historical data is most appropriate. In this respect, they resemble military science very closely. In choosing weapon systems some experimentation is possible but a great deal of analysis is also required. In fact, in the development of weapon systems analysis, one is more handicapped than in most of the sciences, for fully realistic tests come only at infrequent intervals in war, while the development of new weapon systems also takes place in peacetime. But this argues for better analysis and more heavy reliance on analysis where fully relevant experience is not generally available.

Fourth, quantitative aspects are treated quantitatively. This is not to say that all matters can be reduced to numbers, or even that most can be, or that the most important aspects can be. It is merely to say that the appropriate method for dealing with some aspects of problems of choice of weapon systems and strategies requires numbers. Non-quantitative judgment is simply not enough.

What is at issue here really is not numbers or computers versus words or judgment. The real issue is one of clarity of understanding and expression. Take, for example, the statement "Nuclear power for surface ships offers a major increase in effectiveness." Precisely what does that mean? Does it mean 10 per cent better or 100 per cent better? When that sort of question is asked a frequent answer is, "It can't be expressed in numbers." But it has to be expressed with the help of numbers. Budgets are expressed in dollars, and nuclear power costs more than conventional power. If nuclear power costs, say 33 per cent more for some ship type, all factors considered, then, no matter what the budget level, the Navy and the Secretary of Defense have to face the choice of whether to put the nation's resources into four conventional or three nuclear ships, or for a larger budget, eight conventional or six nuclear ships, and therefore whether by "major increase" is meant more than 33 percent, about 33 percent, or less than 33 percent. Because the Secretary of Defense has to make the decision in these terms, the statement "major increase" is not particularly helpful. It must be replaced by a quantitative analysis of the performance of various missions, leading to a conclusion such as, "Nuclear power for surface ships offers something between X and Y percent more effectiveness per ship. Therefore, $1 billion spent on nuclear powered ships will provide a force somewhere between A and B per cent more or less effective than the same dollars spent on conventionally powered ships."

Numbers are a part of our language. Where a quantitative matter is being discussed, the greatest clarity of thought is achieved by using numbers instead of by avoiding them, *even when uncertainties are present*. This is not to rule out judgment and insight. Rather, it is to say, that judgments and insights need, like everything else, to be expressed with clarity if they are to be useful.

Let me emphasize the point about uncertainties. Many people seem to feel that quantitative analysis is not possible if there are any uncertainties. Of course, strictly speaking, if this were true, I suppose we would have no such thing as physics. But this view is incorrect. In fact there is substantial literature on the logic of decision-making under uncertainty going back at least as far as Pascal, Bernoulli, and Bayes in the Seventeenth and Eighteenth Centuries. Morover, there are simple practical techniques for dealing with uncertainty which make it possible to do analyses that point up the uncertainties for the decision-maker and indicate their significance. In fact, rather than conceal uncertainties, a good analysis will bring them out and clarify them. If it is a question of uncertainties about quantitative matters such as operational factors, it is generally useful to examine the available evidence and determine the bounds of the uncertainty. In many of our analyses for the Secretary of Defense, we carry three estimates through the calculations: an "optimistic", a "pessimistic", and a "best" or single most likely estimate. If there are uncertainties about context, at least one can run the calculations on the basis of several alternative assumptions so that the decision-maker can see how the outcome varies with the assumptions. This approach is being used to good advantage in studies on nuclear war being done in the Joint Staff by the Chairman's Special Studies Group.

Next, choosing strategies and weapon systems is fundamentally an economic problem, using the term in its precise sense. That is, it is a problem in choosing how best to use our limited dollars and limited resources valued in dollars, such as man hours, materials, plant and equipment, etc. To do this properly, one must think through the purposes of the weapon systems, formulate good criteria of effectiveness, and then consider alternative systems or mixes of systems in terms of their effectiveness and their cost.

Much of the innovation of which I am speaking has been the introduction of techniques of rational economic analysis and planning. One of the purposes of this is to avoid serious imbalances in the Defense program, such as bombers without enough bases and crews, fighter-bombers without ordnance, and Army divisions without adequate equipment or airlift, all of which have occurred in the past several years. Anyone can recognize the grave and obvious imbalances. But a great deal of effectiveness also can be lost through less obvious imbalances, and it takes detailed quantitative analysis to discover and correct them. Another purpose for which economic analysis is being introduced is to discover and avoid further expansion in those program areas which are, if I may oversimplify, out on the "flat part" of the "cost effectiveness curve" where the gain in effectiveness is small in relation to the increase in cost. I am sure that you are all familiar with the cube root law relating horsepower and the speed of ships. It is a classic case of diminishing marginal returns. After a point it takes a very great increase in horsepower to produce a small increase in speed. Of course, this is not to suggest that some increases in speed are not highly desirable nonetheless. But there comes a point at which it no longer pays to go on increasing horsepower, and it makes sense to look for alternative ways of outflanking the problem and accomplishing the mission. We have found that this same general point applies throughout the defense program, both in the design of weapon systems and in the choice of strategies. That is, there comes a point at which small increases in effectiveness can be bought only at the price of great increases in cost. In such circumstances, it may lead to a great waste of resources to insist on maximum performance at any price. After all, our objective is not to break world speed records or to maximize the range of our surface-to-air missiles. Rather, our real objective is to use our resources as best we can to keep ourselves and as much as possible of the rest of the world alive and free. And this may not coincide with buying the fastest airplane. Of course, the other side of this coin is the expansion of programs for which the extra effectiveness associated with increases is large in relation to the extra cost.

A corollary of this point is that the allocation of the budget between different missions, and the choice and design of weapon systems should ordinarily change as conditions change. Curiously enough, this point is widely understood if one is talking about putting jamming gear on board a bomber in response to improvements in enemy defenses. But it is frequently missed if the required change is to build up non-nuclear forces in response to the build-up of protected enemy nuclear retaliatory power. In the business of choosing weapon systems, as opposed to conducting military operations, one should not be "offense minded" or "defense minded", "air minded", or "for or against bombers," or any other such approach. Whether a good offense is the best defense will depend on the character of the forces, on costs, as well as the important psychological factors. Just as the commander in the field or the admiral at sea must decide when to attack and when to assume a defensive posture, so a man can be for a particular doctrine or weapon system in one set of circumstances, and against it in another without being guilty of self-contradiction or indecisiveness or being wrong. It is the man who does not change his mind as conditions change who bears special watching.

I will admit that all this sounds like a pretty antiseptic prescription, perhaps unreal, certainly far from the controversial world we know in which some individuals are fighting for their favorite weapon system because it symbolizes a way of life and in which others are indulging whatever prejudices they may have. But these factors we have always with us, and they are not in danger of being excluded. What is in danger of being excluded is the effective pursuit of our national security objectives. In the balance between reliance on authority and experience, the tug of vested interests, and the scientific method, I believe that we need more scientific method, that is, more objectivity, more logic, more open explicit analysis.

THE ROLE OF JUDGMENT

Do judgment and experience have no place in this approach to the choice of weapon systems and strategy and design of the defense program? Quite the contrary. The suggestion that the issue is judgment versus computers is a red herring. Ultimately all policies are made and all weapon systems are chosen on the basis of judgments. There is no other way and there never will be. The question is whether those judgments have to be made in the fog of inadequate and inaccurate data, unclear and undefined issues, and a welter of conflicting personal opinions, or whether they can be made on the basis of adequate, reliable information, relevant experience, and clearly drawn issues. The point is to render unto computers the things that are computers' and to judgment the things that are judgment's. In the end, there is no question that analysis is but an aid to judgment and that, as in the case of God and Caesar, judgment is supreme.

Perhaps some of these ideas may be made more clear and definite by the use of an example. Two years ago, some people in my office became interested in the problem of choice of air-to-ground non-nuclear ordnance for fighter-bomber aircraft. They observed that there had been great advances in the performance of the aircraft, as well as great increases in their cost, but they found that one of the Services was procuring essentially the same ordnance as had been procured ten years earlier. They did a few calculations suggesting that it would pay to go to more accurate weapons having greater lethality, even though it cost more, and they went to the Service to ask about it. The first reaction they seemed to get was, "We fought World War II with iron bombs and we know best. Leave us alone." My men persisted. Among other things, it turned out that these particular Service people were calculating only a portion of the relevant cost. They were calculating ordnance cost per target killed instead of complete system cost. The point here is that the cost to kill a target or to suppress movement in an area by weapons delivered from aircraft is dominated by the cost of buying and operating the aircraft, training and maintaining the pilot, and the cost of the actual ordnance delivered tends to be small in comparison. Complete system cost is the appropriate measure of cost in such cases. It measures what it really costs to do the job. The fact that this was the case encouraged us to press our views all the harder. As we did so, the resistance increased, apparently based on a belief that we lacked operational experience and therefore that the question of choice of ordnance was none of our business.

But there are important aspects of this and similar problems requiring backgrounds other than military operational experience. Much of our job in the Office of the Secretary of Defense is to help the Secretary to reach balanced decisions by helping him to bring to bear a broad range of other equally relevant considerations including economic, scientific, technical, and diplomatic aspects. Most of the civilians in the Office of the Secretary of Defense have considerable professional training and experience in one or more of these areas. But these other factors interact with the military aspects in a very intimate way, so that in general they cannot be separated out. For example, the whole point of so-called "cost-effectiveness" analysis is that it does not make sense to consider cost and effectiveness separately. They are opposite sides of the same coin. The conclusion I draw from this is that we must all work together and be willing to make the effort to communicate with and learn from each other. Of course, a part of our job is to see to it that Defense Department programs are chosen and carried out as economically as possible. To do this, there is no alternative to questioning the programs of the Services.

In this particular case, later on it did appear that one of the assumptions used in our calculations was open to question. Though our analysis was corroborated by other military reviewers, it was the case that had used accuracy factors based on test range data, and it was pointed out to us that in combat the effect of enemy opposition would be to degrade the accuracy substantially, although the amount of the degradation is still uncertain and still being debated. We may have placed inadequate weight on what the Services called the "scare factor." So we have revised the assumption and we and the Services are now reworking the calculations.

It is now clear to me that one of the main reasons for the opposition we encountered was the belief that we were neglecting this "scare factor" and that our method inherently overlooked similar important aspects of operational reality. I can only say that I wish that we had been able to have a frank and objective discussion of the problem early in the game so that the time spent in sparring would not have been wasted.

Interestingly enough, the difficulty was first pointed out to me by a man who thought that he was thereby disproving the validity of the whole method. I am happy to report that I was able to bring him around to our point of view by pointing out that the very fact that he could tell me precisely what was wrong with our analysis and how to fix it was strong confirmation of the validity of the method. For this illustrated some important characteristics of the analytical approach we were trying to use, that is, it was self-correcting and verifiable. The trouble with reliance on past experience alone, unaided by analysis, is that it is not self-correcting and verifiable. It might be wrong, and if it is we have no way of knowing it or correcting it.

Incidentally, to say that our calculations proved wrong is not to say that the original Service proposal that we were criticizing proved to be correct. Rather what has happened, I am happy to report, is that subsequently the parties involved did manage to get together and learn to work together and appreciate each other's value, and they are now developing yet another solution which promises to be better in both cost and effectiveness than the ones previously considered.

What kind of problem is the choice of air-to-ground weapons? How should it be analyzed? It has many elements and it is essential that the experts on the various elements recognize that and be willing to cooperate with others in putting together a good analysis. The problem simply cannot be viewed as the sole preserve of the military man, the technician, the production specialist, or the economist although there is no reason why some of these skills cannot be combined in a single person.

A good analysis requires answering many sorts of questions, such as: What are the targets? Why hit them? How important is more or less destruction? What are the criteria of effectiveness? These questions are primarily problems for a military planner, although he can doubtless profit in their formulation from cooperation with operations researchers and/or economists. I think that this has been widely recognized by the Services and is shown by the fact that for years they have used operations research analysts. Then we must ask what alternative types of ordnance are available, or can be developed. This is a technical question best answered by a person experienced in engineering, using methods appropriate to engineering questions. He is likely to be able to benefit a great deal, however, from collaboration with an experienced military man who can suggest to him which characteristics would be particularly useful. How much will these alternative kinds of weapons cost to develop and to produce? That is a question for someone experienced in cost estimation and production, and for someone experienced in the management of research and development. Then, how effective, how accurate, how reliable and how lethal will these weapons be? This is very complicated. Some relevant data can be obtained on the test range. But the judgment of an experienced military planner is required to establish how the tests can be made to approximate operational conditions and also to estimate how the operational factors derived from test data need to be adjusted for operational conditions.

Then, how are the weapons to be used? Again, a question for a military man who is likely to be able to do a better job on this if he is assisted by an operations research analyst. Finally, for any given amount of resources spent on the complete system, including the aircraft, pilot training and everything else, putting all this together into a balanced program is an economic question, solved best by people experienced in the application of economic analysis.

Now, in the real world of deadlines, personnel ceilings, and the thousands of questions that have to be decided by the various staffs in the Pentagon, it won't be possible to break each question down into its smallest component parts and to get an appropriate expert to analyze each one. Moreover, even a problem as simple as this one has gray areas of overlap between specialties. But even so, it is important to bear in mind the fact that there are many different kinds of questions involved in such a problem, each having its own appropriate method of solution. It is also important to maintain a sense of humor and of charity toward others, the practical difficulties of real communication between members of different professions being what they are.

My intention in emphasizing the many different kinds of factors entering into such a problem, and the many different kinds of disciplines and skills that need to be applied, is not to suggest that military men should confine themselves to the purely military aspects of the problems. That would be neither realistic nor desirable. Moreover, many officers are exceptionally well qualified in areas other than purely military matters such as the physical sciences, economics, and the critical matter of judgment of human psychology.

But I do want to suggest two things. First, there is a definite place for representation from other backgrounds and disciplines in the planning of forces and strategies; and second, it is wrong to cover the whole area of defense planning with the mantle of "military judgment" or "operational experience". Military judgment, if by that is meant specifically the experience and knowledge gained by military men in combat or conducting military operations, is something very precious indeed. Unlike most of the things we know and have which are earned at the price of hard work, the military profession has had to pay in blood for its combat experience. This valuable currency is cheapened by attempting to apply it to things to which it does not apply. Military judgment should not be the basis for a view with respect to technical feasibility. Nor is it fair to suggest, when the Secretary of Defense makes a decision contrary to that of his military advisors on the procurement of a weapon system, that military advice and experience are being ignored or that military judgment is being downgraded. Rather, the problem is that the Secretary of Defense has to balance many other factors in his decisions. I am sure we all agree to that in theory. The problem is that it is sometimes forgotten when practical examples come up.

A few years ago there was a very hot political issue on the ballot in the State of California. Someone proposed to remove the tax exemption from parochial schools. As the campaign progressed, it became apparent that the issue might not be resolved on its merits, but could easily divide the State into Catholics and non-Catholics because the Catholic Church operated most of the parochial schools in the State. However, at this point, the Seventh-Day Adventists, who also operate parochial schools, made a major contribution to clearing the air by coming out with the slogan, " It's *what's* right, not *who's* right."

Sometimes Defense gets to be a pretty emotional business. Many people involved have strong feelings about it, and that is not at all surprising. Defense involves our lives, our survival, the livelihood of many people, the livelihood of districts, and above all our precious freedom. Our military Services have seen and made a lot of history and they are the bearers of many of our most glorious traditions. Although inevitably some people will resent the application of dispassionate, cold analysis to something as rich in meaning and tradition as warfare and strategy, there is no sensible alternative in the nuclear age. Our national survival depends on our ability to come up with good answers as consistently as possible. Therefore, we must make defense planning and the selection of weapon systems an intellectual rather than an emotional process. To do so, we must all turn our attention to the question of *what's* right, not *who's* right.

15

OPERATIONS RESEARCH AT THE NATIONAL POLICY LEVEL*
By Alain C. Enthoven

Operations Research at the national policy level, or Systems Analysis as it is sometimes called, is a systematic approach to the problems of national security policy and the design of the defense program. It differs in scope from Operations Research in the conventional sense, and is not performed exclusively or even primarily by people who might be identified as operational researchers. The work of Systems Analysis is conducted in the Service staffs, the Joint Staff, various operations research groups like OEG, and several offices within the Office of the Secretary of Defense. It is a discipline with a logic of its own, similar in many respects to that of Operations Research, but also different in some fundamental aspects.

To better acquaint you with the logic of this discipline, let me begin by describing for you, in a brief and impressionistic way, the process of analysis and decision underlying the design of one of the major components of the United States defense posture, that is, our posture for thermonuclear war. Having done this, I shall then go on to use this example to illustrate what seems to me to be some of the most important facets of operations research at the national policy level.

I hope to make clear as I go on that the process of analysis of major national security policy choices is a continuing one. It is a cycle of definition of objectives, design of alternative systems to achieve those objectives, evaluation of the alternatives in terms of their effectiveness and costs, a questioning of the objectives and a questioning of the other assumptions underlying the analysis, the opening of new alternatives, the establishment of new objectives, etc. For this reason it would be arbitrary to break into the cycle at any particular point. But the selection of provisional objectives is as reasonable a place to begin as any.

What are the objectives of our posture for thermonuclear war? At least provisionally, let me mention three. First, we want to make war unlikely. In large part, we seek to accomplish this by attempting to deter deliberate Soviet attack on ourselves and our

*From address before the Operations Evaluation Group Vicennial Conference, Washington, D. C., 16 May 1962.

allies. We can hope to achieve this by assuring them that, if they attack us, they will suffer some combination of devastating damage to their civil society and to their military forces. A system designed for deterrence does not necessarily have to be designed exclusively to retaliate against civil society. Assurance of a decisive military defeat may in fact be the most effective deterrent. Secondly, in event that deterrence fails and a war does break out, we are interested in limiting the damage inflicted on ourselves and our allies. But, of course, that objective is interdependent with a third one; that of achieving a favorable military outcome and a favorable political settlement of the war. Therefore, the damage limiting objective must be pursued subject to the constraint that we achieve our political objectives at the same time.

Starting with these broad objectives, let us consider the design of the major components for our posture for thermonuclear war: that is, the continental air and missile defense system, the civil defense program, and the strategic retaliatory or long-range nuclear striking forces. Those responsibile for each of these components might quite reasonably begin by selecting criteria of performance consistent with the broad objectives, and then either seeking to maximize the effectiveness of the system in terms of those criteria, given a fixed cost, or alternatively, what is logically the same thing, attempting to minimize the cost of achievement of a particular level of those objectives.

For example, those responsible for the continental air defense system will examine alternative mixes of interceptors, surface-to-air missiles, and control systems, and, within each of these subsystems, will consider various types: area defense missiles versus local defense missiles, short-range versus long-range interceptors, and the like. They might begin provisionally by asking how they can best spend, say, two billion dollars a year in order to inflict the maximum attrition on penetrating enemy bombers and warheads, or to minimize the weapons or megatons falling on U.S. and Allied territory. Or, they might turn it around and define the problem as one of minimizing the cost of limiting the expected damage caused by enemy attack to a specified level.

There are interesting problems of criterion selection here. The broad objective, or higher objective, if you like, is limiting the damage, measured in terms of population and floorspace destroyed. Minimizing weapons or megatons detonating on our territory is an intermediate objective, and pursuing it may or may not be a good way of pursuing the higher objectives. Whether or not it is should itself be the subject of analysis.

The problem facing those responsible for the civil defense program is similar. For example, they might take as their objective to provide a certain amount of fallout protection to some percentage of the population, and then seek the minimum-cost way of providing it.

Those responsible for the design of the long-range nuclear striking force are likely to look at targets, and to ask, under varying circumstances of outbreak and conduct of the war, what forces would be required to assure destruction of some given percentage of the targets at minimum cost.

At this point, if successful, those responsible for each of the major components will have produced efficient designs in terms of their own particular problems. The designer of the continental air defense system will have maximized the attrition of penetrating enemy vehicles, given that he can spend two billion dollars a year. The designer of the strategic offensive force will have established as his requirements that force which can assure the destruction of, say 83 or 92 percent of the targets under a wide range of contingencies at a minimum cost. But this is only the beginning. Many key questions remain. First of all, there is the question of allocation between major components. Perhaps it would be better to take a hundred million dollars a year away from one component, and spend it on another. For example, perhaps the tasks of deterrence and limiting damage to the U.S. and its Allies could be better done by spending less on continental air defense and more on strategic retaliatory forces capable of destroying enemy bases. Perhaps 92 per cent is too low, or too high. It is the responsibility of the systems analyst to assist those who must decide this by translating the percentage of target destruction into its implications in terms of more meaningful criteria, such as civil damage and the balance of military forces.

All three components of our posture for general war contribute to the same objectives, and there are trade-offs or substitution possibilities between them. MINUTEMAN is a substitute for AICBM, both in the sense that, under some circumstances, it can destroy enemy ICBM's on the ground, and also under certain conditions it will draw the enemy's fire away from other targets, i.e., MINUTEMAN can be both "fly swatter" and "fly paper." Moreover, the desirability of making these various substitutions will depend upon questions of cost and effectiveness. They are not doctrinal matters that can be settled in the absence of technology.

Another question that has to be asked is that of budget level. Would it be better to put another hundred million dollars into our posture for general war, or would it be better to put that money somewhere else? Is the extra gain, in terms of the broad objectives of deterring attack, limiting damage and achieving a favorable military outcome worth the extra cost?

Another set of questions have to be asked about the correctness and validity of the assumptions and criteria that have been used. For example, "What assumptions have been made about the circumstances under which the war begins?" The assumptions on which an analysis of this kind is based ought themselves to be the objects of analysis.

Decisions as to the proper mix between the various components, and as to the size of the program as a whole involve a great many judgments which are the proper function of the legally responsible decision-makers—the President, the Secretary of Defense, the Joint Chiefs of Staff, the Congress—and not the systems analyst. Judgments have to be made about U.S., Allied, and Soviet lives lost or saved under various contingencies; about dollars for defense versus dollars for other things; on risks to be taken; on the effects of alternative postures on our diplomacy; on the morale of our own population; and on many other things. The job of the analyst is to bring his findings about alternative postures, their costs and their effectiveness to the legally constituted decision-makers, who in turn will make judgments, suggest revisions of criteria, and the like. These judgments and decisions will then be translated into instructions for the various components of the system. For example, perhaps a decision will be made to modify the objectives and requirements of the continental air defense system to take into account the constraints placed on the enemy attack size by our own offense, and instead of assuming that we have to shoot down the whole enemy attacking force, rather to assume only that we have to shoot down that part which has survived the action of our own offensive forces. And, the designer of the strategic retaliatory system may be instructed as to how he should take into account the effects of the active air defenses. Perhaps under certain conditions the decision-maker will find that a capability to destroy certain enemy forces on their bases is not worth the cost because at the margin, the job of destroying those forces can better be performed by our active defenses.

SOME REMAINING PROBLEMS

Analysis of problems of this kind is full of uncertainties: not only uncertainties about technical and operational parameters, but also conceptual uncertainties. In some cases, our whole way of understanding a particular problem area may be mistaken. The only way that we know of to deal with conceptual uncertainties is to do more and better analysis, and to proceed cautiously. For example, the fact that we do not have a solid clear-cut analytical basis for reaching the conclusion that we should have exactly 15 attack carriers, as opposed to some much larger or much smaller number, does not mean that a decision should therefore be made to stop building carriers. Perhaps if it were, we would find out too late why we needed them. As far as the technical and operational parameters are concerned, we have found that the best way to deal with these uncertainties is to explore their limits, and to do our calculations in terms of the range of uncertainty. It is generally useful to begin with a best guess for each of the key parameters and then to introduce into the calculation an optimistic or upper bound estimate, and a pessimistic or lower bound estimate. Although it is usually sensible to design the defense posture primarily on the basis of the best estimates, the prudent decision-maker will keep asking himself, "Would the outcome be acceptable if the worst possible happened, i.e., if all the pessimistic estimates were borne out?" Carrying three numbers through all of the calculations can increase the workload greatly. For this reason, a certain amount of judgment has to be used as to when the best guesses are satisfactory and when the full range of uncertainty needs to be explored.

Another important point is that the relevant criteria of effectiveness are not usually single-valued. Each of the components of our posture for general war, and the posture for general war itself, does a number of things for us, and it is not possible to assign one single measure of effectiveness to either the system as a whole or to the components. For example, our continental air defense system protects both people and strategic forces, and the strategic forces protect people and destroy enemy forces, and possibly enemy people. I would like to emphasize this point because many of the misgivings that people have about the application of operations research or systems analysis to national policy questions, seem to be based on the misapprehension that systems analysts believe that effectiveness can be measured in terms of a single number or scale.

This, then, is the work of operations research or systems analysis in support of decision-makers at the national policy level. It is a continuous cycle in which the analyst explores alternative courses of action, their cost and their effectiveness, and presents them to the policy-maker who brings to bear value judgments, rejects some alternatives, makes decisions, and asks for more alternatives within the framework established by the decisions already made.

THE BROADER CONTEXT OF DEFENSE DECISIONS

This view of operations research at the national policy level has several fundamental implications. First of all, defense policy problems are much more than purely military problems, that is, involving only questions of military operations, or cause and effect relationships between military forces. These questions are also political and economic. Such matters as the size and composition of our forces for nuclear war, and the mix of nuclear and non-nuclear forces, have a pervasive influence on our whole foreign policy, on the kinds of initiatives our leaders can and cannot take. The character of our military posture determines how forceful and unyielding our diplomats can reasonably be in particular international crises. It also has a major impact on the kinds and amounts of activity in our domestic economy, and on the balance of international payments. Therefore, the number of ICBM's, carriers, or divisions that we buy, is not strictly a military problem. It is a national policy problem, with both military and other elements and implications.

My second main point about operations research at the national policy level is that ends and means interact. The traditional formulation of operations research problems in terms of ends and means—how can I maximize the achievement of an objective or a set of objectives for a given cost, or alternatively, how can I minimize the cost of achieving a certain set of objectives?—is proper, but limited. At the national policy level, the major part of systems analysis is the exploration of the interaction of ends and means. By that interaction is meant that what are objectives from one point of view are means from another; that what is worth trying to do depends on what is possible to do, or on how effective the means for doing it are; and that any given objective is likely to be one of a number of alternative ways of achieving a still broader objective.

In terms of our posture for general war, for example, those responsible for the continental air defense system might take as their objective the capability to achieve a 95 per cent attrition rate against all of the enemy forces that could possibly be launched at us. This might or might not be a reasonable objective. Whether it turns out to be a reasonable objective will depend upon how much it costs to achieve it, and upon whether there are other ways of achieving the "higher" or "broader" objective of limiting damage. For example, it might be the case that a capability to inflict 95 per cent attrition would cost an inordinate amount, and it might be that a combination of a lesser amount of air defense, combined with civil defense and a very effective strategic offense might do the damage limiting job much better.

There are several lessons that can be drawn from this point. First of all, it means that military requirements should not be regarded as absolute. Whether or not the destruction of 83 or 92 percent of the targets is a desirable goal depends on how much it costs to achieve it. There are always other ways to skin a cat or to defend the country. If left to their own devices, those in charge of one of the components might set their requirements in order to do the whole job themselves, independently of the fact that other people are doing the job too. Requirements at any level are means to a broader objective. But there are almost always alternative ways of achieving the broader objectives.

The same point applies to the various objectives themselves, on which the requirements depend. For example, the objective of shooting down enemy aircraft and missiles at all might or might not be a worthwhile objective, depending upon the state of technology and the alternative ways of achieving the broader objectives. It is at least conceivable that, under certain conditions of technology and U.S. postures, it would be reasonable to have a posture for general war that had no continental air defense in it, or alternatively no civil defense. Therefore, the objectives, and also the assumptions on which each ends-means formulation are based, should themselves be the subject of analysis.

All of this is to suggest that analysis in support of decision-makers at the national policy level is different from operations research as traditionally viewed. Like operations research, this kind of analysis can and must be honest, in the sense that the quantitative factors are selected without bias, that the calculations are accurate, that alternatives are not arbitrarily suppressed, and the like. But it cannot be "objective" in the sense of being independent of values. Value judgments are an integral part of the analysis; and it is the role of the analyst to bring to light for the policy-maker exactly how and where value judgments enter so that the latter can make his own value judgments in the light of as much relevant information as possible.

Again, analysis at this level cannot prove the optimality of any national security policy. I don't doubt for a moment that, given a specified set of ships and aircraft and equipment, and a particular task such as tracking down and killing submarines in a given area, operations analysis can indicate the optimal way to go about doing it. There, only one value judgment enters in. That is, that it is desirable to kill enemy submarines. You cannot do that at the national policy level. Rather, at that level, analysis can only trace out implications of alternative policies.

National security policy decisions are based on the interaction of values, on the one hand, and the costs and effectiveness of military forces and weapon systems on the other. The latter are largely, though not exclusively, quantitative matters. And this is my next main point: the quantitative aspects of national security policy problems are of the first order of importance. Defense policy involves numbers of ships, men, divisions, missiles, bombers, and dollars. The significance of these forces for achieving our broad objectives is a quantitative matter. This is not to imply that all relevant factors can be quantified. Rather, it is to say that only in rare and exceptional cases is it possible to do a sensible job of formulating national defense policy without careful consideration of the relevant numbers.

Let me give an illustration. For the past several years, there has been a great deal of public debate between two alternative strategies for general war known sometimes as "finite deterrence" and "counterforce." Much of this debate has proceeded in the complete absence of quantitative analysis of the cost and effectiveness of the two alternative strategies. By "finite deterrence," I understand a posture for thermonuclear war that is limited to providing only a secure retaliatory force capable of destroying enemy cities in a second strike. By the "counterforce" strategy, I understand the provision of offensive forces capable of destroying a very high percentage of the enemy's strategic offensive forces, combined with active and civil defenses able to limit the damage caused by the enemy's retaliation. Now, which of these two postures represents a sensible choice depends, among other things, on the numbers. That is, it depends on the costs of weapon systems, on their yields, their accuracies, and their reliabilities, on the hardness and dispersal and concealment of the enemy forces, and the like.

For example, if each of the two sides in a bi-polar nuclear world had strategic retaliatory forces consisting of 100 POLARIS submarines, and nothing else, the prospects for a counterforce strategy would be likely to be very dim indeed. If on the other hand, one side had a posture consisting of a few soft and concentrated missiles and bombers while the other side had a large force of accurate, reliable, and well-protected missiles, then the prospects for the latter to pursue successfully a counterforce strategy would be relatively good.

Now this is not to say that these quantitative relationships uniquely determine the answer. The finding that a counterforce capability is feasible, or even cheap, does not prove that we should adopt that strategy. That depends on the value judgments placed on the costs and effectiveness of that strategy by comparison with the alternatives. But I am saying that, with rare exceptions, a quantitative analysis of the alternatives is essential to a good decision.

Or, to take another example, we plan to defend Europe by a combination of conventional forces, tactical nuclear forces and strategic nuclear forces. What mix of forces will be rational for us to pursue depends on the kinds of capabilities the enemy has, on how much they cost him, and how much alternative capabilities would cost us and how effective they would be in meeting various threats.

I make this point because so many people seem to believe that it is possible to debate national strategy intelligently in the absence of the relevant numbers. One gets the impression that many supporters of the counterforce view would support it no matter what the yields and CEP's, hardnesses and dispersals of the two sides were; and similarly for some believers in the finite deterrence strategy. But, in fact, one simply cannot decide rationally on a national security policy independently of the quantitative aspects of enemy capabilities.

But as I criticize the non-quantitative approach to defense policy-making, I also want clearly to dissociate myself from the other extreme. Analysis cannot supplant decision-making. Defense policy decisions cannot be calculated. No set of calculations alone can logically imply that the United States should have "X" divisions or "Y" ICBM's; no set of calculations alone can logically imply that we should follow a "finite deterrence" or a "counterforce" strategy. I want to make that point because I have gotten the impression that some operations researchers believe that such calculations can be made.

I emphasize this point also because there seems to be so much misunderstanding about the quantitative analysis being done in the Department of Defense. Some critics seem to believe that defense policies are being made on computers and that "optimal strategies" are being calculated on slide-rules. Nothing could be further from the truth. Our approach is simply based on a belief that quantities are relevant and have to be considered carefully in the making of policy decisions. As far as I know, no responsible Defense official believes that it is possible to calculate the answers to major national security policy questions.

LIMITATIONS AND BENEFITS

To the extent that major national security policy problems are quantitative in character, calculations are relevant. Of course, there are many things that simply cannot be calculated; for example, the reliability of an ally, or the psychological and political consequences of a military operation. And these non-quantitative factors may dominate the problem. But there are also many things that cannot be done intuitively or based entirely on experience. Intuition and experience unaided by calculations will not tell us how many ICBM's are needed to destroy a target system, nor will they tell us how many C-141's are required to move a division. For most of these questions a mix of calculations, intuition, and experience is required. One of the biggest challenges facing us today is how to find ways of blending these factors better in those areas in which unaided calculation is weakest.

This matter of calculation brings me to computers and their use in the analysis of national security policy problems. I want to set the record straight on this because there is so much nonsense written on the use of computers in making national defense policy decisions.

First of all, computers are very useful—indeed essential—for the analysis of problems requiring large scale data handling or many repetitive calculations; for example, calculation of fallout patterns, or the damage to populations and industry caused by the use of nuclear weapons in various ways. But what the computers are doing here is calculation, or the transformation of data from a less usable form to a more usable form so that it can provide the basis for the application of value judgments and the making of decisions. Whether or not it is desirable to use a computer in a particular problem will depend on the amount and character of the data and calculations. Actually, we make rather little use of computers in the Programming Office, but I would not want to suggest that this implies that they shouldn't be relied upon more heavily elsewhere.

But as far as I know, computers are not "running the wars of the future" as one magazine recently put it. Rather, when sensibly applied, they are handling and presenting to flesh-and-blood decision-makers the data that they require so that they will have a basis for making the judgments they will have to make if they are to do a good job of running a war. Nor were computers the basis for the Secretary of Defense's decision to increase Army guerrilla forces, airlift, and tactical air forces. Those decisions were based on judgments about the relationship of the value of the extra capabilities attained and the extra costs incurred. Another journalist has claimed that it was a computer, and not the judgment of the Secretary of Defense, that prevented the RS–70 from being put on full weapon system status. Now this claim is simply wrong. I don't doubt that someone on the Secretary's staff may have required an adding machine to add up all the costs, or that possibly a computer was used in the combining of the kill probabilities that showed that forces already programmed can kill a very high percentage of the strategic targets. But to argue from this that the RS–70 was "done in" by computers is worse than foolish. It is dangerous. It does the country a great disservice by obscuring the nature of defense policy decision-making and confusing the thinking of the public. If there is anything we badly need in the national security business it is greater, not less clarity of thought about the nature of our problems and how to solve them.

Personally, I happen to be rather skeptical of most attempts that I have seen to do systems analysis by means of large computer war games. Obviously, any calculation that can be done by hand can be done on a computer. The difficulty is that computer games tell you the outcome of the war, based on the many assumptions made, but most of them are not constructed to tell you why the outcome came out the way it did and not some other way. Yet that is the really important information. In studies based on large scale computer models, there is a serious risk that most of the time will be spent on developing the computer model, leaving little time for developing an empirical understanding of the real problems. But, in fact, it is necessary to understand the problem before a good model can be constructed. The computer approach risks not helping to develop the quantitative insight of the decision-maker. But every method has its risks, its advantages and disadvantages, and every tool has its proper uses.

Where does this leave us? What is operations research or systems analysis at the national policy level all about? I think that it can best be described as a continuing dialogue between the policy-maker and the systems analyst, in which the policy-maker asks for alternative solutions to his problems, makes decisions to exclude some, and makes value judgments and policy decisions, while the analyst attempts to clarify the conceptual framework in which decisions must be made, to define alternative possible objectives and criteria, and to explore in as clear terms as possible (and quantitatively) the cost and effectiveness of alternative courses of action.

The analyst at this level is not computing optimum solutions or making decisions. In fact, computation is not his most important contribution; he is helping someone else to make decisions. His job is to ask and find answers to the questions: "What are we trying to do?" "What are the alternative ways of achieving it?" "What would they cost, and how effective would they be?" "What does the decision-maker need to know in order to make a choice?" The analyst collects and analyzes this information for those who are responsible for deciding what the defense program ought to be.

16

SYSTEMS ANALYSIS AND THE NAVY*

By Alain C. Enthoven

The past 18 months have seen a great increase in the amount and quality of weapon systems analysis in the Navy, and in the range of problems studied. The Navy's efforts have been successful in clarifying the issues and in laying the foundations for further progress. The work that has been completed has been good for the Navy and good for the United States. It has made it possible to obtain a more effective Navy and to do so at less cost than would otherwise be necessary. Some of the best studies yielded the added return of greatly improved mutual understanding between the Navy and the Office of the Secretary of Defense about force and resource requirements for the Navy. Gloomy predictions that the systematic application of analysis would prove to be disastrous to the Navy were shown to be untrue.

What is systems analysis? I have not been able to produce a good brief definition. I would describe the art, as it has evolved in the Department of Defense, as a reasoned approach to problems of decision. Some have defined it as "quantitative common sense." Alternatively, it is the application of methods of quantitative economic analysis and scientific method, in the broadest sense, to the problems of choice of weapon systems and strategy. It is a systematic attempt to provide decision-makers with a full, accurate, and meaningful summary of the information relevant to clearly defined issues and alternatives.

Systems analysis is not synonymous with the application of computers. There is no essential connection between the two. Certainly the development or utility of the former in no way depends on the latter. Some researchers, working within the limits of the systems analysis approach, try to do their analyses by means of large-scale computer simulations, and sometimes this causes the uninformed to identify systems analysis with computers. Actually, the computer simulation approach so far has not been particularly fruitful as a method of weapon systems analysis. However, the potential advantages offered by high-speed electronic computers are sufficiently great that I would not want to suggest that systems analysts will never make them useful servants of informed judgment. When that day comes, I may be persuaded to modify my preferences for the slide rule and "back of the envelope."

Moreover, systems analysis is not arcane, mysterious, or occult. It is not performed with the help of a mysterious black box. Stories that speak of "slashing equations and whirring computers" are fiction, and poor fiction, at that. A good systems analyst should be able to give a clear nontechnical explanation of his methods and results to the responsible decision-makers.

APPLIED ECONOMICS

The systems analysis approach, as it is being applied today in the Office of the Secretary of Defense, is a systematic attempt to bring to bear on the problem of planning the defense program many relevant disciplines, and to do so in an integrated way. The list includes traditional military planning, economics, political science and other social sciences, applied mathematics, and the physical sciences. Perhaps because I am an economist by professional training, I like to emphasize systems analysis as applied economic analysis. What does that mean?

Economics is the science of the allocation of limited resources; the study of both how our economic system actually allocates limited resources and how it might be done more efficiently. Thus, economics is not really concerned just with money. It is concerned with limited resources of all kinds. Economists give particular attention to money simply because it is the common denominator our society uses to measure the relative value of material things.

What does economics have to do with weapon systems, strategies, and military requirements? Many people say the answer to that question is "nothing;" that our military security, which is one of the foundations of our freedom, is so important that one should not put a price tag on it; that no price is too high to pay for freedom. Another view concedes that economics and military requirements are related in peacetime, but holds that in wartime, when military budgets are "unlimited," economics is irrelevant. These views are wrong.

Whether we like it or not, we have only a limited amount of goods and services available at any one time. Our gross national product, though large, is limited. We have only a finite number of man-hours available for all forms of productive activity. Moreover, there are other needs besides defense: feeding, clothing, and housing our population, educating our children, cultivating our minds, fighting disease, and so on. Therefore, in peace or in war, only a limited amount of resources is available for defense. And if we wish to assure our freedom, it is important that we use those resources well.

A lack of understanding of these fundamental facts shows up often in discussions of practical problems. For example, CVA–67 will cost about 280 million dollars to build. Had it been decided to make her nuclear-powered, she would have cost over 400 million dollars. For roughly 400 million dollars, one can buy either a nuclear-powered carrier or a conventionally-powered carrier plus four 3,500-ton destroyer escorts. Responsible Defense officials must face the choice between the alternative ways of spending the $400 million. People may disagree on which is the better way to spend that money, but there should be no disagreement that it is necessary and correct to pose the problem in this fashion.

Unfortunately, there is such disagreement. Some argue that we should buy the "best" carrier available, cost not considered and then, if they are needed, buy the four destroyer escorts also. This argument is usually combined with exhortations about "nothing but the best" which ignore the crucial difference between "best, given our limited resources," and "best, assuming hypothetically that there is no limitation on resources." Or, it is combined with attacks on "arbitrary budget ceilings." But the man who wants a nuclear carrier plus four destroyer escorts cannot escape the fact that for the same cost one could have a conventional carrier and eight destroyer escorts. Therefore, he cannot escape the question "which is the best way to spend the money?"

The difficulty arises out of a confusion between budget *level* and the *allocation* of any given budget. The nuclear power issue is primarily a budget allocation question: How should we spend four billion dollars per year (or whatever figure one might choose) on attack carrier forces? The question cannot be avoided by arguing that we should add 120 million dollars to the shipbuilding budget to make the carrier nuclear-powered, unless one is prepared also to argue that the extra money is better spent on nuclear power than on the four extra DEs, or on some other 120-million dollar program.

I emphasize the inescapability of the limitation of resources, and the resulting necessity for choice, because it is the basis for the relevance of economics to weapon system choice. Out of this limitation of resources stems the need for systematic thought on the problem of getting the most out of them.

What are the principles of economics? I cannot condense all of the elements into a few pages. But it is possible to indicate briefly some of the fundamental notions that are relevant to systems analysis.

First, in the economist's world there are always alternatives, alternative ways of using resources or alternative ways of doing a job. His theories are built on that assumption, and clearly it is a good one. Thus, if an economist hears that it is required that an airplane be able to fly at Mach 2, he naturally thinks, almost in spite of himself, "I wonder whether Mach 1.9 or Mach 2.2 would be better." Or, if he is told "400 missiles are required to destroy the targets," he instinctively thinks about 350 and 450, and other alternatives. A great deal of economic theory is concerned with the comparison of alternatives.

Of particular interest to economists is the *marginal comparison;* for example, a comparison between the costs and target destruction capabilities of a force of 400 missiles and one of 399 missiles, or some other number not far from 400. The reason for this is that it is often possible to derive a clue as to whether 400 is a sensible force level from a comparison of forces of 399 and 400 missiles.

Let me illustrate. Suppose that, all operational factors considered, our missiles each have a 50 percent chance of destroying a target, and that we must commit all of our missiles to their targets before the firing begins. Suppose there are 100 targets. How many missiles are "required" to destroy the targets?

One approach is to assume, arbitrarily, that we must be able, on the average, to destroy, for example, 90 percent of the targets. Then determining the "required number" becomes a simple arithmetic matter. If we program one missile per target, on the average we can expect to destroy 50 targets (50 percent of 100 targets). If we program two missiles per target, we can expect to destroy 75, and so forth.[1] On the average, a force of 340 missiles can be expected to destroy 90 targets. The answer seems simple and clear enough.

But if one considers the force of 340 missiles in the context of a range of alternative forces, some deeper questions emerge. The following table shows the average number of targets destroyed for several different forces.

---

[1] If we fire two missiles at a target, there are four possible results, each equally probable: (1) both missiles hit the target, (2) the first hits and the second misses, (3) the first misses and the second hits, and (4) both miss. Only if both miss, an event whose probability is 25 per cent, will the target survive. In the other three cases, having a combined probability of 75 percent, the target is destroyed.

Number of Missiles	Average Number of Targets Destroyed
200	75
300	87.5
308	88
324	89
340	90
356	91
380	92.5
400	93.75

The question immediately arises, "Why 90 percent?" Is it worth the price of 16 extra missiles to raise the average number of targets destroyed from 89 to 90; or of 140 extra missiles to raise the average number of targets destroyed from 75 to 90? If we keep 90 as our objective, *on the average*, it costs us 3.4 missiles per target aimed at, and nearly 3.8 missiles per target destroyed. But *at the margin*, raising the required average number of targets destroyed by one costs us 16 missiles. This concept, *marginal cost*, is one of the fundamental notions of economic theory. Its twin is *marginal product*: the 341st missile will add one-sixteenth of one target to the average number of targets destroyed.

Armed with these concepts, the economist will seek out marginal costs and marginal products and describe them for the decision-maker. Of course, the fact that raising the required damage level from 89 to 90 targets costs 16 missiles carries no necessary implication that we should not do it. It is up to the responsible officials charged with making such decisions, that is, the Secretary of Defense, the Service secretaries, and those to whom they have delegated the authority to make such decisions, to weigh the marginal costs and marginal products and to judge at what point the extra target destruction caused by more missiles is no longer worth the extra cost. Having drawn out what the costs of the various alternatives really are, economic analysis has nothing more to contribute to the problem. It becomes a matter of judgment. But the distinction between *marginal* and *average* costs is important. If it were not made, a responsible official might be misled into thinking that because, on the average, 340 missiles destroy 90 of the 100 targets, whence about 3.8 missiles must be expended for each target destroyed, the 90th target also costs 3.8 missiles to destroy.

This example is a particularly simple one. Few requirements problems in the Defense Department can be described in such simple terms. Still, the example does furnish an important insight that does have application even in the most complicated of problems. If one plots the curve relating effectiveness, which is measured in targets destroyed in this example, and cost, which is measured in number of missiles in this example, one very frequently finds a curve with the following characteristic shape:

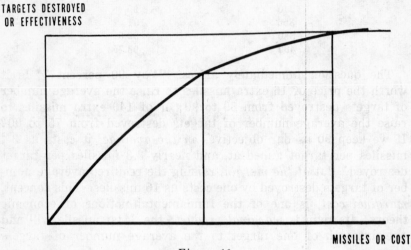

Figure 16

Or, alternatively it may look like this:

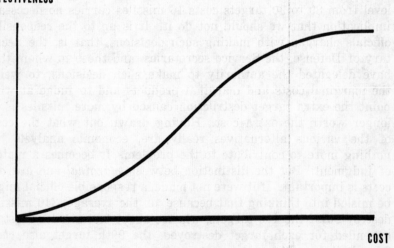

Figure 17

These curves illustrate the widespread phenomenon of *diminishing marginal returns*. That is, as the resources devoted to a mission are increased, after a point the marginal products of additional resources generally decline, or, put another way, the marginal costs of extra effectiveness rise. An understanding of this point is important because it is the key to the sensible resolution of many requirements issues. Rather than viewing the problem of military requirements determination as one of calculation of the forces required to achieve an arbitrarily selected objective or level of effectiveness, it is often sensible to reduce the problem to one of judging at what point the extra effectiveness resulting from more forces—the marginal product—is no longer worth the extra effort—the marginal cost. Alternatively, many requirements issues have been resolved by observing that, at some point, more forces would put us "out on the flat of the curve," that is, they would put us in the position of paying large sums of money for small increases in effectiveness. For these reasons, I have not been able to resist facetiously calling this simple diagram "the single all-purpose cost-effectiveness curve."

Much economic theory is an analysis of what we often refer to in the Defense Department as "balance." What are balanced forces? Or to put the question into the economist's jargon, how does one determine an efficient mix of forces? Suppose that our problem is one of determining the efficient mix of tactical air and ground forces; that is, for example, the combination of wings and divisions that will permit us to achieve a stipulated military objective at least cost.

First, we must determine the substitution or trade-off possibilities. Suppose that CINCSTRIKE advises us that the objective can be achieved with equal probability or margin of safety by any of a number of combinations of wings and divisions, and that these combinations all lie on the curve shown in the diagram below. This curve then represents the substitution possibilities between wings and divisions. Its slope at any point represents the number of wings we can give up in exchange for one more division, or vice versa, and still just be able to accomplish the objective. For example, if we are at point "v", we can trade the number of wings represented by the distance between points "v" and "w" for the number of divisions represented by the distance between points "w" and "x" and still be able to accomplish the objective. The ratio of those numbers, i.e., the ratio of the distances "v" to "w" and "w" to "x", might be called the "substitution ratio," or the ratio at which we should be just willing to substitute wings for divisions at the wing strength represented by point "v". The shape of the curve reflects diminishing marginal returns. The fewer wings we have, the more divisions are required to compensate us for the loss of another wing.

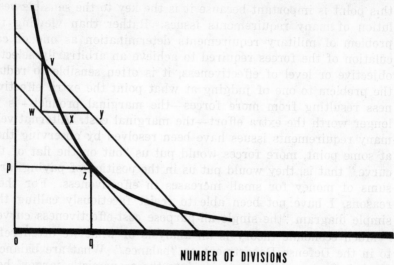

NUMBER OF WINGS

NUMBER OF DIVISIONS

Figure 18

Now, where is the optimum point on the curve? That depends on the relative costs of wings and divisions. Suppose that the relative costs of a wing and a division are in the ratio of the distances "v" to "w" and "w" to "y"; that is, the cost ratio is such that one can trade the number of wings represented by the distance "v" to "w" for the number of divisions represented by the distance "w" to "y" with no change in the total cost. Then consider point "v". Is it the optimum, or can we do better? Well, we have already observed first, that from point "v" we can give up the number of wings represented by the distance "v" to "w" in exchange for the number of divisions represented by the distance "w" to "x", thus moving to point "x", and still do the job. But we have also observed that the relative costs are such that we can give up wings from "v" to "w" and add divisions from "w" to "y" at no change in total cost. Thus, if we can pay for the force combination represented by point 'v", we have the alternative, at the same total cost, of moving to point "x", which does the job equally well, and having the number of divisions represented by the distance from "x" to "y" left over. Therefore, point "x" is more economical or efficient than point "v".

The same process of reasoning can be repeated until we converge at point "z". At this point, the "substitution ratio," or the rate at which we can trade divisions and wings and still just do the job, and the cost ratio, or the rate at which we can trade divisions and wings within any given total budget, are equal. And that is the point that corresponds to the combination of wings and divisions that just does the job at minimum total cost. Thus, for this particular situation and these relative costs, the combination "p" wings and "q" divisions represents a "balanced force."

The same logic can be applied to many problems of allocation of resources; for example, the problem of choice between numbers and quality. One often hears arguments for more numbers at the expense of quality or performance, or for higher performance at the expense of numbers, and the arguments are often in the abstract, independent of the shape of the substitution curves and the relative costs. The important thing is that one cannot decide such matters in the abstract. In the diagram, instead of wings read number of aircraft, and instead of divisions, read individual aircraft performance. Let the job to be done be the destruction of a given set of targets. Then, to determine the optimum combination, one must examine the trade-off curve and the relative costs. At some points like "v", the performance is too low and it would be better to sacrifice numbers to get higher performance. At points below "z", numbers are too low, and performance should be sacrificed to get more numbers. Of course, many other relevant considerations, some of them intangible, must be brought to bear before a final decision can properly be made. One important example would be the safety of the pilots and the impact on morale of heavy loss of life. That is why such problems are matters of decision, i.e., judgments to be made by the Secretary of Defense, the Service secretaries, and those to whom they have delegated authority for such decisions, and not simply matters of calculation to be resolved by the systems analysts.

The issue here is not whether the country should spend more money to get more performance. The level of the budget is a separate question. The point is that one should seek the combination of numbers and performance that would get the most effectiveness out of any given budget. To do otherwise would be wasteful.

CONSTRUCTION OF PARTIAL ORDERINGS

In the discussion of diminishing marginal returns, I mentioned effectiveness but did not define it. What is military effectiveness and how is it measured? That is a very complicated question and there is no generally satisfactory answer. A great deal of analysis must be done before we begin to get a reliable grip on that elusive concept "military effectiveness." But a part of the work of systems analysis is to develop criteria that will permit us to rank alternative mixes of forces in terms of their military effectiveness.

Let me illustrate with an example. The designer of the guidance system for POLARIS can make a variety of trade-offs between accuracy, cost, reliability, and weight. On what basis can he choose one combination of these characteristics over another? If he chooses accuracy as his measure of effectiveness, he might make a choice in favor of maximum accuracy, but at a great cost in terms of the other characteristics. He might pursue accuracy to the point that he is "out on the flat of the curve." Therefore, he needs criteria that will help him to make a good compromise between accuracy and other characteristics. To get them, he must study the purposes of the POLARIS system as a whole.

The POLARIS system is a part of our Strategic Retaliatory Forces whose purposes include making nuclear war unlikely by deterring direct attack against us, and should that fail, helping to limit the damage caused to ourselves and our allies by destroying as many as possible of the enemy's force before they are launched. The extent to which our Strategic Retaliatory Forces can be effective in achieving the second purpose depends on the circumstances of outbreak of the war, that is, on the relative timing of the launching of enemy forces and our own. However, because of "rate of fire" limitations on bombers and some kinds of missile systems, we may expect, even in circumstances in which we are striking second, to be able to destroy a substantial part of the enemy's nuclear delivery forces on the ground. Both of these purposes involve an ability to destroy targets, though different kinds of targets. Thus, the designer of the POLARIS guidance system can begin to derive information on good mixes of accuracy, reliability, weight, cost, and other matters, by looking at the targets. For any particular target, the preferred mix of characteristics can be derived from its hardness, its extent, the desired probability of destruction, and so on. If the objective were to destroy as many as possible of an unlimited list of identical targets, the problem would end here.

But, there are more fundamental objectives underlying target destruction. The deterrence objective is served by an ability to destroy, in a second strike (i.e., after the enemy has attacked our forces), things the enemy values. At least in terms of present-day strategic concepts, this means enemy cities, which are soft, extensive targets. The damage-limiting objective is served by an ability to destroy, under various conditions, bomber bases, missile sites, and other military targets, which are more or less blast resistant "point targets."

Thus, the preferred mix of accuracy, reliability, weight, and cost will depend on which targets the POLARIS will be used to attack, and therefore on our strategy and on the availability of other weapon systems. For example, a strategy that emphasizes counterforce targeting would increase the requirement for accuracy; the availability of large numbers of highly accurate MINUTEMAN missiles would lessen the requirement for accuracy in POLARIS.

The extent to which a large investment in a counterforce posture makes sense depends on the effectiveness of our forces in limiting the damage to ourselves and our allies. Under any given set of assumptions about circumstances of outbreak, war plans, and so forth, this effectiveness can be measured by the difference between the damage that could be caused by the enemy forces if not attacked by our own, and the damage that could be caused us in spite of our attacks on the enemy forces.

Of course, each of our weapon systems and forces has particular advantages and disadvantages that are measured in other ways than by surviving population and wealth. For example, it is argued by some that a large-scale civil defense program in this country would have significant effects on national psychology and attitudes. Our antiaircraft defense system controls our airspace against peacetime intruders as well as helping to limit damage in wartime. An antimissile defense could protect our cities from isolated accidental missile firings, or from blackmail by small powers. All of these factors should enter into judgments made about our choice of weapon systems and strategies.

Thus, to do a good job of measuring the effectiveness of the POLARIS guidance system, it is necessary to develop a complete analysis of the effectiveness of our whole posture under a variety of assumed conditions. Such an analysis permits us to translate accuracy, reliability, weight, and number of missiles (which depends on costs) into target destruction, and to translate target destruction into surviving military forces, population, and wealth.

For several reasons, it is important to put each weapon system problem in the context of the other problems that surround it, and of the broader problems of which it is a part. First, the test of whether a particular set of criteria is a good one is its relevance to the broader objectives which the system is intended to serve. For example, accuracy alone is not a good criterion for the POLARIS guidance system; the objective of target destruction might be better served by larger numbers of more reliable missiles even at some cost in accuracy. Second, developing such a hierarchy of criteria makes it possible to aggregate a large number of detailed measures of performance into a few broad criteria of overall effectiveness that are more meaningful to top-level officials who have to deal with so many problems that they cannot consider every accuracy-reliability choice in detail. In the example cited above, the Secretary of Defense and the Joint Chiefs should not have to worry about the weight of the POLARIS guidance package. They will want to concentrate their attention on prospective damage to U.S., allied, and enemy populations and military forces under a range of possible wars, and on many important intangible factors about which they must make the key judgments. A good analysis will leave them free to do that.

Moreover, putting each problem in its larger context helps the analyst and the decision-maker to see the full range of alternatives. Putting POLARIS in the context of the Strategic Retaliatory Forces helps one to see that one alternative to greater POLARIS accuracy is to have more MINUTEMAN ICBMs. Another alternative is to have more bombers. Considering the Strategic Retaliatory Forces in the context of our whole posture for general nuclear war helps one to see that, in addition to the foregoing, the alternatives to more POLARIS accuracy or to more Strategic Retaliatory Forces include Continental Air and Missile Defense, Civil Defense, and anti-submarine forces. To take but one of these, unless we can easily and surely destroy enemy ICBMs on the ground, perhaps it would be better to plan to destroy their warheads in the air.

Viewing each problem of analysis and decision in this way also helps one to understand the important fact that ends and means interact. Too often, analyses of military requirements will be limited to determining one feasible way, or perhaps the best way of achieving a particular objective. The problem is that whether any particular military objective is worth pursuing will depend on how much it costs to achieve it, because there are almost always alternative ways of achieving the broader or higher objective.

For example, it would be extremely difficult to find and destroy a substantial number of enemy missile submarines in the few minutes between the outbreak of a nuclear war and the time by which they could fire most of their missiles. One approach to the problem of ASW force requirements for this mission is to insist on ever larger forces, even though the one we now have would not be able to destroy very many submarines before they had launched their missiles, and even though a large expansion in the forces would not make us appreciably better off. Proponents of this approach ignore the fact that we have alternative ways of keeping those missiles off our cities: these include active anti-missile defenses, better Strategic Retaliatory Forces to improve our deterrent to nuclear attack, and improved conventional forces to deter limited aggressions or at least keep them from escalating into nuclear war.

A frequent but mistaken view of the determination of strategy and force requirements is that the complete process is one of starting at the top with broad national objectives and then deriving a strategy, and from the strategy, force requirements, and from the force requirements, a budget. It is mistaken because the costs must be considered in choosing strategies and objectives. There are alternative objectives and alternative strategies. And it may be that the advantages of a somewhat more ambitious strategy are worth its somewhat greater cost. And, of course, the cost and effectiveness of each strategy will depend on the cost and effectiveness of the weapon systems used. Thus, the line of causation should not be thought of as running one way, from the strategy to the forces, or, for that matter, from the budget to the strategy. Rather our objectives, strategy, forces, and weapon systems should be thought of as interdependent. And a "requirement" for a particular force level or weapon system cannot be established independently of its cost.

Important as it is to develop a hierarchy of criteria for ordering alternative mixes of weapon systems and forces, it is clear that the best we can ever hope for is a *partial ordering*. For example, it seems doubtful that we can ever develop criteria that will permit the effectiveness of POLARIS and airlift to be measured in the same terms. In fact, the criteria of damage to population and wealth that we use to compare alternative Strategic Retaliatory and Continental Air and Missile Defense Forces cannot establish a complete ordering. Each kind of force will offer a number of "by-products" that cannot be measured in these terms. For example, suppose two postures offer exactly the same number of U.S. and allied survivors in a particular set of circumstances, but one posture does it by a larger Strategic Retaliatory Force and no anti-missile defenses, while the other contains an anti-missile defense but fewer Strategic Retaliatory Forces. Although the two forces may be identical in terms of prospective damage to the alliance in a thermonuclear war, they would have important differences. Presumably, the one with larger Strategic Retaliatory Forces would offer a stronger deterrent to deliberate attack, while the one with the anti-missile defenses would offer some peacetime protection against accidental missile firings. Thus, we cannot and should not expect ever to be able to develop a complete set of numerical criteria to measure "military effectiveness" in general.

SCIENTIFIC METHOD

(For Mr. Enthoven's discussion of the relevant characteristics of scientific method as applied to the problem of choosing strategies and selecting weapon systems, see his address to the Naval War College, selection 14, above, pages 138–148).

ASSUMPTIONS AND UNCERTAINTIES

In order to calculate or analyze a problem, one generally must make assumptions about a variety of factors, some of which will involve substantial uncertainties. Critics of the systems analysis approach like to point out that the results are no better than the underlying assumptions. Though true for any individual calculation, this statement may not be true of a complete study. Good systems analysts have acquired some wisdom in dealing with this problem over the years.

As to assumptions in general, let me make two observations. First, a good systems analyst will do sensitivity tests on his assumptions in order to identify which ones really affect the outcome, and by how much. This will enable him to isolate for further research and evaluation those assumptions that prove to be the most important, and to call them to the attention of the responsible decision-maker.

Second, generally speaking, there is no single "right" set of assumptions. There is often a variety of sets of relevant assumptions, each more or less equally defensible. It is unfortunately the case that this important point is not widely understood. Far too many people keep looking for the "right" set of assumptions the way ancient alchemists looked for the philosophers' stone. Their prospects for success are no better. This is unfortunate, because some people find a set of assumptions that leads to the conclusion they believed all along or hoped would emerge, and they then put forward their conclusions as soundly established, not realizing that the opposite conclusion could have been derived from equally defensible but different assumptions. A good systems analysis will describe the significant alternative sets of assumptions and their implications in such a way that the responsible decision-maker can make his judgment based on the full range of relevant assumptions.

This point was well illustrated by the controversy over the comparative costs of a nuclear-powered and conventionally-powered aircraft carrier. It might seem that comparing the costs of a CVA and a CVAN ought to be a straightforward matter; that one should be able simply to add up the costs of each and compare them. But, in fact, in order to make a cost comparison, one must first make assumptions about a number of relevant factors, each debatable, and each able to have a noticeable effect on the outcome.

For example, should one include the costs of the escort ships, or not? I have heard senior naval officers argue reasonably on both sides of this question, though the balance of the judgment seems to favor including them. It matters because the relative cost increase associated with using nuclear power in the smaller escort ships is much greater than it is for the carrier.

Should one make the comparison on the basis of estimates of the costs of two wholly new task forces identical in all respects but propulsive power? It would seem reasonable to do so. But that would bias the comparison in favor of nuclear power because, at the moment, we have all or most of the conventional major fleet escort ships we need. One could argue that the nuclear force should have to bear the costs of both construction and operation of its nuclear-powered escorts while the conventional force should be charged only with operating costs of the conventional escorts. That, in turn, would be "unfair" to nuclear power because eventually the conventional escorts will have to be replaced. But "eventually" now seems off in the uncertain future. Therefore, although we know that they should lie between these two extremes, good sets of assumptions seem difficult to identify.

Moreover, the assumptions made about the "scenarios" in which the carrier forces are to be used can influence the cost comparison by influencing the fleet support requirements. For example, a cold war deployment involving a long, high-speed transit, little flying, and no consumption of ordnance, will favor the nuclear task force because fleet logistic support requirements will be minimal. If oil is not required, the task force will be able to operate without replenishment for a relatively long time. On the other hand, in a limited-war situation involving heavy flying and delivery of ordnance, the advantage of not requiring black oil will be considerably reduced; both nuclear and conventional forces will require substantial resupply. Which is the "right" assumption? Neither by itself would be completely "right" or "fair." A good systems analysis will describe the situation for the decision-maker, and provide him with whatever information is available that might help him to make a judgment as to the frequency and value of both types of mission in the future.

I mentioned earlier that rather than conceal uncertainties, a good analysis will bring them out and clarify them. This is important. A best guess is not the same as certain knowledge. If it is a question of uncertainties about quantitative matters such as operational factors, or uncertainty about enemy strategies, it is desirable to examine the available evidence and determine the bounds of uncertainty. In many of our analyses for the Secretary of Defense, we carry three estimates through the calculations: a "best" or single most likely estimate, an "optimistic," and a "pessimistic" estimate. One admiral calls this procedure "bop (for best, optimistic, pessimistic) estimates."

"Bop" estimates have produced some unexpected benefits. For one thing, the concept of "bop" estimates has led to some valuable clarity of thought on the whole question of comparing our forces to those of our opponents. There has been a widespread belief that, in cases of doubt, the safe thing to do is to pick from the high end of the range of uncertainty in estimating one's opponent's capabilities and to pick from the low end in estimating one's own. If uncertain about the reliability of the enemy's missiles and ours, according to this belief, one should be sure not to underestimate the enemy's or to overestimate ours. This might be a conservative or safe approach if we did not have limited resources. But, in fact, we have learned that it can be just as dangerous to overestimate the enemy's capabilities relative to our own as it is to underestimate them. Overestimates do not necessarily lead to insurance and safety. They are just as likely to lead to despair, to pricing important capabilities out of the market, and to strategies of desperation.

Perhaps the best example of this has been the persistent gross overestimates of the effectiveness of the Soviet Army. In the United States we get 16 combat-ready divisions (plus a variety of other units) out of an army of about 960,000. Under existing concepts of organization and existing missions and commitments (e.g., Continental Air Defense, Vietnam, to name but two), we could probably get the equivalent of about 18 divisions out of a one-million-man army. It is generally agreed that the Soviet Union has an army of roughly two million men. Yet one often hears and reads statements to the effect that the Soviets have over 100 divisions, each one presumably as effective as one of ours. In fact, numbers like 160 and 175 still appear in print. How can this be? Unless the U.S. Army is very inefficient in its use of manpower (which it is not), surely the Soviets could not get from their army of two million a great deal more than the equivalent of twice the 18 divisions we could get out of a one-million-man army. The overestimate can be traced to the omission of two key factors: first, the important distinction between combat-ready units and units of low readiness; and second, the fact that our divisions, with their non-divisional combat support, such as engineers and heavy artillery, have about twice as many men as their Soviet counterparts. The main reason for the overestimate is doubtless the widespread belief that no harm could come from over stating the strength of the Soviets. But the plain fact is that these over-estimates have led to an attitude of hopelessness about the prospects for a successful non-nuclear defense against non-nuclear attacks in the NATO area, and to an unnecessary and excessive reliance on the early first use of nuclear weapons by NATO. Yet, without an adequate non-nuclear force, we could be forced by Communist aggression into the horrible dilemma of suicide or surrender.

Another benefit of the use of "bop" estimates has been a greater measure of agreement in joint requirements studies. It may well be impossible for two officers from different services and with different points of view, to agree on a single estimate of an uncertain magnitude, or on a single "right" set of assumptions when in fact such does not exist. In the past, such failure to agree has sometimes been erroneously labeled as parochialism. But failure to agree is not surprising when one realizes that there are genuine uncertainties—cases in which we simply do not know where a magnitude will fall between certain limits—and that there often is no single "fair" or right set of assumptions. We have found that an approach that acknowledges that there can be alternative assumptions saves a great deal of otherwise wasted time.

SYSTEMS ANALYSIS AND OPERATIONS RESEARCH

It may be helpful to an understanding of the systems analysis approach to have it contrasted with the discipline traditionally known as operations research. The Navy has a strong tradition in operations research and has every right to be proud of it. But sometimes I fear that when I talk to Navy men about the need for more systematic quantitative analysis, some may interpret this to mean more operations research. There are significant differences between the two. Of course, in reality there is a continuum between them, just as there is between physiology and medicine and between physics and engineering. One necessarily must artificially divide a continuous spectrum into discrete segments in order to define the different disciplines. However, I do think it would be useful further to clarify the sense of the systems analysis approach.

In doing this, I would not want for a moment to suggest that systems analysis is in any sense, intellectually or otherwise, superior to operations research. That would be like suggesting that medicine is superior or inferior to biology. Both have their place. I am reminded of a statement contained in the Carnegie report on excellence to the effect that if a society doesn't respect both its plumbers and its philosophers, neither its pipes nor its theories will hold water.

Let me contrast operations research and systems analysis in several ways.

Operations research techniques are applicable to problems such as calculations of optimum inventory levels for spare parts for an SSBN, calculation of the optimum search pattern for ASW forces seeking a submarine in a given area, calculation of the most efficient blend of aviation gasoline, and the like. Systems analysis, on the other hand, is an approach to broader problems such as determining the preferred characteristics for a new attack aircraft, the design of the POLARIS system, a determination of how many POLARIS submarines are required, or the study of the number of antisubmarine ships or the number of attack carriers that should be included in the Navy force structure.

Generally speaking, operations research accepts specified objectives and given assumptions about the circumstances, the hardware, and the like, and then attempts to compute an optimum solution, usually maximizing or minimizing some objective, given the available resources. Operations research attempts to do an optimization in the small. It may be necessary for the operations researcher first to define the problem, but the operations research techniques themselves are intended for the solution of well defined problems, that is, problems in which all of the relevant relationships can be specified. Operations research then attempts to select an optimum solution from a predetermined range of alternatives.

Systems analysis, on the other hand, has a broader orientation. It analyzes alternative objectives and explores their implications. It is focused more on exploring the implications of alternative assumptions than on analyzing in extensive detail the implications of a single set of assumptions. Systems analysis ordinarily is not concerned with computing an optimum solution. If there is optimization involved, it is optimization in the large, rather than in the small. Systems analysis is concerned with avoiding gross error and with giving the decision-maker a menu of choices representing different mixes of effectiveness and cost so that he can make his choice. It is part of systems analysis to question the objectives.

Systems analysis takes problems that are not defined and attempts to define them. If the problem cannot be well defined, that is, specified in all its aspects, systems analysis techniques are still useful in helping the decision-maker by attempting to define those aspects of the problem that can be defined and quantified. Systems analysis emphasizes design of new solutions and widening of the range of alternatives, rather than selecting the best alternative from among a predetermined range. Rather than trying to select a precise maximum or minimum, a motto of the Systems Analysis Office in the Office of the Secretary of Defense is, "It is better to be roughly right than exactly wrong."

The epistemology of operations research is the epistemology of the exact sciences; that is, operations research assumes that the empirical data are accurate, at least accurate enough to make refined and precise calculations worthwhile. On the other hand, the epistemology of systems analysis is the epistemology of the inexact sciences. Statistics may be used, although in most major weapon system problems the uncertainties are greater than the statistical variations, so that extensive use of mathematical statistical techniques is not likely to produce useful results. Systems analysis emphasizes techniques for dealing with uncertainty, such as sensitivity tests, the use of ranges, alternative scenarios, and the like.

Operations research technique emphasizes applied mathematics, such as linear programing, queueing theory, search theory, and inventory theory; that is, a collection of mathematical techniques for maximizing or minimizing something subject to constraints. Also operations research emphasizes the use of computers because its emphasis is largely on efficient and accurate computation of optimum solutions. In effect, operations research is oriented toward problems in which the element of calculation is dominant, and therefore, in which mathematics can be thought of as a substitute for rather than as an aid to judgment.

Systems analysis, on the other hand, emphasizes basic economic concepts, mostly the simple concepts of marginal product and marginal cost. The systems analysis approach has developed a variety of techniques for analyzing complex problems of decision in such a way as to make calculation the servant of informed judgment. It has, therefore, made use of calculation, but it puts much less emphasis on it than does operations research.

Who, then, are systems analysts? I am unable to hazard a satisfactory definition of them as a group. There are few courses and no degrees in the subject, and that is doubtless a good thing because it helps to minimize appeals to authority. The main attributes of a good systems analyst, other than those, such as good character and imagination, that are valuable in most professions, are an understanding of scientific method, economic intuition, some facility with mathematics which is the language of science, and an appreciation of the limitations as well as the capabilities of his methods. Some very effective systems analysts are officers, some are civilians. No one professional background has proved itself to be best. Representation from a variety of professions and disciplines is clearly beneficial.

LIMITATIONS AND BIASES

What's wrong with systems analysis? What are its particular limitations and biases? One criticism I have heard is that emphasis on quantitative analysis risks ignoring those factors that cannot be reduced to numbers, or at least over-emphasizing those that can.

Suppose, for example, that the problem is to choose between two alternative ways of destroying a certain set of targets. The less costly way is to base short-range missiles on the territory of an ally; the more costly way is to cover the targets with long-range missiles based in the United States. But suppose basing the missiles on the ally's territory would lead to political difficulties, to the embarrassment and possible fall of a friendly government. How does one take account of such political aspects in a quantitative analysis? The answer is that one doesn't. There is no way of "grinding in" the potential political difficulties of an ally. The most the analysis can do is make clear to the decision-maker the differences in cost and effectiveness between the two approaches so that he can make an informed judgment about their weight in relation to the political problems.

I would not want to deny that there is potential danger here, even though there is nothing about the systems analysis approach that prevents an assessment of the political or other non-quantitative factors from being included in the staff work. I am confident that the top-level leaders of the Department of Defense who use systems analyses as one of their sources of information are careful to give balanced consideration to all factors, whether quantitative or not.

Another criticism sometimes made is that application of the "flat of the curve" argument to force or performance requirements may lead people to ignore the decisiveness of a narrow edge in superior performance. There is a danger here if an unwary analyst confuses *performance* and *effectiveness*. There is no question but that, in some cases, a narrow edge in performance may have a very great impact on effectiveness. The performance advantage of the Japanese Zero fighter over American aircraft at the beginning of World War II is a good case in point. But there are other cases in which even a substantial increase in performance, purchased at a high price, may have a small impact on effectiveness. For example, many Navy aviators believe that under today's conditions, a substantial speed advantage in attack aircraft may mean rather little in terms of increased effectiveness. It is easy to confuse performance and effectiveness. But this mistake is clearly not peculiar to the systems analysis approach. The only way to avoid it, and to relate performance to effectiveness properly, is with the help of good analysis. The "single all-purpose cost-effectiveness curve" I drew earlier has effectiveness and not performance on the vertical axis.

Next, it is argued that the systems analysis approach may be biased against the new and in favor of the old. I am sometimes concerned that our analyses may be subject to such bias, but I think that the method of open explicit analysis is much less likely to be so biased than is reliance on judgment or intuition or experience unsupported by analysis. The reason for the bias is that we all tend to compare the old and the new in the current mission that happens to have been optimized for the old. For example, in comparing the effectiveness of the conventional- and nuclear-powered carriers, there is a danger that the studies may, in effect, be trying to answer the question "How well can the nuclear-powered carrier do the conventional carrier's job?" The answer to that question is likely to understate the gain in effectiveness associated with nuclear power.

A similiar argument has it that cost-effectiveness analysis is biased against new systems to replace those already in operation because the new system is charged with its initial investment as well as operating cost, while the old system is only charged with its operating cost. I would plead guilty to this accusation but insist that this is not an unfair bias. Rather, it is the correct procedure for a rational equipment replacement policy. The point is that our objective, in selecting the rate of replacement of weapons and ships, should not be to maximize the degree of newness in the forces. It should be to maximize the total effectiveness we get out of the resources available for defense. And sometimes that objective is best served by replacing the old with new; sometimes by continuing to operate the old. The "breakeven point" comes when the new system, in relation to its costs including initial investment costs, is more effective than the old, in relation to its operating costs. Part of the proof that the cost-effectiveness approach is not biased against modernization is that the past three years have seen a rate of modernization in our armed forces unprecedented in peacetime, and it has generally been justified on cost-effectiveness grounds.

Finally, sometimes it is said that systems analyses oversimplify complex problems. Of course, we have to simplify the complex problems we face; no one could possibly understand most problems of modern weapon systems and strategy in all their complexity. And it is a natural human failing to oversimplify. But I believe the facts are that the systems analysis approach is much less prone to oversimplification than any alternative approach. For it is part of systems analysis to bring to bear all of the best of modern analytical techniques for organizing data and summarizing clearly its most relevant aspects. Moreover, reliance on the method of open, explicit analysis is our best guarantee against persistence in harmful oversimplification. For if I must lay out clearly all of my assumptions, objectives, factors, and calculations, my critics can see what I have done and point out where I have oversimplified, if indeed I have done so. But if I am allowed to keep it all in my head and appeal to experience or judgment, others have no way of knowing whether or not I have oversimplified the problem.

SYSTEMS ANALYSIS AND THE NAVY

Some people have feared that the systems analysis approach would do violence to the Navy because of the latter's multipurpose and flexible character and because of the subtlety and complexity of many of the missions of naval forces. Some predicted that the growth of systems analysis would lead to the decline of the Navy.

This pessimistic view has proved to be wrong. Systems analysis has been beneficial to the Navy, and the Navy's top leadership has given it strong support. Systems analyses done by the Navy, in collaboration with the Office of the Secretary of Defense, have identified and substantiated requirements for an improved light attack aircraft, for accelerated modernization of the amphibious fleet, for development of a new surface-to-air missile system, for more antisubmarine destroyer escorts, and many other improvements in our naval forces.

Systems analysis will prove beneficial to the Navy for another reason also. Many of the traditional reasons for maintaining a large surface Navy do not fit today's conditions. There is no major enemy surface navy for ours to fight. For this reason, one of the main original missions of the attack carrier no longer exists. Nor is the carrier an efficient competitor for the MINUTEMAN and POLARIS systems in the strategic retaliatory mission. But an important part of systems analysis is relating our various military forces to our broad national security objectives. Systems analysis can help and is helping the Navy to find new ways of using our sea power to protect American security, to define new missions best performed by naval forces, and to help Navy men articulate the reasons for maintaining a modern, effective Navy.

Rapid change is a major characteristic of our times. There is rapid change in technology, weapon systems, and the relationship between nations. As these conditions change, the relationship between our military forces and our broad national security objectives, that is, our military strategy, must change. If the Navy is to continue to make a vital contribution to American security, it must keep re-thinking its purposes, re-defining its missions, and re-shaping its forces. To do this well, it needs rational procedures of analysis. Therefore, Navy men should welcome and encourage the growth of systems analysis in the Navy.

As for the complex multipurpose character of naval forces, rather than acting as a barrier to systems analysis, it has been an intellectual challenge, a problem clearly worthy of the best efforts of our most talented analysts, both officers and civilians. Many important problems remain unsolved. The criterion problem for those forces we refer to as "Antisubmarine Warfare, Ocean Surveillance and Control Forces" is an example. We have not so far been able to develop completely satisfactory quantitative standards of adequacy. That is, we do not yet know how, in principle, to answer the question "What is the right amount?" But it would be hard to find a more interesting problem.

Because the systems analysis approach tries to relate military force to our broad national security objectives, it quite naturally leads to emphasis on *usable* military force. By that I mean force that can be applied in a selective and controlled way to achieve those limited objectives necessary to preserve our freedom and that of our allies, without causing unnecessary damage or loss of life and while holding to a minimum the risk of escalation to a more destructive level of conflict. Put alternatively, military force is usable if it can reasonably be expected to bring about a better rather than a worse situation; peace and freedom rather than widespread destruction. Thus, in the past three years, systems analysis has contributed to a shift in U.S. military strategy away from reliance on the "trip wire" and "massive retaliation" to a strategy that emphasizes flexibility, options, deliberation, and control. At the nuclear level, this has meant a requirement for Strategic Retaliatory Forces that can be used with deliberation and control. POLARIS has proved to be an ideal weapon system for this strategy. But even more important, the shift in strategy has led to a buildup in conventional or non-nuclear forces that can be used selectively and with control to bring military force to bear against a wide range of aggressions and crises on the Sino-Soviet periphery and elsewhere. President Kennedy's response to the Cuban missile crisis in October 1962 provides an excellent illustration of this concept. And it is clear that a description of this strategy is a good description of many of the qualities of the Navy-Marine Corps team.

17

COST-EFFECTIVENESS ANALYSIS OF ARMY DIVISIONS*

By Alain C. Enthoven

What is the effectiveness of a U.S. Army Division? How can it be measured? How can it be compared with the effectiveness of another division in any particular mission? How many U.S. and Allied divisions are required to defend successfully against various attacks? How would we know we had enough, short of war? What is the most effective mix of ground and tactical air forces that can be bought and maintained for, say $10 billion per year? How can we know?

These are very difficult, complex, challenging and vital questions to which we now have quite imperfect answers.

We know that many of the most important factors determining the effectiveness of Army units are not susceptible to calculation: courage, quality of training, dedication of the men to the cause for which they are fighting and confidence in its ultimate success, and others. Therefore, although some of these questions call for numerical answers, the answers cannot be produced entirely by calculations.

But some of these questions are inescapable. They will not go away. We may be able to reformulate or transform some of them, or to look at the problem in different ways, but choices from among alternative possible forces of different size and composition and the budgets required to support them have to be made. If we want those choices to be reliably good ones, then we must provide those responsible for making them with the best possible estimates of the effectiveness and costs of the alternatives.

It is important that these estimates be as objective as possible; that is, as free as possible from personal tastes or value judgments. To be so, their derivation needs to be explicit and reproducible rather than based on unanalyzed personal opinion. The method of open explicit analysis in which all parties concerned have an opportunity to review and challenge assumptions and calculations is our best protection against persistence in error.

*From remarks at the Fourth Annual U.S. Army Operations Research Symposium, Redstone Arsenal, Huntsville, Ala., 30 March 1962, revised 9 April 1965. Mr. Enthoven gratefully acknowledges the assistance of Mr. William K. Brehm of the Systems Analysis Office, who collaborated with him in the preparation of this talk.

Moreover, to be useful, the estimates of effectiveness must be able to be related meaningfully to our national security.

It has become possible to do this in several important parts of the Defense Program such as Strategic Offensive and Defensive Forces, Anti-Submarine Forces, and Airlift and Sealift Forces. Although the uncertainties are substantial, we are able, in these areas, to perform cost-effectiveness calculations having these properties.

This is especially true in the case of Strategic Offensive and Defensive Forces. While there are still major uncertainties about the circumstances and conditions under which a strategic nuclear war might be fought, we do have well-defined objectives, as well as a model with which we can do meaningful and useful calculations. Even granting the fact that weapon system performance parameters themselves are not always precisely known, our analyses are valuable in giving decision makers an insight into the cost and effectiveness of alternative programs, and—most important—a feeling for the sensitivity of the effectiveness of various systems and employment strategies to uncertainties in the assumed parameters. With respect to the different circumstances which might precipitate or surround the war, it is possible to analyze alternative postures under various assumed scenarios, and to indicate the outcomes under a range of optimistic and pessimistic assumptions. All of this has permitted us to develop what might be described as a useful economic theory for these forces and, thereby, to reduce greatly the disagreement over what facts are really relevant and what criteria actually ought to be employed in the decision process.

Much progress has been made . . . in analyzing certain individual weapon systems for the General Purpose Forces. However, by comparison with the Strategic Forces, the state of our analysis of the effectiveness of large combat units involving a mix of weapons and mobility is still inadequate. We do not seem to have any objective way of determining, for example, whether another billion dollars would yield more effectiveness in a particular situation if spent on F-4's or mechanized divisions, long-range artillery rockets or armored divisions, or what a reasonable apportionment might be if we were to add a mixture of all four. We are quite certain that the available measures of effectiveness such as the firepower index do not account properly for several important attributes of such forces—attributes for which we pay a great deal and which we believe intuitively must contribute to overall effectiveness. We are speaking of such basic things as readiness, mobility, and logistics support, as well as such less tangible things as training and leadership.

WHY MEASURE EFFECTIVENESS?

While at first glance one might conclude that these shortcomings would at worst result only in a small deviation from "optimum" force allocations, and that in any case the enemy has the same problem, one need only examine the recent history of our deliberations over NATO strategy to discover that our inability to assess the capabilities of General Purpose Forces (on both sides) can, in fact, have potentially dangerous consequences.

Four years ago, the belief was widespread in the West that the Soviet Union had something on the order of 160–175 divisions in its Army, most of which, it was assumed, were fairly readily transportable to the Central Front in Europe, and each of which, it was assumed, had an effectiveness roughly equal to a NATO division. This large force was opposed by some small number of divisions, on the order of 18–20, on the NATO side. This strength ratio of nearly 10-1 made the job of effective non-nuclear forward defense seem hopeless. It is not surprising, therefore, that the United States Government in the 1950's fell back on the strategy of "massive retaliation"—that is, the early use of strategic nuclear weapons, even in case of limited non-nuclear attack—because there seemed to be no possibility of an effective alternative. Whatever else one might say about this strategy, it certainly entailed major risks, for it meant threatening an all-out nuclear response, with all its attendant tragedy and destruction, to counter even quite limited acts of aggression. Moreover, as the Soviets built up their strategic retaliatory forces, our apparent relative weakness at the non-nuclear level left them considerable freedom to initiate piecemeal aggression.

This problem has been studied intensively over the past four years, and some very substantial changes in our thinking have resulted. In fact, it has turned out that the true picture is very different from this pessimistic one. In November of 1963, Secretary McNamara summarized the results of this intensive reexamination up to that time in these words—

> The announced total of Soviet armed forces for 1955 was indeed a formidable 5.75 million men. Today that figure has been cut to about 3.3 million; the Warsaw Pact total including the Soviets is only about 4.5 million. Against that, it is today the members of NATO whose active armed forces number over five million. The ground forces of NATO nations total 3.2 million, of which 2.2 million men are in Europe, as against the Soviet ground combat forces total of about 2 million men, and a Warsaw Pact total of about 3 million. Both the

Soviet Union and the U.S. forces of course include units stationed in the Far East. In Central Europe, NATO has more men, and more combat troops, on the ground than does the Bloc. It has more men on the ground in West Germany than the Bloc does in East Germany. It has more and better tactical aircraft, and these planes on the average can carry twice the payload twice as far as the Soviet counterparts.[1]

Moreover, although there are uncertainties in the details, we know that the strength of NATO has improved in relation to that of the Bloc since that time. Therefore, although it may be that various factors, such as the possibility of surprise or geography or maldeployment, leave us in an inadequate position in certain local circumstances, it certainly cannot be said that we are hopelessly out-manned or out-gunned.

Why were there such very pessimistic estimates so recently? There appear to be two main reasons. First, many people believe that, in the face of uncertainty, the safe thing to do is to overstate enemy strength relative to our own. Second, the count of the number of divisions has been erroneously accepted as a measure of ground force strength and effectiveness. Let me discuss these two questions in turn.

On the first point, we have learned that it can be just as dangerous to overstate enemy strength relative to our own as to understate it. The history of war contains many examples in which one side could have attacked or defended successfully had it realized the true strengths on both sides, but failed to do so because it overestimated the enemy, probably in an attempt to be "safe." What has happened is that the same kind of mistake has been made at the strategic level, in the peacetime planning of our forces. In fact, the overstatement of the strength of the Warsaw Pact armies relative to our own during the 1950's led, not to an increase in our conventional strength, but to a substantial reduction, as the U.S. Army well knows. The argument was made that we could not possibly afford enough new divisions to overcome the 10–1 disadvantage and that there would be no point in building up our armies at all when they were bound to be defeated anyway. The argument was made again and again: "What point is there in increasing the number of NATO divisions on the Central Front from 20 to 30 if the Russians have 100?" Thus, the practical effect of overstatement of the enemy has not been insurance and safety; it has been smaller forces and greater risk. The same kind of error was also being made in several other areas; the Army was not the only one to have this problem.

---

[1] Remarks of Secretary of Defense Robert S. McNamara before the Economic Club of New York, Waldorf-Astoria Hotel, New York, N.Y., November 18, 1963.

The overstatement of enemy forces relative to our own can lead to hopelessness and to strategies of desperation. It can lead to the pricing out of the market of rational strategies that would be effective and, in fact, preferable under realistic assumptions. In short, it can be the dangerous unsafe thing to do. We have made progress in developing better estimates, but there is still a strong tendency—doubtless born of natural inclinations, reinforced by experience in peacetime budgetary battles—to overstate enemy capabilities relative to our own, to emphasize our difficulties and to ignore his; and thus to apply what is, in effect, a double standard when evaluating forces.

The second cause of the overstatement of Soviet forces relative to our own is more difficult to untangle. If we use the resources that we devote to our Army divisions as efficiently as the Soviets use theirs, then the effectiveness of Soviet divisions, in relation to our own, was greatly overstated. This is the practical point of this talk. How do we measure the effectiveness of a Soviet division force relative to one of our own?

We know how to ask and answer this kind of question for a MINUTEMAN ICBM and for a nuclear-powered attack submarine, using such parameters as range and payload, accuracy, detection probabilities and the like, and calculating the probabilities of achieving various events. For the Ground Forces, however, the tendency has been to assume that the basic unit of combat power is a "division" and that all divisions have approximately equal effectiveness. Most of the analyses of forces done in the past few years in the Pentagon have used the assumed number of divisions as the measure of strength at the beginning of the calculation. The results have been very misleading in terms of the force comparisons produced.

Could we do better? Our studies as early as three years ago indicated that there was something paradoxical about merely counting divisions. At the time, we were spending an average of $2.2 billion a year to equip the Army 22 Division Force. At that rate, if the Russians were equipping 160 divisions, they would have to be spending the equivalent of $16 billion a year; or even if they were equipping half that number they still would have to be spending $8 billion a year—roughly four times what we have been spending. This seems most improbable in view of the other demands placed on the Soviet economy. This is the "PEMA² Paradox."

---

² Procurement of Equipment and Missiles, Army.

Subsequently, a similar paradox emerged on the side of personnel strengths: we have nearly a million men on active duty in the United States Army, organized into 16 combat division forces, seven independent brigades, and various other smaller units. The Soviet Army—numbering roughly two million—was estimated to have 160 divisions or more. By our standards, two million men would be enough for about 40 division forces.[3] This disparity of a factor of four is the "People Paradox."

Part of the reason for these paradoxes was that the very important distinction between combat-ready and reserve or cadre divisions had not been drawn clearly enough. There is little doubt that some of the 160 Soviet divisions were in about the same condition as some of the low-priority U.S. National Guard divisions, of which we had about 29. Counting only the useful, combat-ready divisions permits us to reduce the force with which we must contend to less than 80. This is still a large number, but it is certainly an improvement over 160.

The standard planning factor for describing the effectiveness of a U.S. division force relative to a Soviet division force of like type was one-to-one (though higher ratios have been used recently as it has become apparent that the Soviet division was not nearly as strong as its U.S. counterpart). Yet, recent Army studies have shown that the manpower strength of a division "slice" of a U.S. Corps is about twice that of a division slice in a Soviet Combined Arms Army. Moreover, the cost in U.S. prices of our division force is more than twice that of the Soviet division force. Also, U.S. personnel training practices seem to differ substantially from those of the Soviets; the U.S. has a training base of some 150,000 men, or nearly 10,000 men per division. If this training yields an effectiveness in proportion to its costs, then the fact that we have only trained men in our divisions should permit us to take additional credit in the form of increased effectiveness for that factor as well.

When we say that the U.S. division force costs more than two times as much as a Soviet division force when measured in U.S. prices, we are then allowing for and removing the influence of such disparate factors as the low pay of Soviet soldiers and their lower standard of living; we are saying that this is what a Soviet division would cost if we manned it with U.S. soldiers and manufactured its equipment in the United States. Keeping our standard of living and pay scales we could, in fact, buy more than two

---

[3] Counting an independent brigade as one-third of a division, about 960,000 men give us 18⅓ division equivalents. Another 40,000 would be about enough for another 1⅔ division force.

Soviet division forces with the resources with which we buy one U.S. division force. If we choose to continue to buy U.S. type divisions in preference to the more than twice as many Soviet-type divisions we could buy for the same cost, then it must be because we believe our divisions are more than twice as effective. Otherwise we are not getting the most effectiveness out of our resources. Alternatively, to say that our divisions are less than twice as effective is to imply that the organization and equipment of our Army is less efficient than that of the Soviets. If this is the case, then we should reorganize, perhaps along Soviet lines. This is a matter of simple and fairly compelling logic.

Incidentally, these factors do approximately resolve the "People Paradox." That is, if one divides the less than 80 combat-ready division forces in half, reflecting their personnel strength, one obtains a number of "U.S. equivalent division forces" approximately equal to the number we would get from a two million man Army.

Other factors have been offered in partial explanation of the "PEMA and People Paradoxes." There are a great many popular myths such as "we have more medical personnel who don't fight," "half our people are behind typewriters," "the Russians all eat soup but we have to have a lot of cooks," etc. In fact, it is my understanding that we have more doctors but fewer total medical personnel per soldier than the Russians. As for the standard of living items, we have removed them from the problem by pricing the Soviet forces in American prices. They are irrelevant to this particular issue. If one were to believe these myths, one would be driven to the conclusion that the United States is too handicapped by luxury to produce an effective army. I have not been able to find any very convincing evidence for such a conclusion, and I should not think that the U.S. Army would want to argue for it.

Another factor that has been suggested in explanation of the paradoxes is the length of our supply lines. There is no question but that land lines of communication can tie up a substantial number of troops. But Soviet land lines of communication to the Central Front in Europe are clearly no shorter than our own. Moreover, the comparisons of division forces I have been discussing are made from the Corps and Combined Arms Army forward. They do not include the troops in the supply lines.

One factor that has been raised, "staying power," may be much more significant. The Soviets apparently have substantially fewer trucks and trailers supporting their forces than we do. This means that our divisions have more "staying power." But the time profile of the wartime effectiveness of our forces is a matter of choice; we could give up staying power in the second month in exchange for greater combat power in the first month, and perhaps we should. Our staying power will do us no good in the second month if we lose the war in the first month. On the other hand, if we win in the first month, we may not need as much staying power in the second. I am impressed by the fact that in most of the wars in which the U.S. has been involved in this century, the aggressor started with a theory of quick victory. He apparently foresaw great success in the opening months of the war and believed that he could then negotiate an end to the war on terms favorable to himself. The United States and its Allies lost a great deal of territory in the first months, and then spent many months or years fighting to win it back. This experience suggests that we should attach great importance to the effectiveness of our forces in the opening weeks and months of the war. An aggressor is far less likely to attack if he foresees stalemate or defeat in the first few months, even if followed by possible, though uncertain, victory eventually, than he is if he foresees great success in the opening months followed by an uncertain outcome if the war goes on longer. Thus, strength in the opening months may contribute much more to deterrence than staying power or strength in later months. And if deterrence fails, it may contribute more to the reduction of the cost and duration of the war. Therefore, if it is true that we are trading significant amounts of front line effectiveness in the opening weeks for staying power later on, we should reconsider the choice.

EFFECTIVENESS IN RELATION TO COSTS

It seems to me to be very clear that, if we can assume that the net effect of the non-quantitative factors such as morale, courage, terrain, leadership, etc., is not unfavorable to us, the effectiveness of our division forces in relation to those opposing them ought to be in proportion to their costs in U.S. prices. The problem is, are they, and if so, how can we know?

This is really the heart of our problem, and it is not an easy one to solve. First of all, we know that ground forces are not like ICBMs; their effectiveness depends critically on the human element. The decisive factors include the bravery of the men and the ability and judgment of their leadership. When the fighting starts, neither side is likely to claim victory on the grounds that he spent more (or spent less, but more efficiently). Moreover, there are many factors that are difficult to predict or control that affect the outcome, i.e., terrain, weather, the breaks, availability of, or delays in getting, information, and the like. In fact, if one wanted to make a case that it is not possible to measure the effectiveness of Army divisions in any meaningful way, one doubtless could do so convincingly. But the problem is, whether we like it or not, we have to have such a measure. We have to have some way of knowing what our forces can reasonably be expected to do and whether the mix of our forces is reasonably efficient. This measure is essential not only to permit realistic force comparisons and determination of force requirements, but also to allow us to estimate the incremental contributions of new weapons or new organizational concepts.

The argument is somewhat reminiscent of the debates over the possibility of deriving a valid cost-of-living index under conditions of wartime shortages or when new products are being introduced. When the arguments are over, it is clear that the logic of the critics is unbeatable. It is not possible to have a completely valid price index under most realistic circumstances. But as a practical matter, we simply have to have one, and we use the best approximations we can.

Similarly in the case of Army forces. In the absence of some better factor, people will simply count divisions, misleading as we know that to be.

Can we develop the kind of theory of the effectiveness of Army divisions that is required? I sincerely hope so, and with that in mind, offer the following thoughts.

First, the present state of our knowledge of this matter is in a relatively primitive state from a scientific point of view. By that, I mean that it is not generally possible, in this area, for one professional to develop a set of empirical data and calculations supporting conclusions about the relative effectiveness of differently organized and equipped forces that will be generally persuasive to other professionals. The element of personal opinion based, in large part, on personal experience, is very strong. This suggests the desirability of pursuing all approaches to the problem that show any promise of success at all. Nobody is, at this point, in a good position to support a claim for the superiority of his methods or to deny the validity of others, unless, of course, they contravene rules of logic or established principles of scientific method. Rather, an effective dialogue between practitioners of different approaches is needed.

Among the approaches that need to be pursued are field exercises and tests, map exercises, war games, and other simulations, and detailed empirical study of the history of war. I would like to emphasize the last-mentioned of these both because of its importance and because it appears to receive very little attention now. We need studies directed not at the derivation of broad abstractions like the so-called "principles of war," but at empirical propositions with precise quantitative content. In other words, we need to bring experience to bear, not only in an individual personal way, but also in a general and systematic way.

Hopefully, the results of investigations using these methods can be reconciled one to another. The theoretical models must be able to explain both field exercises and historical results.

Second, half of the "cost-effectiveness" problem is cost. We have made some progress in developing methods for estimating the costs of Army forces, but it is clear that there is still much to be done. We must have sufficient detail and flexibility in our cost models to permit the estimating of investment and operating costs for each of the organizational units or weapon systems whose effectiveness we are trying to measure. The costs should include both the direct costs of the unit and the indirect costs of the "overhead" units required to command and support it.

Although a good understanding of cost relationships is only half of the problem, it can be surprisingly useful even in the absence of data on effectiveness. It can illuminate for the decision maker the choices he is making; what alternative opportunities are being foregone when he chooses to apply his resources in a particular way. It defines the judgment that must be made about the relative effectiveness of alternatives. We found, in the analysis of other General Purpose Forces, that careful cost analysis yielded conclusions about where the money was going quite different from what had previously been assumed. This, in turn, has led to revised judgments about preferred combinations of forces.

There is no good reason not to have good cost information. Yet, unfortunately, today, it is still the case that the Army's leaders have to make many of their force decisions in the absence of good cost estimates of the kind I have described. Given good cost estimates, which, as I have said, should be obtainable, a good point of departure in many cases would be to compare the effectiveness of different forces having the same total system costs. The Army has underway some very good work along these lines.

Third, war is a complicated social process. The study of war may be able to borrow some useful methods and insights from the social sciences. For example, economists have found that the gross aggregations of our national economic life—such as national income, gross national product, and total consumption—appear to obey laws that are different from the laws that govern the behavior of the individual person or firm. Consequently, economists have developed theories for both the individual and the firm on the one hand, and the various aggregates on the other. So far, attempts to integrate the two (to solve the aggregation problem) have not been successful. But economists have found that it has been possible to develop a fairly successful theory of national income behavior without building it up from the individual pieces.

This may also be true of the study of ground forces. Although at this stage in our thinking every promising approach should be tried, there are reasons for thinking that an approach that begins with the squad and tries to build up from there is not going to be successful. For one thing, the range of uncertainty around the effectiveness of the squad or other small unit is bound to be large. If one then were to add up the high estimates and the low estimates for each of these, one would get a very large uncertainty for a division as a whole. Results that are quite unpredictable for individual small units may be much more predictable for the larger units into which they are aggregated.

Finally, let me emphasize that the inquiry I am describing should not be viewed as a quest for a simple answer, a single calculation or index, certainly not a substitute for experienced judgment. Judgments will always be necessary to integrate the various indicators that are developed, to evaluate the many factors that cannot be measured and the realism of our measurements of those that can be, and to estimate the relative likelihood of various uncertain events. Rather, we should seek to reveal and make explicit those judgments in such a way that they can be understood clearly and applied appropriately to varying conditions. We need methods that would enable us, when experts disagree, to develop a rational and explicit process for defining the disagreements and for finding a systematic way to resolve them.

PART V

U. S. DEFENSE POLICY FOR THE 1960's

"A man may build himself a throne of bayonets but he cannot sit on it." What, then, is the role of force in the world today and how should force be organized and controlled for the achievement of desired and desirable objectives? Those questions are examined in the single selection of this Part, a speech by Mr. Enthoven. It brings this anthology full circle, back to the issues raised by Secretary McNamara in selection 1. Planning, programming, budgeting, and systems analysis are tools for management and not ends in themselves. Moreover, military policy and military instruments in the final analysis are merely the means through which the United States seeks to establish and maintain a peaceful world order that accords with its ideological concepts. The significance, therefore, of the innovations in Defense budgeting since 1961 is that they have facilitated the process of considering alternative ways to achieve this ultimate objective—rationally, economically, and efficiently.

18

U. S. DEFENSE POLICY FOR THE 1960's*

By Alain C. Enthoven

I am very happy to be here this evening and to have an opportunity to discuss defense policy with you. This is an appropriate forum for such a discussion because we are at a university which is dedicated to the harmonious development of secular learning and moral religious thought, each enlightened by contact with the other, and we are in a city many of whose citizens are daily making a major contribution to the development and production of advanced weapon systems. It is at the intersection where we stand this evening—where our secular and religious thought and our armaments production cross—that we must confront the questions of the reasonableness and the morality of the defense policies that shape our choices of military forces and weapon systems. I would like to address these questions this evening by describing for you the main lines along which our defense policies are now developing, and by explaining some of the reasons for them.

Military force is but one instrument in the hands of the President to be used in the struggle to keep us alive and free. It takes its place alongside diplomacy, economic policy, foreign economic and military assistance, alliances, and many other activities that contribute to our national security. Its ultimate purpose, like that of these other activities, is to enable the President, in cooperation with the leaders of other free nations, to establish and maintain a peaceful world order based on a belief in the worth and dignity of the individual, and on freedom for each person to develop his own capacities in the way he chooses. The role of military force, in the pursuit of this objective, is to prevent would-be aggressors who do not believe in freedom and human dignity from forcing free men to live under a system based on tyranny and coercion. The problem of formulation of defense policy is to select those forces which will contribute most effectively to these multiple objectives.

---

*From address before the Loyola University Forum for National Affairs, Los Angeles, California, 10 February 1963, and before Students, Faculty, and Friends of Seattle University, Seattle, Washington, 11 February 1963.

There are three related themes underlying and uniting our defense policies today. They are, first, deterrence of aggression; second, freedom for the President to select and apply the amount and kind of force appropriate to the threat at hand; and third, the controlled use of force. In the nuclear age, military force will be too dangerous to use if our objectives are not carefully chosen and limited at each step of a conflict, and if the force cannot be used in a controlled and deliberate way to achieve precisely the objectives being sought. To fight for unlimited objectives, or to fight in an uncontrolled way would almost surely bring on almost unlimited destruction.

THE APPROPRIATELY LIMITED USE OF FORCE

In order to give the President the freedom of action required to be able to limit appropriately the use of force, current defense policy emphasizes flexibility, options, and choice. One of its main objectives is to make available to the President a range of military responses appropriate for each threat to our security, so that he can apply force adequate to accomplish the objectives at hand without causing any unnecessary damage or loss of life, and while holding to a minimum the risk of escalation to a more destructive level of conflict.

A few years ago, there was a great deal of public debate as to whether limited war was possible. The theory and practice of strategic bombing in World War II, the use of the atomic bombs, and the unconditional surrender policy left in their aftermath a widespread belief that war could only be total. This belief persisted long after the armed resistance to Communist aggression in Greece and Korea. Of course total war remains possible. But as time goes by, and the size and destructive power of nuclear arsenals increase, more and more, total war between nuclear powers will mean total destruction. It is my own opinion that with the widespread realization of this fact will come the general belief that all wars should be limited. At no time should we deliberately choose to fight an unlimited uncontrolled war. The "limited war—general war" dichotomy that has crept into our language may be harmful if it suggests that there is a kind of war that it makes sense to fight without limits, though of course, the limits that we adopt will have to depend on the threat and on our objectives.

What this means, in practice, is that we are working to acquire a flexible, balanced defense posture giving us capabilities for the selective use of force for all kinds of conflict, from counter-insurgency and antiguerrilla warfare through large scale conventional (non-nuclear) warfare, through major thermonuclear war. Although the choice of the amount and kind of force to be applied in any circumstance is bound to be a difficult one, we would like to make it possible in all cases, if I may borrow a phrase from The Mikado, "to make the punishment fit the crime."

THE CONTROLLED USE OF FORCE

Keeping the use of force appropriately limited requires control. The range, speed, and destructiveness of modern weapons makes this problem both more urgent and more difficult than it has ever been before. More than ever before, this means that the President must have communication and control facilities to provide him with timely and accurate information on the course of events and to permit him to communicate his decisions in a similar manner. It also means that the military forces must be responsive to his direction, even in considerable detail. To use President Kennedy's words, "Our weapon systems must be usable in a manner permitting deliberation and discrimination as to timing, scope and targets in response to civilian authority."[1]

Moreover, when force is being applied, the military action must not be allowed to control events and compel the President's decisions; rather, it should be the other way around. To borrow a term from missilery, our use of military force in the cold war must be command guided, not inertially guided.

This belief may be contrasted to the view that "peace is peace and war is war," and in war military necessity is the only valid criterion for decision. Certainly the requirements of the military commander must be considered very seriously, both because our security requires success in whatever armed conflicts are thrust upon us, and because the lives of our soldiers are involved, but still, the President must be free to weigh them against other requirements and decide what is best for the security of the United States. This principle was important before nuclear weapons; it has taken on added importance in the nuclear age.

This was one of the hard lessons of the Korean War. The United States had to re-learn to fight for limited objectives. There were reasons which the original military commander found very compelling for expanding the scope of the conflict. But in the President's judgment, to expand the conflict would have risked touching off another world war which would have left both the

---

[1] "Special Message to the Congress on the Defense Budget, March 28, 1961," *Public Papers of the Presidents of the United States: John F. Kennedy, 1961* (Washington: U.S. Government Printing Office, 1962), p. 232.

South Koreans and ourselves far worse off than the final outcome that actually was achieved. The President must be in a position to make and enforce such judgments.

The same principle of control was applied in a thorough-going way in the . . . Cuban crisis. Each military move was, in effect, a carefully formulated message from the President to Khrushchev, intended to convince him that the United States would use military force to the extent necessary to achieve removal of the offensive weapons. But each move was also intended to convince him that he could withdraw without armed conflict, if he would withdraw. Because each move was a carefully formulated message, all moves had to be carefully controlled from the White House.

All this was summarized by the President in the words—

> Our arms must be subject to ultimate civilian control and command at all times, in war as well as peace. The basic decisions on our participation in any conflict and our response to any threat—including all decisions relating to the use of nuclear weapons, or the escalation of a small war into a large one—will be made by the regularly constituted civilian authorities.[2]

Because of the importance of such control, a great deal has been done in the Defense Department in the past two years to strengthen and make more secure the means of high level command and control of forces.

CONVENTIONAL FORCE BUILDUP

How have these themes worked themselves out in the development of our defense program? One of the most important ways has been in the recent and large buildup in our conventional or non-nuclear forces.

To understand properly the importance of the buildup of non-nuclear forces, it is necessary first to understand that there is a very great difference between nuclear weapons and non-nuclear weapons. Nuclear weapons are not simply high explosives writ large. Their destructive power makes them a completely new kind of military force which must be understood and related to our national security objectives in new ways. Hiroshima was destroyed by a 20-kiloton bomb. We now have weapons a thousand times that size. Roughly 2½ million tons of TNT were dropped on Germany in World War II. One B–52 can now deliver many times that amount of destructive power, and we have the ability to deliver the equivalent of thousands of millions of tons intercontinentally. As well as the familiar effects of blast and heat,

2 *Ibid.*, p. 231.

these weapons can cover many thousands of square miles with deadly radioactive fallout. All this is familiar.

There has been in recent years the development of small nuclear weapons having yields equivalent to a few thousand tons of TNT or less. The day will come, if it has not come already, when there will be nuclear weapons of smaller yields than the largest high explosive weapons. When that day comes, will there no longer be a distinction between nuclear and conventional weapons? Some have argued to that effect. But they are mistaken. There is and will remain an important distinction, a "fire break" if you like, between nuclear and non-nuclear war, a recognizable qualitative distinction that both combatants can recognize and agree upon, if they want to agree upon one. And in the nuclear age they will have a very powerful incentive to agree upon this distinction and limitation, because if they do not there does not appear to be another easily recognizable limitation on weapons—no other obvious "fire-break"—all the way up the destructive spectrum to large scale thermonuclear war.

Adequate conventional forces are important. It is for this reason that, in the past two years, we have increased the number of active combat-ready Army divisions from 11 to 16, and our active tactical air wings from 16 to 21. It is for this reason that we have more than doubled the annual rate of procurement of Army equipment, that we have speeded up the tempo of modernization of our tactical air forces, and that we have increased our outlays on naval ship building. Moreover, it is for this reason that we are now urging our NATO allies to increase the size and effectiveness of their conventional forces. Why?

The reason strong conventional forces are required is that there are many situations in which the use of nuclear weapons would be inappropriate. For the same reasons that a sledge hammer does not make a good substitute for a fly swatter, nuclear weapons are not a good substitute for non-nuclear forces against a wide range of military threats. Even if they could be used to apply the minimum force required to achieve our objectives, their use would risk triggering escalation to a more and unnecessarily destructive level of conflict.

A nation or an alliance which maintains a strong nuclear posture combined with weak conventional forces thereby puts itself at a great disadvantage in the confrontation with another power that has both strong nuclear and strong conventional forces. This will be true no matter how strong and effective are its nuclear forces, provided that the other power maintains a secure second-strike nuclear retaliatory capability. Because nuclear war is so destructive, the use of nuclear weapons must be reserved only for the most desperate circumstances. But if the nuclears have to be reserved for vital issues, the side with the strong conventional forces is likely to be able to have its way on all issues less than vital. The side without adequate conventional forces will have no means for effective resistance in such confrontations. The side with conventional forces can use "salami slice" tactics, or make its aggression piecemeal in the confidence that it will be able to have its way on all but life and death matters. This is the kind of threat we have been facing in Berlin. The danger in piecemeal aggression is that erosion in the position of the free world over the years can end in world domination by the Communists.

Put alternatively, the President will be in a weak bargaining position indeed if he is confronted by the Communist bloc with a choice between suicide or surrender, holocaust or humiliation. In order to resist aggression and defend our freedom, the President must have more attractive alternatives. Without conventional forces, our choice when faced with aggression may be "red or dead;" conventional forces help to deter aggression, and if deterrence fails, they can give us the opportunity to fight to stay alive and free.

Nevertheless, the buildup in our conventional forces has been costly and controversial. Two main lines of argument have been advanced against it. The first is that it weakens our nuclear resolve. In effect, it is a message to Khrushchev telling him that we are afraid or unwilling to use nuclear weapons, and that he can commit aggression against us with the expectation that we will not use them. Of course, pushed to an extreme, such an argument would say that we ought to abolish the United States Marine Corps. But the argument is defective. The important thing is not to convince an aggressor that we will use nuclear weapons. The important thing is to convince him that we will use whatever force that is necessary to preserve our freedom. In many cases, that will be non-nuclear force. Sole or excessive reliance on nuclear weapons may tempt him to believe that we will not fight for less than vital issues. The danger is that each issue can be made less than vital. Aggression can be made piecemeal and in small enough pieces so that succumbing always looks attractive by comparison with thermonuclear war. Isn't Berlin Khrushchev's "last territorial demand in Europe"?

In fact, reflection on the problem should convince most reasonable men that the threat of the ultimate use of nuclear weapons, if required, is much more credible to an aggressor who sees that to accomplish his objective he must first defeat a large and effective conventional force. If he succeeds in doing that, the issue at stake is likely by then to be vital for the defender.

Still some argue that we should try to convince our adversaries that we would use nuclear weapons even in situations in which it is irrational to do so. Interestingly enough, Khrushchev himself has recently attacked this principle as a policy for the Communist Bloc, and in attacking him, the Chinese Communists have nonetheless acknowledged the enormous destructiveness of nuclear war. When it is clear that the Communists know the facts of nuclear destructiveness, it would seem foolish for us to base our strategy on the pretense that we do not. The trouble with trying to exploit "the rationality of irrationality," as theorists of bargaining and conflict call this, is that it simply is not a viable policy in the long run for a democracy, especially a democracy with allies. We must have defense policies that make sense to the American people and to our allies. Moreover, threats to blow ourselves up along with the aggressor are not likely to be credible. Rather, the most credible kind of threat is the threat that we will do what in the event will be most in our interest to do. In the case of piecemeal non-nuclear aggression, that will be to apply conventional forces.

The other main line of argument against the buildup of our conventional forces is that it will be fruitless, extremely costly, and unable to achieve the objective of adequacy because we are so badly outnumbered by the Communist hordes. These arguments, though widely believed, are not supported by the facts. Conventional military strength requires fighting men; it also requires that the men be fed, clothed, and equipped with effective weapons and other materiel. Equipping and supporting armies requires wealth and industrial production. The NATO allies outnumber the members of the Warsaw Pact in population, men under arms, and even foot soldiers in active army forces. In the dire straits into which mismanagement has plunged their economy, the Chinese Communists appear to be far from being able to provide modern and effective equipment for an army the size of our own. Moreover, the gross national products of the United States and our allies are more than twice the same total for the Soviet Union and its allies; in terms of industrial production, the ratio is more than two and one half to one. What all of these facts suggest is that although substantial sacrifice may be involved for us and our NATO Allies in equipping ourselves with adequate conventional forces, proportionally the sacrifice is much smaller for us than it is for our adversaries. Although we do need to strengthen our conventional forces some, the extra costs are not large. We have already paid the entry fee into the "non-nuclear club." It is now largely a matter of making fully effective the force levels we have already agreed to provide.

A related argument has it that limiting conflicts to non-nuclear weapons puts us at a disadvantage because of our numerical inferiority, and that we need to use nuclear weapons as an equalizer in all but the smallest of armed conflicts. Leaving aside the undesirable character of the equalization they accomplish, and the unresolved question of whether the use of nuclear weapons is to our military advantage if the other side replies in kind, let me point out that our wealth and technology confer on us some important advantages in non-nuclear combat. Indeed, the effectiveness of modern non-nuclear arms is so great that they can offset substantial numerical inferiority in isolated situations in which we might be numerically inferior. The ability to produce such armaments in large quantities is a key determinant of the effectiveness of a nation's non-nuclear forces.

In summary, conventional military force is usable force. In Korea and in the Cuban crisis, we found that the non-nuclear forces were the cutting edge of our military power. We can use conventional force with a minimal risk of self-destruction. Therefore, it provides a more credible deterrent to non-nuclear aggression. As the destructiveness of nuclear war increases, and as nuclear weapon systems become less vulnerable to sudden attack, the effectiveness of the threatened use of nuclear weapons as a substitute for conventional forces will diminish, and we will have no sensible alternative to building up our conventional forces to the point at which they can safely resist all forms of non-nuclear aggression. Our forces will be adequate if we can never be forced because of weakness to be the first to have to resort to nuclear weapons.

U.S. POSTURE FOR THERMONUCLEAR WAR

But if nuclear forces are not an effective substitute for adequate conventional forces, neither are conventional forces an effective substitute for adequate nuclear forces. Rather, the relationship between the two is one of complementarity. Now that the Communist Bloc is armed with nuclear weapons, we cannot successfully fight conventional wars except under the umbrella of nuclear strength. This nuclear strength is required to deter the Communists from escalating a non-nuclear conflict which is not going well for them into nuclear war, and to convince them that an act of nuclear aggression would lead to their defeat, and possibly to the destruction of their society.

This then is the most important objective of our nuclear posture: to make thermonuclear war unlikely by deterring deliberate calculated nuclear aggression. We also seek other objectives. We want to make accidental, unpremeditated, irrational nuclear war unlikely also. And if war does occur, we want to be able to bring it to a speedy termination on military terms favorable to ourselves, and we want to do what we can to limit the damage caused to ourselves and our allies. How do we go about pursuing those objectives?

First, we attempt to deter deliberate premeditated attack by maintaining secure second-strike retaliatory capabilities, that is forces that cannot be knocked out in a surprise first blow. This means relatively invulnerable weapon systems like MINUTEMAN, TITAN, and POLARIS, and secure, protected, survivable command and control facilities that will enable our national leadership to survive an attack and direct the use of retaliatory forces against any aggressor.

There is a great deal of literature and there are many approaches to the subject of deterrence. Some argue that, in the event of a nuclear attack on the alliance, we should plan to retaliate strictly against Soviet cities. Others argue that we should plan to strike back only against Soviet military forces. Still others argue for both. Some believe that we should design our posture for an irrevocable commitment to a spasm of massive retaliation. Our approach is based on options, deliberation, flexibility and control. Rather than decide ahead of time which targets must be hit by which weapons, and then commit ourselves to it, our approach is to give the President a range of choices so that he can select the plan whose targets and timing of attacks are most appropriate to the circumstances at hand. I won't speculate here as to which nuclear response might be used in which circumstances. Nothing useful would be accomplished by doing so. But let me make three observations about this policy.

First, it is a policy of strength not weakness. It takes superior nuclear forces to be able to ride out any kind of attack and then retain the option to destroy most of the enemy's remaining military forces should that be appropriate. It would be a policy of weakness to commit ourselves irrevocably to a spasm of nuclear retaliation against Soviet cities.

Second, this policy requires secure forces and secure command and control. It requires weapon systems like MINUTEMAN and POLARIS that are hard and dispersed, or mobile and concealed, and that can ride out a thermonuclear attack and be held in reserve in the environment of nuclear war. This is one of the reasons why the Defense Department's procurement of strategic weapon systems in the last two years has emphasized MINUTE-MAN and POLARIS.

Third, this approach to nuclear deterrence illustrates the principle that across the spectrum of conflict, military force is to be used with deliberation and control. There is, to be sure, a danger of breakdown of control in the environment of thermonuclear war. But, short of complete destruction of Western society, there is no point at which it makes sense to choose to abandon control. Even when it comes to thermonuclear weapons, if our weapons are to be used to keep us alive and free, their use must be controlled.

This emphasis on control has led us, in the past two years, to emphasize the procurement of survivable, secure, redundant, and internetted command, control, and communications facilities. For example, we now have a SAC command post with a general officer on board constantly airborne, 24 hours a day. For the top civilian authorities, we have a National Emergency Airborne Command Post, command posts on ships at sea, and various hardened underground command posts, all tied together by protected communications. As well as making a major contribution to our ability to deter deliberate attack, this strengthened command structure has made an important contribution to reducing the likelihood of such unlikely eventualities as unauthorized, accidental, or other unpremeditated attacks blowing up into large-scale thermonuclear war. And, along with many other safety precautions that we have taken, it is making much less likely the possibility of accidental or unauthorized use of nuclear weapons on our side.

I would like to emphasize this point because some recent literature has suggested that there is a lack of concern among the military and civilian leaders of the Department of Defense for the safety and stability of our nuclear weapons posture. This suggestion could not be farther from the truth. In fact, both our military and civilian leaders take this problem very seriously and they have been willing to accept considerable costs to assure the compatibility of military readiness with the highest possible degree of safety.

But, despite our best efforts a war may still occur. In these dangerous and unpredictable times it would be foolish to base our planning on the assumption that a thermonuclear war could never happen. Despite our best efforts, almost any kind of nuclear war would be an unprecedented disaster. But if such a war were thrust upon us, there are worthwhile things that could be done to mitigate its consequences. We are making preparations whose purpose is, in the event of war, to enable us to maintain a favorable military position, to bring the war to an end quickly, and to hold to a minimum the damage to ourselves and our allies. To limit the damage, we are making a combination of plans and preparations, including Civil Defense, active air and anti-missile defense, and an ability to destroy what we can of the enemy's offensive weapons. Let me explain each one.

The largest part of our Civil Defense program is fallout shelters for our population. One of the most destructive effects of nuclear weapons is radioactive fallout. In a thermonuclear attack on the United States, many millions of people would die, even though they were far from the blast and thermal effects, simply from radioactive fallout. Although there are substantial uncertainties here, and the numbers vary widely depending upon the assumptions made, most studies suggest that whereas several tens of millions might die from the blast and thermal effects of a nuclear attack on the United States, because of fallout the total deaths could well be over a hundred million in the United States alone. In order to prevent this, the President has directed the Department of Defense to undertake an expanded Civil Defense program, which has as its first objective the provision of fallout shelters for all of our population.

Civil Defense is very important for many reasons. Without it, our active defenses and other preparations for survival in a thermonuclear war would be rendered meaningless. For example, if we defended our cities with impenetrable anti-missile defenses, but had no fallout protection for the inhabitants, an attacker could still destroy all the people in those cities simply by surface bursting thermonuclear weapons upwind and killing the people with fallout. If we do have a Civil Defense program, then active air and anti-missile defenses can also make a very important contribution to our survival. Civil Defense is also necessary if we are to have any hope of limiting the effects of a major thermonuclear war and making possible a meaningful strategy of controlled use of nuclear weapons.

As well as these measures, we are also buying strategic retaliatory forces capable of knocking out those vulnerable elements of enemy nuclear striking power remaining after an attack has been launched against us. Of course we are up against the limitation here that after such an attack, our counter attacking forces are likely to be spent destroying many empty bases and launching sites. However, our studies to date suggest that, in such circumstances, it would still be likely that there would remain vulnerable forces that could be used against us in follow-up attacks, and that their timely destruction would help to limit the damage to the United States and our Allies.

Beyond these physical measures, we are also opening up the option of maintaining some effective deterrence after a nuclear war begins. This was described last spring by Secretary of Defense McNamara in an address at the University of Michigan. In his words—

> The U.S. has come . . . to the conclusion that to the extent feasible, basic military strategy in a possible general nuclear war should be approached in much the same way that more conventional military operations have been regarded in the past. That is to say, principal military objectives, in the event of a nuclear war stemming from a major attack on the Alliance, should be the destruction of the enemy's military forces, not of his civilian population.
>
> The very strength and nature of the Alliance forces make it possible for us to retain, even in the face of a massive surprise attack, sufficient reverse striking power to destroy an enemy society if driven to it. In other words, we are giving a possible opponent the strongest imaginable incentive to refrain from striking our own cities.[3]

Doubtless questions will arise in your minds as to whether nuclear war can and should be limited and controlled. First, can it? The answer depends on our will to make it so. With the protected weapon systems, command posts and communications we are now acquiring, there is no technical reason why the use of nuclear weapons cannot be controlled in a nuclear war. The destructive power of their uncontrolled use should give all participants a strong incentive to find ways of avoiding it. Moreover, as both sides acquire protected forces like MINUTEMAN and POLARIS, the prospects are that neither side will be able to improve its military position by a sudden attack on the forces of the other. Then, if massive thermonuclear attack ever did make sense, it will do so no longer.

The other question is, "Should we try?" The argument against trying, one that has been used against Civil Defense, is that it weakens the "fire break" between nuclear and non-nuclear war. But any thermonuclear war would be such an unprecedented disaster that it is difficult to see how anything we could do to mitigate its consequences would effectively weaken the "fire break." And the disaster of an unlimited nuclear war would be too great to permit us not to take whatever measures we can to minimize its likelihood. Moreover, the principle of controlled and limited use of military force is indivisible. If we believe in control

---

[3] Commencement Address at the University of Michigan, Ann Arbor, 16 June 1962.

in some circumstances and not in others, it will become more difficult to maintain it in those circumstances in which we should.
An emphasis on control and limitations in the use of force is
desirable across the spectrum of conflict.

MORAL ASPECTS

I am sure that you are all concerned, as I am, about the moral
problems raised by our military preparations. Is it right or
wrong for us to be buying hundreds of inter-continental ballistic
missiles, fighter-bomber aircraft, and equipment for many Army
divisions? Can we justify weapon systems and war plans that
would enable us, if a nuclear war were thrust upon us, to fight
back even though doing so might lead to the deaths of many
millions of people?

These are extremely complex and difficult problems that we can
neither escape nor hope to understand fully. Their moral solution
cannot come from artificial simplification. Tonight what I would
like to do is offer you some questions and some reflections that
may illuminate some of the issues. A proper appreciation of the
moral aspects of defense policy requires an understanding of
theology as well as the alternative strategies and their implications. A dialogue is required, and I offer the following remarks
in that spirit.

According to traditional Christian doctrine, the use of force to
repress evil can be justifiable under certain conditions including
the following: First, the use of force must have a reasonable
chance of success. Second, if successful, it must offer a better
situation than the one that would prevail in the absence of the
use of force. Third, the force that is used must be proportional
to the objectives being sought (or the evil being repressed). For
this to be satisfied, peaceful means of redress must have failed.
Fourth, the force must be used with the intention of sparing non-
combatants and with a reasonable prospect of actually doing so.

It is interesting to observe that the potentially catastrophic
character of thermonuclear war has forced practical decision-
makers, reasoning in a secular context, to adopt a set of criteria
very much like those of the traditional Christian doctrine and to
apply them to the design of the military posture of the United
States. Now, much more than in the recent past, our use of force
is being carefully proportioned to the objectives being sought,
and the objectives are being carefully limited to those which at
the same time are necessary for our security and which do not
pose the kind of unlimited threat to our opponents in the cold
war that would drive them to unleash nuclear war. In the past,

before nuclear weapons, deliberate limitations in the use of force did not present much of a practical problem because of the limited destructive power of non-nuclear weapons. Nuclear weapons have now given such contraints great practical importance.

Within the broad policy of armed resistance to aggression, which is one of the alternatives open to us, and in terms of the moral criteria of the traditional Christian doctrine, I think it is fair to say that we have made considerable progress. This is not to say that we have gone as far as we can go. But it does suggest that all the moral questions are not concerned with whether or not armed resistance can be justifiable.

During the past fifteen years, a number of commentators, theologians and others, have taken the position that although in former times the traditional doctrine was valid and, under appropriate conditions the use of armed force could be justified, now, in the atomic age, there can be no justifiable war. The argument has been made that nuclear war does not and cannot offer a reasonable chance of bringing about a better situation than that which would have prevailed in the absence of the use of force; that the thermonuclear force, being essentially unlimited in its destructive effects, cannot be proportioned to reasonable objectives; and that with it the non-combatants cannot be spared. Therefore, many argue that the traditional doctrine is obsolete and that a new doctrine must be found. Some argue that the only morally acceptable course is to renounce nuclear weapons; others believe that we must renounce the use of force altogether.

I would not want to suggest that this line of thought is not based on good and compelling reasons, even though I have not found it convincing myself. It may prove to be the case that the danger of escalation is so great that future limited non-nuclear wars will bring with them an intolerable risk of massive thermonuclear destruction. However, experience in the past 15 years has shown that non-nuclear wars can be kept limited and that freedom can be defended from Communist aggression without massive destruction.

A question to consider in one's critical thought on this problem is whether the view that the traditional doctrine is obsolete is based on an overremphasis on unlimited nuclear war, perhaps an identification of all armed conflict with it. An unlimited nuclear war is an extreme on a broad spectrum of possible armed conflicts. Of course, it is a very important extreme because of its disastrous consequences, but it is not the whole spectrum. In fact, it is only one among many possible kinds of thermonuclear war. It can be a mistake to apply reasoning based on this extreme to all kinds of armed resistance to aggression and injustice. I think it is important to recognize this, for if our thinking is unclear on this point, and if we identify any use of armed force with unlimited destruction, we are likely unnecessarily to disarm ourselves and leave ourselves victims of Communist aggression.

It is clear that we have elected to retain the threat of use of nuclear weapons in our own defense and that of our allies. We thereby consciously accept the risk that we will have to use them. Some people believe that we should reject the use of nuclear weapons. Before accepting such a judgment, one should consider carefully the full implications of such a decision. We do have worldwide responsibilities. Many millions of people depend for their lives and freedom on our military strength. In this respect, the United States is in a very different position from any other country in the free world.

The question I would like to leave with you . . . is whether current U.S. defense policy, which emphasizes deterrence, control, and the use of the appropriately limited amount of force, represents a good reconciliation of the traditional doctrine with the facts of life in the nuclear age. We have achieved some success with the controlled use of force. We are still alive and free today, and the missiles are out of Cuba. We are running great risks, to be sure, but would the risks be ameliorated by laying down our arms? It is tragic that nations must at times resort to armed force to resolve their differences. War is destructive and it has evil consequences. But our defense posture is being designed to make war less likely and less destructive. I am not suggesting that we can make war and violence desirable. The question is whether we have a better alternative.

. . . I have defended our policies on the grounds that they make sense. Can they also be defended on the grounds that they are moral? Viewed with perspective, the two should be the same.

APPENDIX I

INTRODUCTION OF NEW GOVERNMENT-WIDE PLANNING AND BUDGETING SYSTEM*

By President Lyndon B. Johnson

I have asked you to meet with me this morning to discuss the introduction of a new planning and budgeting system throughout the Government.

The objective of this program is simple: to use the most modern management tools so that the full promise of a finer life can be brought to every American at the least possible cost.

This program is aimed at finding new ways to do new jobs faster, better, less expensively; to insure sounder judgment through more accurate information; to pinpoint those things we ought to do more, and to spotlight those things we ought to do less; to make our decision-making process as up to date as our space-exploring equipment; in short, we want to trade in our surreys for automobiles, our old cannon for new missiles.

Everything I have done in both legislation and the construction of a budget has been guided by my deep concern for the American people—consistent with wise management of the taxpayer's dollar.

In translating this principle in action, and with the help of an outstanding Congress, we have passed more progressive legislation than in any comparable period in history.

We have been compassionate. We have also been prudent.

But we can and must do better if we are to bring the Great Society closer to all the people.

Good Government demands excellence.

It demands the fullest value for each dollar spent. It demands that we take advantage of the most modern management techniques.

---

*Statement by the President to Members of the Cabinet and Heads of Agencies, 25 August 1965, *Weekly Compilation of Presidential Documents*, vol. I (30 August 1965). On 12 October 1965, the Bureau of the Budget provided general instructions for the establishment of planning-programing-budgeting systems by all major Federal departments and agencies; see BOB Bulletin No. 66-3, 12 October 1965; and Supplement dated 21 February 1966.

This is what I want to introduce today—a new planning-programming-budgeting system developed by our top management experts led by Budget Director Charles Schultze. Once in operation, it will enable us to—

(1) Identify our national goals with precision and on a continuing basis.

(2) Choose among those goals the ones that are most urgent.

(3) Search for alternative means of reaching those goals most effectively at the least cost.

(4) Inform ourselves not merely on next year's costs—but on the second, and third, and subsequent year's costs—of our programs.

(5) Measure the performance of our programs to insure a dollar's worth of service for each dollar spent.

This system will improve our ability to control our programs and our budgets rather than having them control us. It will operate year round. Studies, goals, program proposals, and reviews will be scheduled throughout the year instead of being crowded into "budget time."

To establish this system and carry out the necessary studies, each of you will need a Central Staff for Program and Policy Planning accountable directly to you. To make this work will take good people, the best you now have and the best you can find.

I intend to have the 1968 budget and later-year programs presented in this new form by next spring.

With these programs will go the first studies produced by your planning and policy staffs.

It is important to remember one thing: no system, no matter how refined, can make decisions for you. You and I have that responsibility in the executive branch. But our judgment is no better than our information. This system will present us with the alternatives and the information on the basis of which we can, together, make better decisions. The people will be the beneficiary.

The Budget Director has already talked to most of you about the need for this new approach. He is now preparing plans for setting it up. He is ready to help you in any way he can.

Within the next several weeks he will send out detailed instructions for incorporating fiscal year 1968 and later-year programs into this system. But to make this new plan a success, he will need your full support. I know that you will give him that support.

APPENDIX II

AN ILLUSTRATIVE EXAMPLE OF SYSTEMS ANALYSIS*

By William P. Snyder, Major, Infantry

In contrast to his predecessor of a few years ago, the professional officer of the mid-1960's is at least familiar with the term "systems analysis." Most, however, lack a genuine understanding of the matter. The situation is somewhat analagous to America's tradition of a bipartisan foreign policy: in foreign affairs, politics stops at the water's edge; knowledge of systems analysis stops with the term itself.

One of the reasons why there is so little genuine understanding of systems analysis is because the term has never been adequately defined. The lack of a precise definition, in turn, is explained by the eclectic nature of systems analysis itself. The practitioners of systems analysis have not confined their activities to limited problem areas; they have, rather, attacked a wide variety of problems, drawn from every possible area of public or private concern. In addition, the concepts and techniques of systems analysis have been pirated from several academic disciplines which has made it impossible to tie it firmly to any single intellectual field.

While these features contribute to an understanding of our difficulty, they also make it necessary to approach the subject of systems analysis inferentially. One way is to outline the traits which characterize systems analysis generally and good systems analysis in particular. The first and most important characteristic is the use of scientific method. This means that the data utilized are capable of verification, either by observation or by deduction from plausible premises. Scientific method also means that the procedures adopted in the analysis conform to accepted rules of logic. Systems analysis is characterized, in the second place, by the use of quantifiable data and mathematical techniques. That

---

*Editor's note: This material was prepared in the spring of 1964 for instructional purposes at the United States Military Academy. It is used with the permission of the Professor of Social Sciences, U. S. Military Academy, West Point, New York.

is not to say that systems analysis is simply decision by computer or multiple regression theory. Computers are sometimes useful, especially in analyses which require extensive calculations of a repetitive or iterative nature; in many cases, however, nothing more complicated than simple arithmetic is needed. Explicitness is the final common denominator of systems analysis. The criteria and assumptions are always specified, and incommensurables and areas of uncertainty are carefully delineated.

Systems analysis can also be explained by noting what it is not. It is neither a panacea nor a Pandora's box. Quite the contrary. Many problems are highly complex, and the difficulty in quantifying the key variables limits the applicability of systematic analysis. In addition, systems analysis is neither easy nor time free; it requires hard work, long hours, and highly qualified analysts. Finally, systems analysis seldom answers all the questions which must be solved before a decision can be made. It may provide some useful answers and some insights into the problem, but there remains substantial room for judgment. In short, systems analysis is a useful aid to, but not a substitute for, judgment and decision-making.

This article adopts yet a third method for understanding systems analysis—the case study. Although the setting, problem, and data are hypothetical, the techniques, purposes, benefits, and shortcomings of systems analysis are illustrated in the example which follows. The case study has several limitations—but if these are clearly understood, the example loses none of its value as a teaching device. Some of the methods of good systems analysis have been deliberately violated, primarily to stress their importance. The analysis is also simplified in places, not because the computation involves unfamiliar techniques but because the problem would otherwise be too long. Finally, certain aspects of the problem are given less detailed consideration than they would in fact receive in an actual analysis.

THE BACKGROUND

Military operations in The Republic of Vietnam took a turn for the better in the summer of 1965 when Vietnamese forces began to have greater success in locating and defeating Viet Cong units. These successes were attributed by American military advisers to the vastly improved Vietnamese political situation. Under General - - - the Vietnamese government had become more responsive to the needs of the countryside, and no less important, Saigon demonstrated a marked improvement in administrative efficiency. There was also a noticeable improvement in economic conditions: the country's balance of payments position returned to surplus, and the rapid inflation which had plagued The Republic of Vietnam between 1962–1964 was finally stopped. Communications within the country were slowly re-established, and by 1966 it was again possible to travel safely on the main roads.

By late 1966 the remnants of Viet Cong forces had been driven into the inaccessible and mountainous country between Binh Dinh and Hue. While their defeat and withdrawal from the Southern and central parts of the country was a major setback, their orderly withdrawal demonstrated the very considerable potential of these forces. Their location near the Laotian border and the 17th parallel (the border between North and South Vietnam) makes it possible for them to receive supplies and reinforcement from Communist sources outside the country. The immediate objectives of Viet Cong leaders is to consolidate their defensive positions northwest of Binh Dinh, to retrain and re-equip their forces, and, as units are reorganized, to embark on limited operations against The Republic of Vietnam.

The South Vietnamese government has deployed three infantry divisions in the area Binh Dinh-Hue. (See map I, p. 218) The - - - Government plans to keep the Viet Cong forces under severe pressure, in the hope that they will be unable to recover from their defeat in the South. Active operations are also necessary to minimize the possibility of raids and infiltration in those areas which have been returned to South Vietnamese control.

The Vietnamese Army units deployed against the Viet Cong forces are well-trained and commanded by experienced and competent officers. Their combat effectiveness was demonstrated during the operations which led to the defeat of Viet Cong forces in the southern and central areas. The most pressing problem presently facing the Vietnamese Army is supply—the road network north of Binh Dinh is extremely poor, and throughout much of the year heavy rainfall makes existing roads impassable.

The U.S. Army engineers have examined the resupply problem and conclude that construction of an all-weather road from Saigon to the area of operations is impracticable. Although the estimated cost of an all-weather road is only about $75 million, construction would require approximately fifteen months, sufficient time for Viet Cong forces to effect their recovery. Moreover, such a project would impose a heavy burden on the civilian economy and seriously limit other road construction, flood control and reclamation projects, and agricultural improvement activities badly needed elsewhere in South Vietnam. One major alternative, road con-

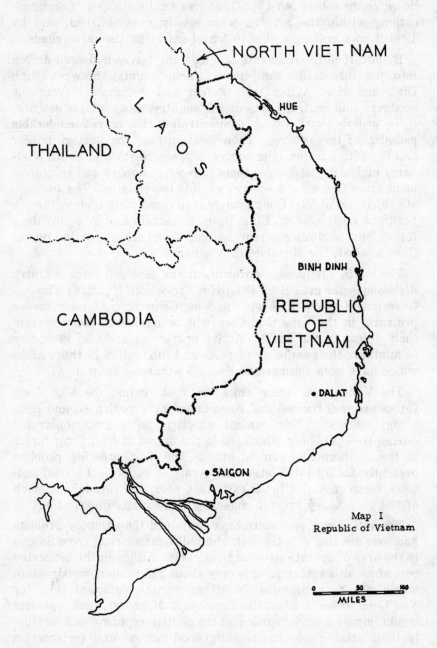

NORTH VIET NAM

LAOS

THAILAND

HUE

BINH DINH

CAMBODIA

REPUBLIC
OF
VIET NAM

• DALAT

• SAIGON

Map I
Republic of Vietnam

0   50   100
MILES

struction by U.S. forces, has been ruled out for political and economic reasons. Five engineer battalions would be needed, and these units would probably be involved in frequent, small-scale contact with Viet Cong forces. Finally, this area of Vietnam is thinly populated and has only limited agricultural potential; there would be, therefore, little use for such a road after defeat of Viet Cong forces.

The U.S. Military Commander in Vietnam has proposed to the Department of Defense that all Vietnamese Army supply requirements for the three division force deployed north of Binh Dinh be provided by an American operated intratheater airlift. It is estimated that Vietnamese forces will require about 725 tons of supplies per day. Between 85 and 90 per cent of that amount is consumption items—gasoline and petroleum products, food, ammunition, fortification materials, and medical supplies. The remainder will consist of equipment, light vehicles, weapons, and communications sets.

The proposal of the U.S. Commander in South Vietnam concluded with these paragraphs—

> One of the major lessons we have learned as a result of our operations in South Vietnam is the vital necessity of tactical air lines of communications. In counterinsurgency campaigns, combat units are widely dispersed, constantly moving, and separated by large distances. It is always impracticable and frequently impossible to resupply forward units by means of ground transportation. If the United States is to fight in areas such as Vietnam—or, indeed, in Africa, the Middle East, or Latin America—an intratheater air resupply capability responsive to the needs of the theater commanders is an absolute must. However adequate our equipment, organization, or training for this type of war, we will fail without an adequate logistics system. Air transport is our only hope in many parts of the world.
>
> Considering our past efforts in South Vietnam, the costs of air resupply for Vietnamese forces seem a small price to pay to insure the successful termination of this war. Although the distances and tonnages involved are limited as compared to those which would be encountered by U.S. forces operating in other areas of the world, this situation nevertheless provides an excellent opportunity for the Army to develop appropriate techniques and organizations for this capability. Upon completion of operations in this command, the U.S. Army would then possess sufficient aircraft to form the nucleus of an intratheater air logistical system capable of world-wide deployment.

The proposal of the U.S. Military Commander, Vietnam, after its receipt by the Joint Chiefs of Staff, was referred to the Department of the Army. At a subsequent meeting of the Joint Chiefs, the Army Chief of Staff recommended that the Army be authorized to purchase a light transport aircraft. "The Pioneer has just recently completed its acceptance tests," the Army Chief of Staff explained to his colleagues, "and it is a very fine aircraft indeed. In the tests conducted by Continental Army Command, the Pioneer was able to exceed its rated payload, while retaining its superior take-off and landing characteristics. Our studies indicate that about 50 aircraft will be necessary to meet the requirement proposed by the U.S. Military Commander, Vietnam. The procurement costs of the Pioneer will be about $75 million." The Chief of Staff, USAF, did not concur in the Army's recommendation. "The Air Force can do the job easier and cheaper," he declared, "and the mission is properly our responsibility. We can move that amount of tonnage easily with twenty-five or thirty of our new Freighter transports. Procurement cost of these aircraft would be about $90 million. Although slightly more expensive, the Freighter has a heavy drop capability, which the Pioneer lacks. This alone is worth the difference in price. Moreover, the Freighter, because it has better radio and navigation equipment, can operate in weather which will ground the Pioneer." "That may be," replied the Army Chief of Staff, "but your aircraft cannot take off and land on short runways; furthermore, the Freighter is an Air Force aircraft, and a logistics system using that aircraft would not be as flexible or as responsive to local Army commanders as one using the Pioneer. These factors, coupled with less cost, more than balance off the slight technical advantages claimed for the Freighter."

At this point the Chairman intervened and suggested that the Special Study Group of the Joint Staff examine the problem and present to the Joint Chiefs a more thorough examination of the Army recommendation. The Secretary of Defense agreed, and indicated that the study should center on the relative merits of the various aircraft which might be utilized: "I agree with the proposal that we provide an air line of communication in South Vietnam. The question which must now be answered is: Which aircraft should we procure to provide a flexible and responsive intratheater air resupply system capable of supporting U.S. Army forces deployed in a variety of circumstances, with varying distances and tonnage requirements?"

Some two months later the Chiefs were presented with the following paper:

TACTICAL AIR LINE OF COMMUNICATIONS:
A COMPARISON OF ARMY AND AIR FORCE PROPOSALS

I. PURPOSE

This paper presents a cost-effectiveness analysis of the Freighter and Pioneer aircraft in tactical air line of communications (TALOC) operations. Although the analysis is limited to the specific tactical deployment described in JCS #736,* the results will be applicable to any TALOC support of deployed U.S. forces. The justification for this assumption rests on the fact that Vietnamese forces employ the same doctrine and organization as U.S. forces.

II. THE MODEL

1. The logistical system necessary to support Vietnamese forces requires deliveries to Corps, Division, Regiment, and forward units. This analysis is confined to units of regimental size or larger, since it is assumed that deliveries to units smaller than regiment can be provided by other means. A second assumption is that the aircraft employed in the logistical system will be utilized only for resupply activities. The aircraft utilized for TALOC could, of course, be employed in other duties; the daily resupply mission is of such massive importance as compared to these other roles, however, as to require individual analysis. (These assumptions apply both to deployed U.S. forces and to Vietnamese forces, with the exception that the supply requirements of Vietnamese Army units approximate the tonnages consumed by U.S. organizations one echelon smaller, e.g., the daily consumption of a Vietnamese Corps approximates that of a U.S. division.)

2. The critical variables in the logistical system are the following:

    Routes of supply.
    Tonnage requirements.
    Distance.
    Aircraft type.

In the model these factors are treated as major variables, and the results depend on assumptions regarding these factors.

3. The total systems costs which appear in this analysis include both the number of aircraft and airfield construction costs. The equation for total systems costs is:

---

*An identification number assigned by the Joint Staff to the request from the U.S. Military Commander, Vietnam.

Total systems cost=
number of aircraft $\times$ cost/aircraft+
number of ft^2 of airfield surface $\times$ cost/ft^2

4. *Design and Cost Assumptions*

a. The logistical system includes sufficient aircraft to carry anticipated loads, over expected distances, at normal utilization and availability rates, under expected conditions of weather, terrain, and altitude encountered in South Vietnam.

b. System life is assumed to be five years.

c. System operating costs are calculated on the basis of peacetime operations for a five-year period.

III. DEPLOYMENT AND ROUTING LEGS

1. The tactical situation described in JCS 736 is depicted on map I (page 218). Under normal operating conditions one full division is maintained in reserve in the Corps area; similarly, one regiment is retained as a reserve in each division area. Reserve units will be employed where required by the tactical situation, but normally only during periods of heavy combat. Since transportation, including aircraft, will normally be available from Vietnamese sources to effect deployment or rotation of reserve units, it is assumed that the logistical system is unaffected by changes in the disposition of local reserves.

2. The schematic illustration (diagram 1, p. 223) depicts the logistical system and indicates the portion segregated for analysis. The tonnage required daily at each echelon in the system are indicated in table I below:

Table I. Resupply Loads*
(Tons per Day)

Units	Unit Requirement	Total T/D
Corps (Corps Hq, Support Units & Reserve Division)	375	375
Division (Division Hq, Support Units & Division Reserves)—2 Divisions deployed	125	250
Regiments—4 Regiments deployed	25	100
Daily Total		725

*Tonnage requirements for deployed units are based on average resupply requirements of Vietnamese Army units engaged in tactical operations during a 12-month period in 1964–65.

It should be noted that the load delivered to division and regimental level is multiplied by the number of units deployed. The total tons/day is thus the amount which must be delivered at that echelon.

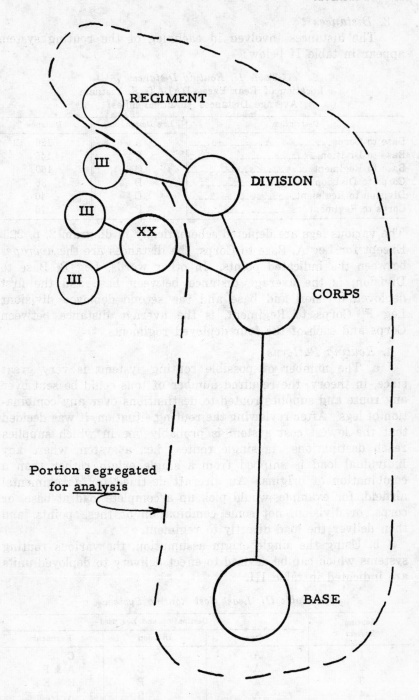

DIAGRAM #1

3. *Distances*

The distances involved in each leg of the routing system appear in table II below:

Table II. Routing Distances.
Location of Rear Base—DALAT, S. Vietnam
Average Distances (nautical miles)

Description	Leg Designation	Distance
Base to Corps_____	A	120
Base to Division_____	B	145
Base to Regiment_____	C	160
Corps to Division_____	D	35
Division to Regiment_____	E	40
Corps to Regiment_____	F	70

The various legs are depicted schematically in diagram 2, p. 225. Except for Leg A, Base to Corps, the distances are the *averages* between the indicated points. In other words, Leg B, Base to Division, is the average distance between base and the first deployed division and base and the second deployed division; Leg F, Corps to Regiment, is the average distance between Corps and each of the four deployed regiments.

4. *Routing Patterns*

a. The number of possible routing systems is very great since, in theory, the required number of tons could be sent over any route and supplies routed to destinations over any combination of legs. After reviewing the routing situation, it was decided that the lowest cost system is probably one in which supplies reach destinations via single routes; i.e., a system where any individual load is shipped from a single origin rather than a combination of origins. An aircraft destined for a regimental airfield, for example, would pick up a complete load at base, or corps, or division, not some combination of these points, and then deliver the load directly to regiment.

b. Using the single origin assumption, the various routing systems which can be devised to effect delivery to deployed units are indicated in table III.

Table III. Least Cost Routing System.

Routing System	Destination and Leg used		
	Corps	Division	Regiment
1	A	B	C
2	A	B	A & F
3	A	B	B & E
4	A	B	A, D, & E
5	A	A & D	C
6	A	A & D	A & F
7	A	A & D	B & E
8	A	A & D	A, D, & E

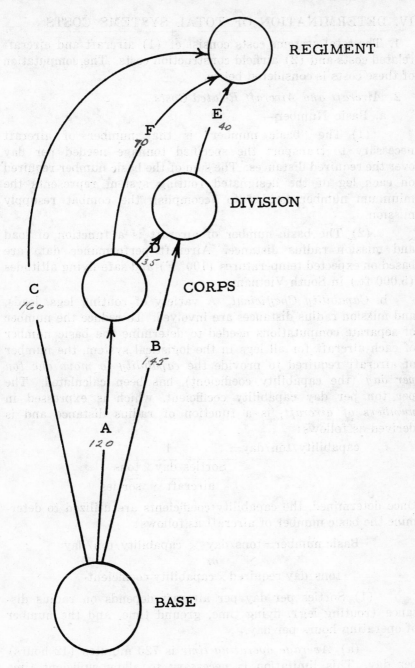

REGIMENT

E
40

F
70

DIVISION

D
35

C
160

CORPS

B
145

A
120

BASE

DIAGRAM #2

IV. DETERMINATION OF TOTAL SYSTEMS COSTS

1. The total systems costs consist of (1) aircraft and aircraft related costs and (2) airfield construction costs. The computation of these costs is considered below.

2. *Aircraft and Aircraft Related Costs*

   a. Basic Number—

   (1) The "basic number" is that number of aircraft necessary to transport the specified tonnage needed per day over the required distances. The sum of the basic number required on each leg of the designated routing system represents the minimum number needed to accomplish the combat resupply mission.

   (2) The basic number of aircraft is a function of load and mission radius distance. Aircraft performance data are based on expected temperatures (100° F) and safe flying altitudes (5,000 ft.) in South Vietnam.

   b. *Capability Coefficient.* A variety of routing legs, loads, and mission radius distances are involved. To reduce the number of separate computations needed to determine the basic number of each aircraft for all legs in the logistical system, the number of aircraft required to provide the *capability to move one ton per day* (the capability coefficient) has been calculated. The per ton per day capability coefficient, which is expressed in *numbers of aircraft*, is a function of radius distance and is derived as follows:

$$\text{capability/ton/day} = \cfrac{1}{\cfrac{\text{Sorties/day}}{\text{aircraft}} \times \cfrac{\text{tons}}{\text{sorties}}}$$

Once determined, the capability coefficients are utilized to determine the basic number of aircraft as follows:

$$\text{Basic number} = \text{tons/day} \times \text{capability/ton/day}$$
or
$$\text{tons/day required} \times \text{capability coefficient}$$

   (1) Sorties per day per aircraft depends on radius distance (routing leg), flying time, ground time, and the number of operating hours per day.

   (a) *Average operating time* is 720 minutes (12 hours) per day. This limitation is necessary to allow sufficient time to perform maintenance on both the Pioneer and Freighter. Operating time for an individual aircraft will vary from day to day, of course, depending on the number of hours of daylight, airfield conditions, weather, aircraft maintenance status, the intensity of enemy activity, and the length of time required to fly a given sortie.

(b) *Ground time* is a function of the aircraft design, the expected load, and the availability of loading equipment. The estimated times are indicated below:

Table IV. Estimated Ground Time[1]
(minutes)

Activity[3]	Leg A[2]		Legs B, C, D, F		Leg E	
	Freighter	Pioneer	Freighter	Pioneer	Freighter	Pioneer
Loading initial cargo	25	15	25	15	50	30
Unloading initial cargo	15	10	45	30	45	30
Loading return cargo at destination	10	5	20	10	20	10
Unloading return	5	5	5	5	15	10
TOTAL	55	35	95	60	130	80

[1] Estimates were furnished by appropriate Army and Air Force staff agencies.
[2] It is assumed that materials handling equipment will be available at Base and Corps.
[3] Refueling is performed simultaneously with unloading at origin.

(c) Average cruising speed for the Freighter is 180 knots; for the Pioneer 150 knots. Warm up and taxi times are included in cruising speed. Round trip flying time, as a function of radius distances, is depicted in graph I, p. 228.

(d) Sorties per day is computed by dividing total operating time (720 min.) by total elapsed time per sortie. Elapsed time per sortie is the sum of ground time and flying time.

Table V. Sorties Per Day.

Aircraft	Leg	Flying Time (a)	Ground Time (b)	Sorties/day (720÷a+b)
Freighter	A	80	55	5.3
	B	97	95	3.7
	C	107	95	3.5
	D	24	95	6.0
	E	27	130	4.5
	F	47	95	5.1
Pioneer	A	96	35	5.5
	B	116	60	4.1
	C	128	60	3.8
	D	28	60	8.1
	E	32	80	6.4
	F	56	60	6.2

GRAPH I

ROUND TRIP FLYING TIMES

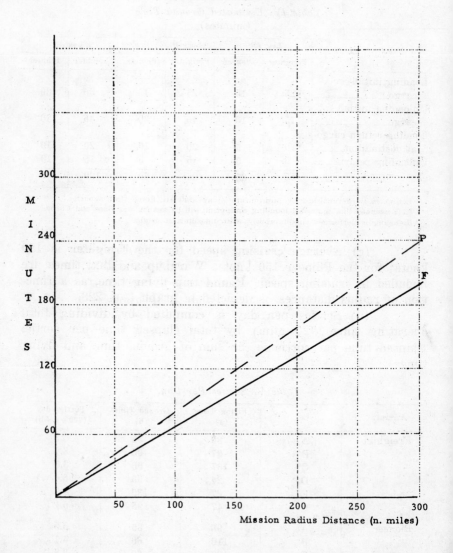

Mission Radius Distance (n. miles)

(2) *Tons per sortie* is a function of the allowable gross take-off weight, the empty weight, and the weight of fuel required for the radius distance. Weight and load data are as follows:

	Gross Take-Off Weight	Empty Weight
Freighter	105,000	75,000
Pioneer	35,000	22,000

(a) Fuel consumption curves are indicated on graph II, p. 230. Payload curves are computed by subtracting from gross take-off weight the sum of empty weight and round-trip fuel requirements. The curves are displayed on graph III, p. 231.

(b) Tons/sorties for the two aircraft on the various routing legs is as follows:

Table VI. *Tons/Sorties, Routing/Legs.*

Leg	Distance	Tons/Sortie	
		Freighter	Pioneer
A	120	11.3	5.3
B	145	11.0	5.1
C	160	10.9	5.0
D	35	12.4	6.0
E	40	12.3	5.9
F	70	11.9	5.8

(3) Utilizing the data in paragraphs 2b (1) and 2b (2), the ton/day capability coefficients for the various routing legs can be calculated.

Table VII. *Capability Coefficients*[1]

$$\text{Capability/ton/day} = \frac{1}{\text{sorties/day x ton/sortie}}$$

Aircraft	Leg[2]	Sorties/day	Tons/sorties	Capability Coefficient
Freighter	A	5.3	11.3	.0167
	B	3.7	11.0	.0246
	C	3.5	10.9	.0262
	D	6.0	12.4	.0134
	E	4.5	12.3	.0181
	F	5.1	11.9	.0165
Pioneer	A	5.5	5.3	.0343
	B	4.1	5.1	.0478
	C	3.8	5.0	.0526
	D	8.1	6.0	.0206
	E	6.4	5.9	.0265
	F	6.2	5.8	.0280

[1] The unit is number of aircraft.

[2] If the distances were not fixed—as would be the case if a variety of locales were considered—the capability coefficient could be depicted graphically as a function of radius distance for each aircraft.

GRAPH II

ROUND TRIP FUEL REQUIREMENTS

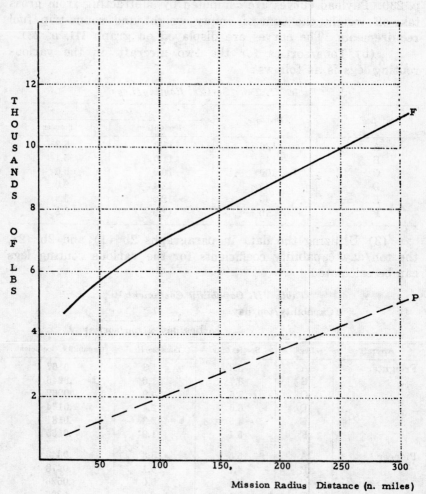

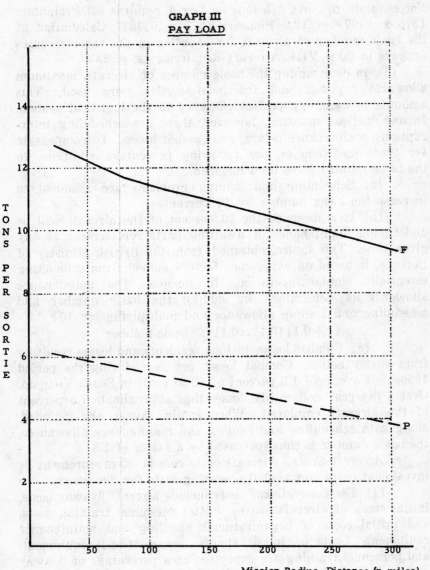

GRAPH III
PAY LOAD

(4) The basic number of aircraft required for a given tonnage on a specified routing leg is calculated by multiplying the coefficient indicated in table VII by the tonnage required. For example, to move 375 tons on Leg A requires 6.3 Freighters (375 x .0167) or 12.9 Pioneers (375 x .0343). Calculation of the basic number of aircraft for each leg in the various routes appears in table VIII, Aircraft Requirements, p. 233.

(5) In determining the basic number of aircraft, maximum allowable payloads and fractional sorties were used. This amounts to assuming perfect efficiency in the logistical system. In any tactical situation, however, there are scheduling interruptions, maintenance delays, and combat losses. To compensate for these inefficiencies, the following percentage additions to the basic number have been included.

(a) Scheduling and loading problems are assumed to increase the basic number by 10 percent.

(b) It is assumed the 10 percent of the aircraft will be undergoing maintenance or awaiting parts replacement at any given time. This figure, obtained from the British Ministry of Defence, is based on experience factors gained from conducting essentially similar operations in Borneo. The maintenance allowance is determined by adding the basic number and scheduling and loading allowance and multiplying by .10:

$$(1+0.1)(0.1)=0.11 \times \text{basic number}$$

(c) Combat losses include accidents and losses resulting from enemy action. Combat losses per year during the period 1960–1964 averaged 1.5 percent of all aircraft in South Vietnam. Over a five-year system life, losses thus approximate 7.5 percent of the aircraft employed. When combat losses are included, along with scheduling and loading and maintenance allowances, the basic number is thus increased by a factor of 1.3:

c. *Aircraft Costs.* Aircraft costs consist of procurement or investment costs and annual operating costs for five years.

(1) *Total investment costs* include aircraft flyaway costs, initial stock of aircraft spares, initial personnel training costs, and initial costs of organizational handling and maintenance equipment. Costs of initial spares, organizational equipment, and personnel training are expressed as a percentage of flyaway costs. Since neither aircraft has been produced in quantity, costs have been estimated by the manufacturer or service department, rather than based on operating unit experiences. Flyaway costs were determined on the basis of a production order of sufficient size to meet the tonnage delivery requirements established in JCS 736 (Freighter: 0–50; Pioneer: 0–50).

Table VIII. Aircraft Requirements.

Leg	t/d	(a) Basic Number	Allowances* (b) S&L	(c) M	(d) CL	Total (a+b+c+d)
			FREIGHTER			
A	375	6.3	.63	.69	.58	8.2
	475	8.0	.80	.88	.72	10.4
	625	10.5	1.05	1.15	1.00	13.7
	725	12.1	1.21	1.33	1.06	15.7
B	100	2.5	.25	.28	.27	3.3
	250	6.2	.62	.68	.60	8.1
	350	8.6	.86	.94	.80	11.2
C	100	2.6	.26	.29	.25	3.4
D	100	1.3	.13	.14	.13	1.7
	250	3.4	.34	.37	.29	4.4
	350	4.7	.47	.52	.41	6.1
E	100	1.8	.18	.20	.12	2.3
F	100	1.7	.17	.19	.14	2.2
			PIONEER			
A	375	12.9	1.29	1.42	1.19	16.8
	475	16.3	1.63	1.79	1.48	21.2
	625	21.4	2.14	2.35	1.91	27.8
	725	24.9	2.49	2.74	2.27	32.4
B	100	4.8	.48	.53	.39	6.2
	250	12.0	1.20	1.32	1.08	15.6
	350	16.8	1.68	1.85	1.47	21.8
C	100	5.3	.53	.58	.49	6.9
D	100	2.1	.21	.23	.16	2.7
	250	5.2	.52	.57	.51	6.8
	350	7.2	.72	.79	.69	9.4
E	100	2.7	.27	.30	.23	3.5
F	100	2.8	.28	.31	.21	3.6

*Notes:
   S&L: Scheduling and Loading Allowance—10% of basic number.
   M: Maintenance Allowance—10% of basic number and S&L Allowance.
   CL: Combat Loss Allowances—7.5% of aircraft employed—1.21 x basic number or
          a+b+c.

Table IX. Investment Costs per Aircraft.
(Thousands of dollars)

Cost Category	Pioneer	Freighter
Flyaway Costs	$1,470	$3,125
Aircraft Spares (@ 20% Flyaway)	294	625
Organization Equipment (@ 3% Flyaway)	44	94
Personnel Training (@ 25% Flyaway)	367	782
Total Investment Costs	$2,175	$4,626

(2) Annual operating costs include personnel costs, flight pay costs, aircraft spares, organizational equipment spares, fuel costs, and, a residual category, other operating costs. Operating cost factors were furnished by Army and Air Force Comptrollers, and are based on expenses incurred by similar aircraft. These costs (in thousands of dollars) are derived as follows:

(a) *Personnel Costs*

Personnel Costs=10 × Number of Officers + 3 × Number of Enlisted Men.

(b) *Flying Pay Costs*

Flying Pay Costs=2.0 × Number of Rated Officers + 1.0 × Number of Rated Enlisted Men.

(c) *Aircraft Spares*

Aircraft Spares=1.5 × Annual Fuel Costs.

(d) *Organizational Equipment Replacement and Maintenance*

Organizational Equipment R & M=.15 × Cost of Initial Organizational Equipment

(e) *Fuel Consumption*

	Annual Peacetime Flying Hours	Fuel Costs Per Flying Hour $	Annual Fuel Cost Per Aircraft (Thousand $)
Pioneer	600	38	22.8
Freighter	600	90	54.0

(f) *Other Operating Costs*

This category includes annual consumption of operating supplies and services and other miscellaneous costs not included in the above categories. The equation is:

Other Operating Costs=4.4 × Annual Fuel Costs

(g) Manpower requirements, one of the two major variables in operating costs functions, are estimated on the basis of anticipated peacetime workloads using appropriate Army and Air Force manning and maintenance factors.

Aircrews

Number of Men Per Crew

	Crews/Aircraft	Pioneer	Freighter
Pilots	2	2	2
Navigators	2	0	1
Flight Engineers	2.5	0	1
Flight Crew Chiefs	2.5	1	1
Totals per Aircraft		4 Off/2.5 EM	6 Off/5.0 EM

Maintenance Personnel (EM)

Manpower Per Flying Hour

	Pioneer	Freighter
Unit	5)	20
Support	4)	
Depot	2	4
	11	24

Annual Maintenance Personnel Requirements

	Pioneer	Freighter
Total Man Hours	11 x 600 = 6600	24 x 600 = 14,400
Total Man Years	3.37	7.35
(Total Hours/Man Year = 1960)		

Support Personnel. Service-wide support requirements, including personnel in administrative, training, logistical, and maintenance activities, are calculated at 2 times the crew and maintenance manning requirements per aircraft. Current Army and Air Force planning factors form the basis for this estimate.

(3) Annual operating costs per aircraft are computed below:

Table X. Annual Operating Costs per Aircraft
(Thousands of dollars)

Cost Category	Pioneer	Freighter
Personnel Costs	173.0	291.0
Flying Pay Costs	10.5	17.0
Aircraft Spares	34.2	81.0
Organizational Equipment, Replacement & Maintenance	6.6	14.1
Fuel Consumption	22.8	54.0
Other Operating Costs	91.2	216.0
Total Annual Operating Cost Per Aircraft	338.3	673.1
Times 5 Years	1,691.5	3,365.5

(4) Total systems costs for a five-year period are indicated in table XI.

Table XI. Total Systems Costs.
(Thousands of dollars)

	Pioneer	Freighter
Investment Costs	$2,175.0	$4,626.0
Five-year Operating Costs	1,691.5	3,365.5
Total	$3,866.5	$7,991.5

3. Airfield Construction Costs*

a. *Some General Considerations.* Additional airfields are needed at corps, the two deployed divisions, and at each deployed regiment, it being assumed that the base was selected because of the existence of an airfield of adequate size to handle anticipated traffic. The required size in sq. ft. of prepared surface area of an airfield at any location varies with the amount of traffic arriving and departing per day, which in this instance depends on the location and routing system. In addition, runways are of different lengths depending on the aircraft employed; the width of taxiways and the size of unloading areas are a function of both the number of arrivals and departures per day and the aircraft required to operate the system.

b. *The Coefficient of Construction Requirement.* The airfield area in ft² can be calculated by means of the following formula:

$$Ft^2 = k + aC + bN, \text{ where}$$

k is a constant which accounts for the length and width of the minimum runway needed to accommodate an aircraft at its destination. k varies with the type of aircraft. The minimum runway length for the Freighter is 2,500 ft.; the Pioneer is 1,500 ft.; the runway width is 50 ft. for both; thus k=125,000 for the Freighter and 75,000 for the Pioneer.

aC is a term which accounts for additional space or quality above the minimum runway and taxiway requirements. It applies to runways and taxiways at both destination and origin and to loading and unloading space at the destination. "C" is the number of cycles per day (a cycle is a one-way trip, and includes one landing and one take-off) and "a" is a coefficient which depends on the type of aircraft and leg.

bN is a term which accounts for the parking space required at the origin. "N" is the basic number of aircraft and "b" is the parking space required per aircraft (Freighter=19,500ft²; Pioneer=11,100ft²).

c. Airfield construction costs are of two types, fixed investment costs and variable costs. Fixed investment costs include expenditures for installed equipment—items such as communication, navigation, safety, and airfield marking devices. This equipment must be available at every airfield. If the Freighter is used, total investment costs are $1.5 million per airfield; with

---

*This discussion of airfield construction costs is intended only to suggest the general procedure—in contrast to the complete description of aircraft costs. The treatment is abbreviated to keep the illustrative example within the limitations imposed by study time. For the purposes of the problem, airfield construction costs may be assumed as given.

the Pioneer these costs amount to $0.9 million per airfield. Variable costs are directly related to the size of the airfield, and include the costs to the United States of supplying Vietnamese Army units with construction equipment, supplies, and military advisory personnel. Cost per ft^2 is estimated at $4.10. Cost/ft^2 is based on expenses incurred in supporting similar construction by indigenous forces in South Korea and was provided by the Deputy for Military Assistance, Office of the Chief of Engineers.

d. Airfield construction costs for each airfield employing the various routing systems is shown in table XII.

Table XII. Airfield Construction Costs.

	Routing Systems				Construction Costs Per Echelon (Millions of dollars)	
Designation	Delivery Point	Leg	Tons/ Day	Airfields Required	Freighter	Pioneer
1	Corps	A	375	1	2.05	1.48
	Division	B	250	2	4.36	2.95
	Regiment	C	100	4	8.73	5.27
2	Corps	A	475	1	2.07	1.56
	Division	B	250	2	4.36	2.95
	Regiment	F	100	4	9.61	5.99
3	Corps	A	375	1	2.05	1.48
	Division	B	350	2	4.86	3.16
	Regiment	E	100	4	9.73	5.90
4	Corps	A	475	1	2.07	1.56
	Division	B	250	2)	5.54	3.42
	Division	D	100	2)		
	Regiment	E	100	4	9.73	5.90
5	Corps	A	625	1	2.08	1.67
	Division	D	250	2	5.73	3.60
	Regiment	C	100	4	8.73	5.27
6	Corps	A	725	1	2.10	1.74
	Division	D	250	2	5.73	3.60
	Regiment	F	100	4	9.61	5.99
7	Corps	A	625	1	2.08	1.67
	Division	D	250	2)	6.07	3.81
	Division	B	100	2)		
	Regiment	E	100	4	9.73	5.90
8	Corps	A	725	1	2.10	1.74
	Division	D	350	2	6.40	3.97
	Regiment	E	100	4	9.73	5.90

V. ROUTING AND AIRCRAFT SELECTION

Based on the aircraft and airfield construction costs calculated in Section IV, above, both the least-cost routing system and the least-cost aircraft can be selected.. These computations appear in table XIII, Routing and Aircraft Selection Sheets (pp. 238–239).

Table XIII. Routing and Aircraft Selection Sheets.

Routine Systems				Systems Costs per Leg (millions)						Lowest Systems Cost with F. and P.		
Desig-nation	Delivery Point	Leg	Tons/Day	FREIGHTER (79915)			PIONEER (88665)					
				Aircraft	Airfield	TOTAL	Aircraft	Airfield	TOTAL	Aircraft	Leg Cost	Total Cost
1	Corps	A	375	65.5	2.05	67.55	65.0	1.48	66.48	P	66.48	
	Division	B	250	64.7	4.36	69.06	60.4	2.95	63.35	P	63.35	
	Regiment	C	100	27.2	8.73	35.93	26.7	5.27	31.97	P	31.97	
		T				172.54			161.80			*161.80
2	Corps	A	475	83.2	2.07	85.27	82.0	1.56	83.56	P	83.56	
	Division	B	250	64.7	4.36	69.06	60.4	2.95	63.35	P	63.35	
	Regiment	F	100	17.6	9.61	27.21	13.9	5.99	19.89	P	19.89	
		T				181.54			166.80			166.80
3	Corps	A	375	65.5	2.05	67.55	65.0	1.48	66.48	P	66.48	
	Division	B	350	89.5	4.86	94.36	84.4	3.16	87.56	P	87.56	
	Regiment	E	100	18.4	9.73	28.13	13.5	5.90	19.40	P	19.40	
		T				190.04			173.44			173.44
4	Corps	A	475	83.2	2.07	85.27	82.0	1.56	83.56	P	83.56	
	Division	B	250	64.7) -- 13.6)	5.54	83.84	60.4) -- 10.5)	3.42	74.32	P	74.32	
	Division	D	100									
	Regiment	E	100	18.4	9.73	28.13	13.5	5.90	19.40	P	19.40	
		T				196.24			177.28			177.28
5	Corps	A	625	109.4	2.08	111.48	107.8	1.67	109.47	P	109.47	
	Division	D	250	35.2	5.73	40.95	26.3	3.60	29.90	P	29.90	
	Regiment	C	100	27.2	8.73	35.93	26.7	5.27	31.97	P	31.97	
		T				188.34			171.34			171.34

#	Unit	Code	Qty						P	Total
6	Corps	A	725	125.4	2.10	127.50	125.4	1.74	P 127.14	
	Division	D	250	35.2	5.73	40.93	26.3	3.60	P 29.90	
	Regiment	F	100	17.6	9.61	27.21	13.9	5.99	P 19.89	
			T			195.64			176.93	176.93
7	Corps	A	625	109.4	2.08	111.48	107.8	1.67	P 109.47	
	Division	D	250	(35.2)--	6.07	67.67	(26.3)--	3.81	54.11	
	Division	B	100	26.4			(24.0)			
	Regiment	E	100	18.4	9.73	28.13	13.6	5.90	P 19.50	
			T			207.28			183.08	183.08
8	Corps	A	725	125.4	2.10	127.50	125.4	1.74	P 127.14	
	Division	D	350	48.7	6.40	55.10	36.4	3.97	P 40.37	
	Regiment	E	100	18.4	9.73	28.13	13.6	5.90	P 19.50	
			T			210.73			187.01	187.01

*Least cost route.

VI. SUMMARY

1. For the logistical operations proposed in JCS 736, the Pioneer offers some cost advantages as compared to the Freighter. This advantage exists on every leg in the routing system.

2. The least cost routing system of the eight considered is #1, which is about $6.6 million less costly than the next cheapest alternative, system #2. The Pioneer is approximately $11.0 million less expensive than the Freighter on system #1.

3. Additional considerations: In addition to its cost advantage, the Pioneer would also—

   a. Provide more rapid emergency service to forward units. Although it has a slightly lower airspeed than the Freighter, its lower ground time gives the Pioneer a significant advantage on the short legs of the routing system. Emergency deliveries of one or two tons to forward units could therefore be accomplished more quickly.

   b. The Pioneer requires considerably less airfield area than the Freighter. In the event of damage to a forward airfield, especially at regimental bases, airfield repairs could be accomplished more quickly if the aircraft employed in the logistical system were the Pioneer.

   c. The radio communications equipment currently utilized by Vietnamese Army units is compatible with the radio equipment installed on the Pioneer. The Pioneer would thus be able to establish voice contact with employed units of battalion size or lower. Installation of compatible equipment on the Freighter would cost $35,000 per aircraft, a total systems cost of $735,000.

4. Recommendations. If it is decided to provide the logistical support requested by Commanding General, U.S. Forces, Vietnam, it is recommended that the Pioneer aircraft be procured for this purpose.

The Pioneer-Freighter analysis was reviewed by the Department of Defense Comptroller. That office submitted the following report:

MEMORANDUM FOR: The Secretary of Defense

SUBJECT: Comments on "Tactical Air Line of Communications:
  A Comparison of Army and Air Force Proposals"

1. The recommendations advanced in "Tactical Air Line of Communications: A Comparison of Army and Air Force Proposals" are unsound. Procurement of Pioneer aircraft in sufficient quantity to meet the requirements outlined in JCS 736 is

probably the more costly, not the cheaper, of the two possible alternatives examined. Further, the Pioneer provides fewer secondary advantages than the Freighter.

2. Although the cost-effectiveness analysis of the Pioneer and Freighter is excellent in many respects, particularly in the design of the analytical model, it contains an important conceptual error. The analysis is confined to the tactical situation outlined in JCS 736. *The issue under consideration, however, is an intra-theater air resupply system for deployed U.S. forces.* The analyst appears to recognize that two different problems are at issue; but the attempt to examine these problems simultaneously is unsuccessful. Although the assumption that the tonnage requirements of deployed U.S. forces approximate those of deployed Vietnamese forces one echelon higher (i.e., a U.S. division requires the same daily tonnage as a Vietnamese Corps) is quite plausible, it does not account for the crucial difference between forces deployed in varied situations worldwide and those operating in Vietnam. The analysis implicitly assumes, because it does not examine alternatives, that the distances over which U.S. forces would be resupplied will be the same as those over which Vietnamese forces will operate. In point of fact. deployed U.S. forces may be expected to operate over much greater distances than those envisaged in the analysis.

a. The sensitivity of the solution to distance is demonstrated by graph IV (p. 242) which assumes that the requirement is to move 400 tons per day. Aircraft and aircraft related costs (basic number of aircraft plus allowances times cost per aircraft) is depicted as a function of distance. The distances involved in the deployment outlined in JCS 736 are relatively short; the longest route (Leg C) is only 160 miles. With one exception the Pioneer provided the least-cost system to meet the requirements, not because it is the more efficient airplane, but because the analysis was confined to those distances and tonnages in which the Pioneer's design characteristics makes it the more efficient aircraft.* When the distances are increased, the Freighter is clearly the least-cost solution—because at greater distances the design characteristics of the Freighter give it an advantage over the Pioneer.

b. The solution is also sensitive to tonnage changes. This is illustrated in graph V (p. 243), which plots aircraft and air-craft related costs against tonnage moved, with distance held constant.

---

*The possible exception is Leg A in Routing System 6, where very high tonnages (725 tons per day) are involved. See paragraph 2b, above.

GRAPH IV

TOTAL AIRCRAFT & AIRCRAFT-RELATED COSTS
(Fixed Tonnage -- 400 T/d)

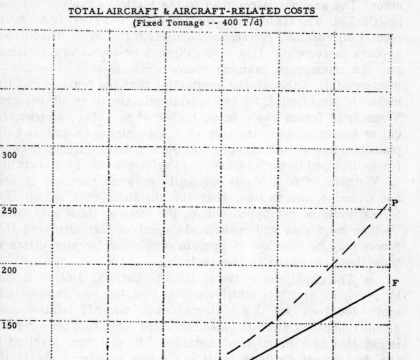

Mission Radius Distance

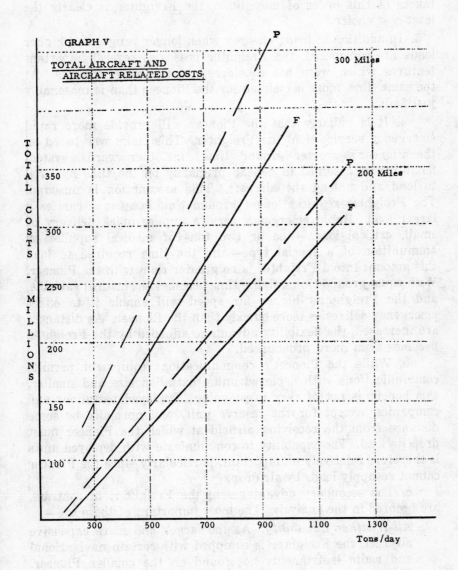

GRAPH V

TOTAL AIRCRAFT AND
AIRCRAFT RELATED COSTS

T
O
T
A
L

C
O
S
T
S
-
M
I
L
L
I
O
N
S

350

300

250

200

150

100

P

300 Miles

F

P   200 Miles

F

300   500   700   900   1100   1300

Tons/day

c. Graph VI (p. 246) suggests the considerable advantages of the Freighter when both large tonnages and long distances are involved. Since an air logistical system supporting deployed U.S. forces would in all probability involve tonnages and distances of this order of magnitude, the Freighter is clearly the least-cost choice.*

3. In addition to being cheaper when longer ranges and higher loads are considered, the Freighter possesses several important features which were not considered in the basic analysis. At the same time, more is claimed for the Pioneer than is reasonably justified.

a. It is unlikely that the Pioneer will provide more rapid emergency service than the Freighter. This claim was based on the Pioneer's shorter ground time; in other words, system flexibility is assumed to depend primarily on the time required to load and unload the aircraft. This assumption is unsound. The Freighter requires longer ground time because it carries a larger load. Rapid emergency service implies quick delivery of small, critical loads—one or two tons of medical supplies or ammunition of a special type—and the time required to load this amount into a Freighter is no greater than with the Pioneer. With equal ground times, flying time becomes the critical variable, and the Freighter's higher air speed will enable it to effect emergency deliveries more quickly than the Pioneer. As distances are increased, the flexibility advantage afforded by the Freighter becomes even more pronounced.

b. While the Pioneer's communications equipment permits communications with deployed units, battalion size and smaller, this benefit is not of very great value. Deployed battalions and companies, except for the reserve unit, will normally be some distance from the receiving airfield at which the Pioneer must drop its load. The capability to communicate with deployed units is therefore relatively unimportant, particularly since the Pioneer cannot resupply loads by air drop.

c. The secondary advantages of the Freighter, in contrast, are ignored in the analysis. The most important of these are—

All-Weather Capability. As the larger and more expensive aircraft, the Freighter is equipped with certain navigational and radio instruments not found on the smaller Pioneer. The Freighter would therefore be able to carry out resupply

---

*Airfield construction costs may safety be ignored. Airfield costs vary directly with C and N (see p. 236) ; with the Pioneer, C and N increase rapidly when tonnages and distance are increased. Thus the advantage in airfield construction costs which the Pioneer enjoys at low levels of tonnage and distance tends to disappear when these are increased.

operations in weather conditions which would ground the Pioneer. Since an intratheater logistical system may be employed in a variety of locales and will be the only method of resupply in some situations, improved all-weather capability becomes a very worthwhile feature.

Outsize Capacity*. Approximately 85% of the equipment standard to the Vietnamese Army division can be transported by the Freighter. Less than one-third of these items can be moved by the smaller Pioneer. Similarly, the Freighter can carry about 75% of the equipment in the current U.S. Army division, versus about one-fifth for the Pioneer.

Air Drop Capability. The Freighter has a heavy drop capability. This will enable it to support isolated units or to continue normal resupply activities in the event airfields in battle zone are damaged. This feature improves considerably the overall flexibility of the logistical system.

These capabilities should have been mentioned in the analysis because they are relevant in any choice between the two aircraft, even in the narrow context of support for Vietnamese forces. The analysis, incidentally, is such that a price tag can be put on these added capabilities. On the least-cost routing system, the extra costs of improved all-weather, outsize, and heavy drop capabilities is $10.74 million (the difference in costs between the Pioneer and Freighter).**

d. The study also did not consider the possibility of some of both types—for example, sufficient Freighter aircraft to operate part of the system, utilizing Pioneer aircraft in the remainder. If the Freighter were utilized on Leg A of Routing System 1, for example, the extra cost would be only $1.7 million—a very small price for the extra flexibility which would be purchased.

e. When larger tonnages and longer distances are considered, the additional capabilities of the Freighter become, of course, part of the extra costs of buying the Pioneer. Put in other terms, in an air logistical system supporting deployed U.S. forces, the extra capabilities of the Freighter are free.

4. The analysis also fails to consider aircraft other than the Pioneer. Strictly speaking, there was no requirement to do so. But the question of the suitability of other aircraft is a nagging

---

*It is recognized that the student was not provided this information.

**Pricing the incommensurables in this manner slightly disadvantages the Pioneer. Its improved short field characteristics may in fact be worth more than the savings which accrue because smaller airfields are required.

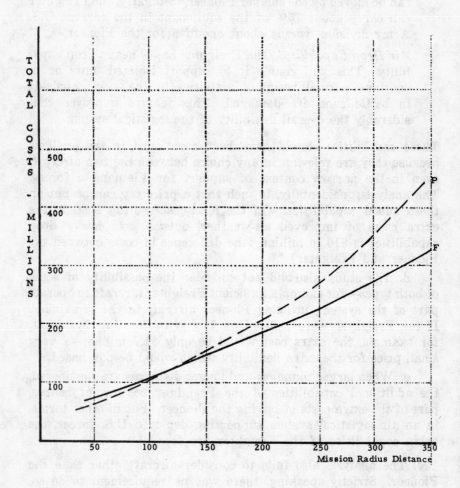

GRAPH · VI

TOTAL AIRCRAFT AND AIRCRAFT RELATED COSTS
(Fixed Tonnage - 700 T/d)

one—and one which needs examination before a decision of this magnitude is made. To illustrate the point, consider the capabilities of the Skyhook helicopter. On a routing leg of 40 miles, the Skyhook carries 4.0 tons. Based on a 10 hour flying day* an average ground time of 6.0 minutes, and a flying speed of 100 knots, it can complete 10.0 sorties per day. The capability coefficient is .0250, and in routing systems incorporating Leg E (systems 3, 4, 7, and 8—100 tons per day), 3.25 Skyhooks are required (basic number plus allowances). With initial investment and five year operating costs totaling $4.70 million per aircraft, total aircraft and aircraft related costs amount to $15.3 million. The cost of the Pioneer on the same leg is $13.5 million; that of the Freighter $18.4 million. With the Skyhook, however, it would be unnecessary to build large, expensive airfields—which would more than compensate for the $1.8 million savings in aircraft and aircraft related costs which the Pioneer allows. Thus the Skyhook would provide the least cost solution on the very short legs of the logistical system. It would, moreover, improve the overall effectiveness of the logistical system since emergency deliveries could be made directly to the deployed units. Finally, emergency medical evacuation from forward units would also be speeded.

5. *Recommendations*

a. The questions which must now be examined are: How many Freighters will be needed? What mix of Freighters and Pioneers—or, as seems more likely, Freighters and Skyhooks— provide the least cost solution? I recommend that these questions be referred to the Joint Staff. My office has been assisted by the Joint Staff in the preparation of this critique, and that group is well equipped to continue the analysis.

b. The problem of TALOC support for deployed Vietnamese forces needs immediate resolution. My office, assisted by representatives of the Departments of the Army and Air Force, is preparing an analysis to determine which of the immediately available aircraft types in the inventory would be most appropriate for the Vietnamese logistical mission. This study will be available in about ten days, and will be forwarded to you at that time.

---

*Limited to this time by maintenance requirements.

/s/

/t/   COMPTROLLER*

Department of Defense

A Concluding Comment:

This fictitious case study was designed to illustrate the techniques of systems analysis. To enhance further its value as a teaching vehicle, mention needs to be made of those parts of the analysis which are capable of refinement. There are three areas, all of relatively minor importance:

1. The computation of allowances for aircraft losses is highly simplified. Aircraft losses are of two types: peacetime accidents, which are a function of hours of flying time; and combat losses, which are associated with the amount of time the aircraft is exposed to attack by enemy ground or air defense forces. An accurate estimate of combat losses should, therefore, be based on the number of hours an aircraft is exposed to enemy defenses, not total flying hours. Exposure time multiplied by loss rates of aircraft flying in the exposed zone would give a more reliable estimate of combat losses.

2. A number of significant costs are ignored in the computation of aircraft and aircraft related costs. The costs of annual training to maintain crew proficiency is an example. Annual operating cost figures employed in the case study are of the right order of magnitude because "Other Operating Costs" was fudged. "Other Operating Costs" would normally amount to one or two times fuel costs.

3. The discussion of system flexibility is somewhat simplified, both in the critique and the original analysis. If greater "flexibility" (and the term demands more precise definition) is desired, a routing system involving all six legs is probably required. Additional flexibility would also be achieved by the simple process of constructing extra airfields.

4. Finally, a good analyst would quickly spot the most sensitive element in the system, ground time. Reductions in ground time, which would increase sorties/day, could be achieved quickly by the addition of simple unloading equipment such as fork lift trucks.

---

*Now Assistant Secretary of Defense (Systems Analysis).

SUGGESTIONS FOR FURTHER READING

Committee for Economic Development, *Budgeting for National Objectives: Executive and Congressional Roles in Program Planning and Performance.* A statement on National Policy by the Research and Policy Committee. New York: Committee for Economic Development, 1966.

Enthoven, Alain C., "Economic Analysis in the Department of Defense," *American Economic Review,* Papers and Proceedings of the 75th Annual Meeting of the American Economic Association, vol. LIII, no. 2 (May 1963), pp. 413–423. Reprinted as "Economic Analysis and Defense Policy" in Morton Berkowitz and P. G. Bock, editors, *American National Security.* New York: The Free Press, 1965, pp. 129–135.

————, "Systems Analysis and Decision Making," *Military Review,* vol. XLII, no. 1 (January 1963), pp. 7–17.

———— and Henry S. Rowen, *Defense Planning and Organization.* (Rand Corporation, Paper P–1640.) Santa Monica, Calif.: The Rand Corporation, 1959. Also available in *Public Finances, Needs, Sources, and Utilization.* Princeton, N.J.: Princeton University Press, 1961, pp. 365–417.

Hitch, Charles J., "National Security Policy as a Field for Economics Research," *World Politics,* vol. XII, no. 3 (April 1960), pp. 434–448.

———— and Roland N. McKean, *The Economics of Defense in the Nuclear Age.* Cambridge, Mass.: Harvard University Press, 1960.

Huzar, Ellias, *The Purse and the Sword: Control of the Army by Congress through Military Appropriations, 1933–1950.* Ithaca, N.Y.: Cornell University Press, 1950.

Kahn, Herman, and Irwin Mann, *Techniques of Systems Analysis.* (Rand Corporation Memorandum RM–1829–1. Revised June 1957). Santa Monica, Calif.: The Rand Corporation, 1957.

Kaufmann, William W., *The McNamara Strategy.* New York: Harper and Row, 1964.

Large, M. P., editor, *Concepts and Procedures of Cost Analysis*. (Rand Corporation, Memorandum RM–3589–PR). Santa Monica, California.: The Rand Corporation, 1963.

Marx, Fritz Morstein, "The Bureau of the Budget: Its Evolution and Present Role," *The American Political Science Review*, vol. XXXIX, nos. 4 and 5 (August and October 1945), pp. 653–684, 869–898.

Novick, David, *Resource Analysis and Long-Range Planning*. (Rand Corporation, Memorandum RM–3658–PR). Santa Monica, Calif.: The Rand Corporation, 1963.

————, editor, *Program Budgeting*. Cambridge Mass.: Harvard University Press, 1965. (Abridged edition, Washington: U.S. Government Printing Office, 1965).

Peck, Merton J., and F. M. Scherer, *The Weapons Acquisition Process: An Economic Analysis*. Cambridge, Mass.: Harvard University Press, 1962.

Quade, E. S., *Military Systems Analysis*. (Rand Corporation, Memorandum RM–3452–PR). Santa Monica, California.: The Rand Corporation, 1963.

————, editor, *Analysis for Military Decisions*. (Rand Corporation, Report R–387–PR). Santa Monica, Calif.: The Rand Corporation, 1964. (Also published by Rand-McNally Co., Chicago, 1964, and North-Holland Publishing Co., Amsterdam, 1964).

Rowen, Henry S., "National Security and the American Economy in the 1960's," Study Paper No. 18, U.S. Congress, Joint Economic Committee, Study of Employment and Price Levels, 86th Congress, 2d Session, Washington: U.S. Government Printing Office, 1960.

Siegel, Irving H., *Allocation of Resources: Problems of Strategic Posture and Readiness*. (Research Analysis Corporation, contract study for Office of the Chief, Research and Development, Department of the Army, November 1963). Washington: Research Analysis Corporation, 1963.

Smithies, Arthur, *The Budgetary Process in the United States*. New York: McGraw-Hill Book Co., 1955.

U.S. Congress. House. Subcommittee of the Committee on Government Operations, *Systems Development and Management*. 87th Congress, 2d Session. Hearings, Part 2. Washington: U.S. Government Printing Office, 1962. (Note particularly testimony by Mr. Charles J. Hitch, pp. 513–547, and Appendix IV, "Program Package," pp. 642–804).

————. Senate. Document No. 11, *Financial Management in the Federal Government*. A Comprehensive Analysis of Existing and Proposed Legislation including Financial Management Improvements Made on a Government-Wide Basis, by the Staff of the Committee on Government Operations. 87th Congress, 1st Session. Washington: U.S. Government Printing Office, 1961.

————. Subcommittee on National Policy Machinery, Committee on Government Operations, *Organizing for National Security*. 86th Congress, 2d Session, and 87th Congress, 1st Session, vol. 1, Hearings. Washington: U.S. Government Printing Office, 1961.

————, vol. 2, *Studies and Background Materials*.

————, vol. 3, *Staff Reports and Recommendations*.

Williams, J. D., *The Compleat Strategyst: being a primer on the theory of games of strategy*, New York: McGraw-Hill Book Co., 1954.

Wilmerding, Lucius, Jr., *The Spending Power: A History of the Efforts of Congress to Control Expenditures*. New Haven, Conn.: Yale University Press, 1943.

U.S. Congress. House. Subcommittee on the Committee on Government Operations. *Automated Systems in Management.* 98th Congress, 2d Session. (Testimony Don E. Wasserman.) U.S. Government Printing Office, 1984. (Testimony by Mr. [Oberkeck]. Hearing pt. 675-567.) Appendix IV. "Program Budget," pp. 495-603.)

———. Senate. Document No. 11. *Financial Management in the Federal Government.* Compiled by April Mayer. Budget and Proposed Legislation Indicated. Financial Management Subcommittee of the Congressional Committee for the Staff of the Committee on Government Operations. 98th Session. Washington: Government Printing Office, 1984.

———. Subcommittee on National Policy Machinery. Committee on Government Operations. *Organization and Management.* 86th Congress, 2d Session and 87th Congress, 1st Session, vol. 1-3. Hearings. Washington: U.S. Government Printing Office, 1960.

———. vol. 2. *Studies and Background Materials.*

———. vol. 3. *Staff Reports and Recommendations.*

Williams, J. D. *The Compleat Strategyst: being a primer on the theory of games of strategy.* New York: McGraw Hill, Book Co., 1954.

Wildavsky, Aaron. *The Politics of the Budgetary Process.* 3d Edition. Boston: Little, Brown, and Company, 1979.

Wlhoundaire, Andris, Dr., PhD. *Speculative Essays of Theory on Aspects of Economic Incentives.* New Haven, Conn.: Yale University Press, 1978.

INDEX

A

Advanced development, defined, 82
Air Force
  General Purpose Forces, 81
  military planning, 67
Airlift and Sealift program, 81
Airlift case study, 215–248
Antisubmarine warfare, requirement for, 172–173
Army divisions, cost-effectiveness analysis
  analysis of staying power, 191–192
  and inaccurate strength estimates, 188–189
  contradictions in estimating strength, 189–190
  cost estimates, 194
  differences in U.S. and Soviet standards, 190–191
  human element, 192
  importance of judgment, 195
  in weapon replacement, 181–182
  intangible factors, 185
  objectivity in, 186
  paucity of ground forces data, 186–187
  primitive state of the art, 193
  U.S. vs. Soviet Army, 176–177, 187–192
  use of social science methodology, 194–195
  (*see also* Systems analysis)
Army General Purpose Forces, 79

B

Balance of payments, and defense budget, 39–41
"Bop" estimates, 176
Budget and Accounting Act of 1921, 2
Budget, Bureau of, 2
  participation in DOD budgeting, 104–105
  review of DOD programming, 54–55

Budgeting, defense
  after 1961, 70–73
  and balance of payments deficit, 39–41
  and governmentwide budgeting, 98, 213–214
  and military effectiveness, 23–24
  basic premises in formulation, 22–23
  before 1961, 66–70
  Budget Bureau participation, 54–55, 104–105
  congressional review, 1, 68, 70, 98, 101–104
  consideration of field commander requests, 62
  disadvantage of annual submission, 108
  effects of tax policies, 41
  evolution of procedures, 113–114
  FY 1964 budget program, 97
  foundations of, 30–32
  functional categories, 95
  impact of political objectives, 27–29
  impact on national economy, 44–45
  increase of defense expenditures, 42–44
  JCS role, 56–61
  major programs, 78–84, 96
  McNamara reforms, 21–24
  military service role, 25, 53–55, 96
  phase in planning-programming-budgeting process, 84–85
  presidential role, 25
  research allocation problems, 38–39
  responsibility of the Secretary of Defense, 24
  (*see also* Programming system; Systems analysis)

C

Centralization, defense decisionmaking, 25–26, 111–112
China, Communist, resource allocation, 38, 39

253